Values

Values

A Symposium

edited by
Brenda Almond

and
Bryan Wilson

HUMANITIES PRESS INTERNATIONAL, INC.
Atlantic Highlands, NJ

First published in 1988 in the United States of
America by
HUMANITIES PRESS INTERNATIONAL, INC.,
Atlantic Highlands, NJ 07716

© 1988 by Humanities Press International, Inc.

© 1988 by the Individual Authors

Library of Congress Cataloging-in-Publication Data
Values: a symposium.

Bibliography: p.
1. Values—Congresses.   I. Almond, Brenda.
II. Wilson, Bryan R.
BD232.V265   1988   121'.8   86–5152
ISBN 0–391–03368–9

All rights reserved. No reproduction, copy or
transmission of this publication may be made
without written permission.

Printed in the United States of America

Contents

Foreword   vii

Introduction   1

I The Notion of Value

Value
    Alan Montefiore   13

II Moral Values in Society

Values and Society
    Bryan Wilson   31
Values and Tradition
    Edward Shils   47
Merit
    J. D. M. Derrett   57
A Comparison Between American, European, and Japanese Values
    Gordon Heald   75

III Values and Institutions

Politics and Value
    Edmond Ions   93
Sophisters, Economists, and Calculators: On the Notion of Value in Economics
    Paul Seabright   105
Values in the Civil Law
    J. K. B. M. Nicholas   119
Justice
    D. C. M. Yardley   131
Investment in Science
    J. D. M. Derrett   145

IV Values in Application

Environmental Values
  Brenda Almond ... 163
The Value of Invention
  John P. Haggart ... 179
Values in Education
  John Wilson ... 191
Values and the Novel
  Bernard Richards ... 207
Language, Literature, and Moral Values
  Barbara Cowell ... 219
Value in Drama (A Prologue, Three Acts, and an Epilogue)
  Charles Lepper ... 233

List of Contributors ... 251

Index ... 253

Foreword

Okada Mokichi, the Founder of M.O.A.

Okada Mokichi was born in 1882 in a poor suburb of Tokyo. He was the fourth child of a second-hand goods dealer who, despite limited means, was nevertheless determined to give his talented son the best possible education. Despite chronically bad health, the young Okada was successful in his early education, and demonstrated artistic ability. On his father's death, he embarked, despite recurrent health problems, on a successful business career, selling and later designing costume jewelry, and eventually becoming well-known for his patented artificial diamond.

Various set-backs and bereavements, including the loss of his young wife, changed Okada's approach to life during his twenties and thirties. During his many illnesses he had lost all faith in medical treatments and, partly for this reason, he began to investigate spiritual approaches to his problems. His personal and business life had become a catalogue of disasters and he sought guidance along a variety of religious avenues. At this time, Japan was experiencing great upheavals under the impact of the West and new philosophies and religions abounded. Okada did not find any of these totally satisfying but he increasingly came to believe that solutions to the human malaise lay in the spiritual and aesthetic rather than in the material realm.

In the early twentieth century, the Japanese authorities were promoting a form of Shinto as the state religion, but it was not to this that Okada turned. Rather, in the 1920s, he became increasingly closely affiliated with Omoto-kyo, one of Japan's new religions. Omoto-kyo had a charismatic founder who claimed powers of healing and who stressed internationalism as the way forward for mankind. Although not all aspects of Omoto-kyo appealed to Okada, he was attracted by its concern to promote world peace and its emphasis on aesthetic appreciation. During this association with Omoto-kyo, Okada was deepening his own religious experience and reading widely in religion and philosophy, ancient and modern. He was convinced that the rising tide of nationalism both in Japan and world-wide would only be destructive and that what was necessary was active work for peace. He believed that only by a radical process of change in humanity's spiritual and moral character would this come about. In one profound religious experience he believed that Kannon, a Bodhisattva who in Buddhist tradition embodied compassion, had chosen him especially to spearhead a movement for the reconstruction of man's spiritual state. From this time, Okada's own powers of healing became notable; he began what was to become a considerable volume of writing; and he founded a religious organization, Sekai Kyusei Kyo (World Salvation Teachings), which, as the name suggests, adopted a distinctly international perspective. This movement was subjected to some harassment by the Japanese authorities and it was not until after the Second World War when the Occupying Forces proclaimed freedom of religion that Okada, who died in 1955, became at all widely known in Japan. Okada encouraged his dedicated following to undertake expansion work outside Japan as soon as this became feasible after the War, and today S.K.K. has significant numbers of members in South America and South East Asia, and has also attracted membership in North America and Europe.

A fundamental element of Okada's vision is that mankind *can* create a better, more harmonious world. He promoted a philosophy of cultural exchange, particularly but not exclusively in the realm of the arts. He believed that an appreciation of beauty, together with deepening realization that spiritually as well as physically man and the forces of nature were interdependent, would promote less materialistic, less competitive dispositions. To this end, he founded M.O.A., an organization that continues to promote exhibitions of works of art, sometimes from its own very impressive collection housed in a modern museum in Atami. M.O.A. also sponsors concerts, promotes the art of flower-arranging and encourages appreciation of poetry. The theme of "Value" was close to the heart of Okada, and his work was dedicated to the attainment of all that would be of greatest value to humankind.

ELIZABETH DERRETT

Introduction

BRYAN WILSON

Of all widely invoked concepts, few are as difficult to specify as the concept of values. The plural form connotes quite different considerations from the singular. Value may be, and is often, expressed at the most rudimentary level as price or in some monetary unit of measure, but values are usually perceived as irreducible, perhaps arbitrary, dispositions or commitments of widely divergent generalizability. Whilst values may at times be compromised, it is assumed that normally they will not be traded. They are indivisible ultimates and to be surrendered or abandoned only under severe duress. Were values too readily displaced we should, in all probability, not recognize them as such. They are taken to be ultimate dispositions or commitments. And *commitments* is a better word than *choices*, since choices suggests something necessarily too conscious and deliberative. It is a better word than *preferences*, which does not sufficiently indicate the non-negotiability of values, which are irreducible, durable, and prescriptive—ideally, even mandatory—for social action.

Values are readily ascribed to different social conglomerates from humankind to individuals, from nation-states or multinational societies (as in "Western values") to small groups. They may be the organizing principles of self-conscious social units, such as sects, action groups, or political parties; or they may be merely implicit, perhaps no more than latent, in less consciously constructed social entities—tribes, families, and, in certain cultures and historical periods, even in social strata. Certainly in literate, articulate, and self-conscious societies, we recognize that even single individuals espouse values that determine or at least condition behaviour and may differ in greater or lesser degree from any or all of the values of the social groups with which they are affiliated.

We may ask where values finally reside. For strictly individual values that question presents no difficulty, but most of the values embedded in social action are not individual values, are not expressed or experienced as self-conscious individual choices or opinions, but they are the cumulative repository of preferences and prohibitions transmitted in society or in one or another of its subordinate parts. Even so, there must be a sense in which the values of social groups and of society itself entail individual commitment, either conscious or unconscious. The values enshrined in custom prevail, certainly, but only through shared participatory commitment of those concerned. The major institutions of society such as marriage, courtship, initiation, graduation, and taboo are rather complex clusters of required or strongly preferred acts that realize certain values in everyday life. But although these social values are borne by the individual, in a sense they exist, as Durkheim would have said, independently of any individual carrier. The individual need not be conscious of them or offer any formal adherence to them. None the less, we may here speak of values as readily as we may in reference to the conscious commitments that obtain within formal institutional structures such as legal codes, the educational system, redistributive arrangements and social welfare. We may say this, even though in the process of social change it is generally considered that planning procedures and deliberative, formally constituted organizations have increasingly displaced the unconscious, spontaneous, so-called natural social entities exemplified by the tribe or the extended family and the unreflective institutions that functioned for these social units.

Social values, then, ultimately do not reside in individuals, even though they are mediated through individual lives. Certain personal values may be elicited from individuals—at least in advanced societies—as their own self-conscious and deliberative choices, and the realm of these values increases as rational social reorganization occurs; but there remain other values that operate more as social constraints or compulsions to which the individual accedes, more or less consciously, with more or less freedom.[1] The individual in contemporary society often acts in accordance with values without conscious commitment. Such action in traditional societies may simply be seen as "normal" behaviour, yet prescribed procedures and generally shared goals always carry value implications, whether actions be trivial, such as raising one's hat in greeting, or crucial, such as avoidance of public display of sexual excitement. Thus the understanding of values calls for more than a survey of opinions since, paradoxically, operative values do not have their source in individuals. Such values may not be matters of conscious opinion at all or, if so, then often of only unreflective, unchallenged, and uncritical opinion at best.

Once people are made conscious of values, however, the occasion for deliberative assent or dissent occurs, and while most people, most of the time, may choose not to reflect upon, much less challenge, most existing values, the possibility of such challenge, of critical response, and of demands for personal choice and freedom from socially constraining values arises increasingly in advanced society. Such demands are evident even in religion, the primary area of the most explicitly canvassed values, where a process of privatization is widely recognized. Men choose what has been described as an "assortment of ultimate meanings" rather than accept the "sacred canopy" of received and traditional religious ideas and values.[2] Philosophical and political ideologies arise which assert that the amalgam of individual value choices produces the best sort of society, and that people should all be made conscious of the value implications of all social action. That condition, however, is far from being attained and its attainment would no doubt lead to unexpected and unintended consequences. In the meantime, national cultures are seen as the locations of distinctive constellations of values, and even public opinion surveyors, of necessity committed to highly individualistic assumptions, treat national differences as if nations were natural categories according to which values are naturally distributed and are to be appropriately classified.

These reflections are those of the sociologist, for whom society's values are primary data, social facts in themselves. But the sociologist does not have a monopoly on the discussion of values; every academic discipline deals with values and, at some level, may lay claim to values of its own. In applied subjects, values are largely derivative; in the core theoretical disciplines of the academic curriculum values are central assumptions; and in some disciplines they are a significant and deliberate focus of analysis and appraisal. Although values are implicit in all social activities, they belong, more self-consciously and coherently, in the academic interpretation of those activities. Acts and artefacts—the telling of stories, the performance of ritual, the writing of poetry, the painting of pictures, and the procedures of science—and their substantive products—are value-laden. These creative activities, together with the whole tissue of social intercourse and institutions in which values subsist, constitute a culture, a constellation of positively evaluated phenomena. To the values intrinsic to the culture *per se* the values embodied in academic appraisal are an addition. In societies in which academia has evolved, the self-conscious concern about values has itself become a culturally valued activity. The academic in the quest to scrutinize, elucidate, and bring to consciousness the values within a given sphere of activity, becomes the custodian (though not necessarily the conservator) of particular values within a given realm of activity. It is at this level of the scrutiny and assessment of values (not at the level of direct transmission of specific substantive values) that the essays in this volume are pitched.

The contributors to this book have a special reflective concern about the values in a given area of activity as they are pursued in Western society. This volume, providing a commentary on specifically Western values, does not purport to articulate the values of all departments of social life. It examines values that undergird the legal, political, economic, and ecological arenas, yet it does not explore various basic social institutions of Western society such as the values of family life, social cohesion, religion, and sport. (The authors have chosen not to include religion, for example, since although it has prescribed and legitimized behaviour patterns in the past, it now, in a pluralistic and secularized society, presents a congeries of obscure and internally divergent values.) That these originally folk institutions embody and transmit significant value orientations that stem from the inheritance of a communal past is in no way ignored. But here the focus is rather on the values in more consciously constituted institutions. In this pioneering study the authors concentrate on those institutions whose values represent explicit commitments to a conscious order of priorities and concerns, and it is in that spirit that these essays are put forward.

The substantive values that appear to be most widespread in Western society such as competitiveness, money-making and personal enjoyment, and the values that they appear to have displaced such as doing the will of God, maintaining tradition, and altruism (in the Durkheimian sense) engage little of the discussion in this book. Rather, this volume looks at a range of pursuits in which values are more or less consciously transmitted or negotiated, sustained, realized, and communicated in fields such as literature, education, law, science, and the environment. The substance of values is sometimes assumed; at other times, values are taken as part of the charter (to use Malinowski's term) of particular institutional procedures. These essays, then, do not pretend to present a complete picture of Western culture or constitute a cultural analysis in the genre that became celebrated in works like Ruth Benedict's *The Chrysanthemum and the Sword*. They do aspire to contribute to the understanding of a diverse range of values which operate in some of the most fully articulated spheres of contemporary society.

The spirit pervading these chapters, arising without collusion, is that of value-neutrality. The distinction of fact from value is a matter-of-course assumption, which is perhaps the most salient value commitment of the academic disposition of Western society. In other cultures, facts and values are not always sharply distinguished. The normative order is often inextricably enmeshed in the factual understanding of the world and society, and neither sheer facticity nor value-judgement needs to be conceived of apart from this. These societies may have no pressing social need for a distinction that has become basic to the Western scientific mind (whatever qualifications we might acknowledge respecting the infirmity of the frontier between fact and values). Whilst it is well recognized that the choice of an object of study must rest on some fundamental value-disposition, and that rules of value-relevance govern the selection of evidence in scientific work, none the less, self-consciousness on these points only underscores the general determination to maintain, in all other aspects of academic inquiry, the highest level of impartiality and value-neutrality. Only rarely do these essays definitely express value preferences, but they do this most conspicuously in the realm of the arts—disciplines that are often value-committed at much more intrinsic levels than are the sciences and social sciences. The spirit of scientific analysis in these essays—itself a significant element in Western values—reflects the essentially exploratory nature of the symposium for which they were written. There was no preconceived conclusion which this wide-ranging, interdisciplinary discussion was expected to reach. Whatever the value premises the authors may have had, they remained generally unavowed in the symposium.

That such a symposium should have been held at all, and that this present volume has issued from it, is owed to the vision of the sponsors. It is still relatively unusual, even in an age much given to conferences, for representatives of quite diverse disciplines to come together to discuss a common theme. Usually it is the case that people who know about the same kind of facts, use similar methods, and think along much the same sorts of lines come together to confer. Perhaps feelings of insecurity and an unwillingness to be made to think in different ways or to confront inconvenient findings or challenging new techniques induce scholars and others to shy away from participation in interdisciplinary discussions. The very structure of academic life promotes the same tendency: financial grants to confer are available for experts who share closely related bodies of expertise, but are much less readily given, or requested, for meetings of people whose knowledge is drawn from divergent areas of experience, organized in formally quite distinguished subjects, even if their substantive interests must at some important points converge.

It is at this point that pioneering academic ventures benefit from the vision of sponsoring bodies such as the M.O.A. Foundation, which promoted the symposium responsible for these chapters. The goal of the M.O.A. Foundation is to promote new liaisons in the cultural field, between countries as well as disciplines. Its initiative led to the choice of a theme of great importance, both to society at large and to academics in a wide variety of disciplines, as the subject for a symposium of a kind that is probably unique.

The essays here appear in three sections. The first section, devoted to discussion of values at the most general, societal level, begins with a philosophical treatment of the concept and its social location, with the difficulties inherent in seeking to extricate the value element in speech-acts and behaviour, in distinguishing the individual from the social, and in establishing the range and types of evaluation in society. These philosophical concerns are closely related to the sociologist's interest in the functionality of values. This section's second chapter discusses the central themes of value-consensus and value conflict as they relate to the extent to which value consensus may be considered as indispensable to society's functioning and survival, and the limitations on the character of value orientations if values are to subserve this function. Professor Edward Shils takes up a more specific issue on which he is the acknowledged authority, namely, the complexity of the relation of values to tradition (which, in popular usage, are not infrequently confused with each other). Another specific topic which applies in perhaps all societies is the ascription of merit. Since every society differentially valuates its members, ascribing to them qualities such as nobility, honour, or sanctity, such merit may well be a general and significant attribution of values, ascribed or achieved. From it, a society's evaluations might be adduced, but the very practice of ascribing merit lies at the centre of the creation of evaluative order. The final chapter in the first section presents a picture of the distribution in various national populations of the values relative to a wide range of phenomena as assessed by public opinion polls. Clearly, there are difficulties in applying comparable questions in different cultures (as, for example, questions about God and the Decalogue directed to the Japanese, whose culture lacks both of these concepts as such), but comparative exercises are always arresting and particularly so when they present what appears as hard, empirical data.

The second section examines the values that prevail within four of the dominant institutional orders of society: politics, economics, law (treated here in two different respects), and science. In each of these areas, rational procedures are employed to make operational particular value preferences and received normative frameworks of social order. In politics and economics, all advanced societies have constructed an elaborate apparatus for the realization in an orderly way of socially valued ends. In both these areas, values are disciplined, and priorities articulated and organized; values are realized by the imposition of certain strategies of choice, not only for individuals but also in response to certain facets of the general will. Normative order is less open to change by the democratic process or open only subject to much more protracted and elaborate procedures—in the case of regulative institutions, conspicuously law. Law, rooted in and drawing on custom and convention (particularly English law), embodies society's presumed normative codes of conduct in all potentially serious areas of everyday intercourse. Law embraces specific values respecting life, person, property, honour, obligation, and so on, which are assumed to be refractions, in consciously created institutions, of society's values. Law responds slowly and only with the intervention of specialized élites to hypothesized changes in "public opinion" (or, in this case, "the general will") and may indeed resist change where that public opinion is held to be "uninformed." The values enshrined in legal enactments and legal procedures often appear to be received from the past; if not indeed from "on high," and certainly stem from some distilled wisdom that may not be generally understood or appreciated in most sections of the population at large.

If anything, science may appear more autonomous and completely insulated than law from the direct impact of public opinion about values. Modern societies have few if any institutionalized agencies that can transmit the summation of individual attitudes towards scientific processes. The subjects are considered technical, and although science certainly has value implications, the weight of technical obscurity about its operations appears to provide an insulating device to protect it from the impact of external values. Science is a complex of institutional procedures that imply social change, often of an unconsidered or inadequately considered kind. Its potential for unintended consequences, for results that totally transcend the considered evaluations not only of the general uninformed public, but even of concerned and specialized élites, is clearly vast. As Professor J. D. M. Derrett makes clear, decisions respecting science involve immense financial, strategic, and political implications, and the source of values involved in policy may often be hard to locate in the bureaucratic corporate structures by which science is now regulated. The goals of science, loosely identified with an idea of progress, are often assumed to be self-evidently desirable, even inevitable, without recourse to popular sentiment, much less to democratic vote. Only in recent years have the implicit values of the sciences met any challenge (other than those arising from obscurantism). That issue is opened up in the third section of this volume, which deals with the application of values in specific moral locales.

The ecological issue illustrates an area of profound but newly articulated agitation about contemporary values. More than any other issue, this one speaks of the spirit of our times. The routinized, entrenched, self-sustaining, and self-justifying values encapsulated in the corporate apparatus of scientific research, in the provision of government funds, and in the popular demand for solutions to problems of modern living are challenged as the unintended, sometimes horrifying consequences of the application of scientific knowledge are increasingly perceived. New values in defence of life, health, and security (and not merely of the conservation of tradition and treasured life-styles, although they too are values that cannot be ignored) are now articulated in the face of new technology and the technocracy which manages it. The values of science have ceased to be self-evident. One unintended consequence of scientific advance has been to stimulate those who previously espoused their cherished values much less demonstrably and with less awareness of the deep-seated values that were operative in social life. Since it is in the situation of value conflict that awareness is heightened and commitments are sharpened, in such a situation people may also become sensitive to the further potential conflict arising from the possible incongruence of the values embodied in the means science employs and the end values those means are intended to safeguard or promote.

It is not inappropriate in relation to the increasing social cost of science that one perhaps rudimentary method of evaluating new techniques, as reflected in the sphere of inventions and patents, should command the attention of those concerned with values and the quality of life. The chapter by John Haggart contains a practical demonstration of the complexity of considerations that have evolved in the determination of the worth of innovation. The questions implicit in this process are, of course, those of the positive worth of an invention, while the ultimate, and less calculable *costs* of an invention are another and less tractable problem.

It is the arts, rather than the sciences or social sciences, which are most readily recognized as purveyors of values, as they self-consciously present value conflicts and value positions relative, usually, to individual (rather than collective) moral and aesthetic life. Values lie nearer to the surface in these disciplines than they do even in law, although they may be less explicitly normative and have a less rational apparatus to order value priorities or to promote their realization. Literature and drama generally are almost specially constructed vehicles for values, for an almost immediate consideration of values, and at least part of the purpose of this consideration is to awaken in the reader or the spectator the consciousness of moral problems, moral choices, and moral consequences. All of this is, of course, a focus common to education and socialization. In that context, the issues expand: the concern to communicate values raises the question of "which values?" and debate arises about the substantive qualities to which value is attached by positive attitudes prevalent in society, or at least in significant and salient sections within it. Educators and literary critics, acutely alert to the problems of socialization, often become the arbiters of substantive values. Their discourse does not easily sustain separate discussion about the process of the transmission of values from consideration of substantive values in and of themselves (even where these are designated only in the most general and perhaps abstract terms—good will, responsibility, sensitivity, commitment, regard for others, without specification of "for what" or "to whom"). Indeed, if a value-judgement may be permitted, there is no cause for such separate discussion to be sustained where the arts are concerned, since, at some point, it must be acceded that living entails values and the business of the educators and the humanists must, sooner or later, treat the substantive question of how people are to live.

Notes

1. A telling example of the extent to which values inhere in the culture and are not matters of individual choice in less developed societies is apparent from the account provided by David Riesman in the Introduction to Daniel Lerner, *The Passing of Traditional Society: Modernizing the Middle East* (Glencoe Ill.: Free Press, 1958). Commenting on the survey research interview as a cultural form, Riesman observed (p. 3) that in pre-industrial and pre-democratic societies, the respondents who replied "Don't know" to questionnaire items were still a very large number, and he continued:

   "The Turkish peasant who, responding to the question as to what he would do if he were President, declared:

   > 'My God! How can you ask such a thing. How can I . . . I cannot . . . president of Turkey . . . master of the whole world?'

   Correspondingly, many of the tradition-minded in these interviews, asked where they would like to live if they could not live in their native villages, said they would rather die; they could not conceive of living anywhere else, any more than of being somebody else."

2. The phrase comes from Thomas Luckmann, *The Invisible Religion* (London: Collier-Macmillan, 1967) p. 102. The concept of the "sacred canopy" was developed by Peter L. Berger, *The Sacred Canopy* (New York: Doubleday, 1967).

I

The Notion of Value

Value

ALAN MONTEFIORE

"It is understood," stated the circular sent out to the members of this colloquium on value, "that our task is to define Value, and this is obviously a philosophical undertaking." Just what one might expect of a definition of *value* is perhaps less obvious. In fact, the great majority of participants preferred to avail themselves of the licence not to address themselves directly or explicitly to this task granted by the following paragraph of the circular: "Members should not allow themselves to be confused or distracted by overarching considerations. They should avail themselves of the greatest freedom in proceeding, and not hesitate to leave Value implicitly in their work . . . while they state, discuss or criticise the values that prevail in their field(s)." The participants did very largely prefer to take for granted whatever meaning they attached to the terms value or values. That is, they preferred to make use of it in their discussions rather than submit it to any direct analysis.

A titularly professional philosopher, however, called upon to make his contribution under the title of "Value" itself, cannot properly proceed in this way. Does this mean that he should be expected to offer some very general definitional formula? If so, he might very well start with the suggestion, for example, that positive values be taken to be whatever give positive meaning or point to any object, state of affairs, activity, or institution that people, consciously or unconsciously, explicitly or implicitly, individually or collectively, may treat as good, important, useful, interesting, obligatory, beautiful, and so forth, and that value itself be taken as being whatever is the common or family characteristic of these. (Negative values, this reasoning might continue, could be treated in an appropriately mirror-image-like fashion.) The trouble with this or any such suggestion, as John

Wilson in effect points out in his chapter, is not so much that it is somehow mistaken but that it is far too broad and too generally indeterminate to be of any particular use. If, on the other hand, one is seeking to make clear the variety rather than the general structure of value or values, then it seems that any overall problem of definition simply gives way to so many particular problems of what may be involved in counting something as good or beautiful or interesting or important. It is, doubtless, nearly always worthwhile to look for greater linguistic precision. But if we are seeking to learn something beyond the illumination that good dictionaries can bring, we may do better to try a different approach.

Another very respectable opening move might be to present some sort of survey of the latest philosophical works on the general nature of "value." But quite apart from the fact that such a survey might be an exercise of considerable tedium for all those already familiar with this literature, to follow it through with even minimum adequacy would inevitably take up more than all the available space. So let us instead, as a third possibility, start in the classically philosophical way by turning first to the problem of how we should understand the relationship between a conscious subject on the one hand and the world of which it may take itself to be conscious on the other, and then to the further problem of how, in the light of that understanding, we may see "value" as entering into the picture.

It is important, of course, in this philosophical day and age, that major questions should not simply be begged through an abrupt introduction of the subject. The time of pure Cartesian primacy as the ultimate foundation of knowledge and even of meaning has by now almost certainly receded into the past; contemporary questions turn rather on whether, in what sense, and to what degree it may even be altogether eliminable from theories of language, meaning, or knowledge. Nevertheless, we may still begin with this relationship between the conscious subject and the world as object of its conscious awareness inasmuch as it is a relationship within the terms of which we already find ourselves included by virtue of our very raising of any such questions; and it is a leading feature of these already given terms of reference that the conscious subject of experience and of inquiry must presume itself able to pick out, to recognize, and to describe and report (both to itself and to others) certain features or states of the world of which it is thus aware. No recognition (no re-cognition, we might insist in a slightly different context of concern), no consciousness, at any rate, no consciousness aware of itself as such—the argument is at least as old as Kant. Moreover, if acts of recognition are to be possible, it must also be possible to make some very broad distinction between the identification or recognition of some feature or state of the world, in short of a fact, and the formation of affective attitudes that the recognizing subject may have to whatever he or she recognizes. For the ability to handle concepts of any kind, the first and foremost concepts through which items are recognized as being of some sort, depends on the acknowledgement of the existence of certain "objective" constraints on the subject's use or application of them. (This argument, if its origins are at least as old as Kant, has in our century been powerfully renewed by Wittgenstein, with his attack on the idea that a purely private, individual subject-created language might be possible.) Thus the acceptance of some sort of distinction between the facts of how things may be and any attitude that I, the conscious speaker or subject, may or may not have towards them is written into the enabling conditions of any explicit self-consciousness or of any language whatsoever. So if we like, provisionally, to assign the term *value* to everything that stands on the attitudinal side of this distinction, we may now rechristen it the divide between fact and value. And we may further affirm that there can in principle never be any logically compelling passage or inference from the first to any version of the second. Indeed, on this account, the term *value* actually derives its characteristic sense by way of this contrasting comparison with *fact*.

A view of this sort cannot be taken as in any way definitive of Western culture as such. Both this view and this very general, overall use of the term *value* are, on the contrary, distinctly modern phenomena. And although such a view is indeed found vigorously and even dogmatically restated, it has in fact in recent years been brought once again under wide and exceedingly diverse attack. The strength of this reaction has been indisputable. But, it may very well be asked, if the distinction between recognitional diagnosis and affective or prescriptive attitude is indeed a constitutive presupposition of meaningful self-consciousness itself, how can this renewed assault on the distinction be regarded as anything other than a (doubtless very sophisticated) retreat towards a state of more or less wilful confusion?

The rest of this chapter offers a sketch of an answer to this question through the use of another classically philosophical device—that is by a story of openly mythical origins. Once upon a time, we may suppose, all the men and women in the world of our story lived in one homogeneous community—they all spoke the same language, lived and worked within the common institutions of a shared socio-economy, followed the same religion, and observed the same customs in their dealings with one another. The children of this community, of course, at a very early stage of their lives, and like the children of any other society, had to learn its language as a necessary condition of being full social participants in it. As a condition of their acquisition of language and of the ability to communicate with others through the use of meaningful symbols, at the same time they had to learn to distinguish between their purely personal inclination to produce any given mark or sound on any particular occasion and their recognition of its acceptability to others as appropriate to the relevant context of would-be communication—to distinguish, as one might say, between ("subjective") will or desire and ("objective") reality with all its constraints. There were, moreover, other reasons why this was a lesson which they could not avoid learning. Some were reasons of evolutionary survival: those who cannot distinguish between reality and their own desires are in no position to adapt to the "reality" of the situations in which they may find themselves, and those who cannot adapt are in no long-term position to survive. For reasons of psychological survival, those who cannot distinguish between their own desires and the "reality" of their situations are in no position, even in the short term, to pursue the deliberately effective satisfaction of their own desires. And as to further conceptual reasons, to repeat the reference to Kant and Wittgenstein, it is a presupposition of any form of conceptualized self-awareness that the conscious subject should be able in principle to distinguish between its own conscious "perceptions" and that "objective reality" to which most of those perceptions will refer, a "reality" the "objectivity" of which must consist in its being whatever it is in at least relative independence of however it may appear to "the subject" at any given moment of its conscious awareness.

The language of our "original" homogeneous community had, of necessity, to allow for a distinction between the recognition and report of states of affairs or "facts" and the expression of desire—whether positive, negative, or indifferent—that the state of reported conditions should or should not obtain. The members of the community had to learn, as they learnt their own language, not only to recognize the difference between wanting something to be the case and acknowledging that it was or it was not, but and also and by the same token, to realize that their own ("subjective") preferences were logically independent of the ("objective") existence or non-existence of any state of affairs to which they might or might not be directed. The "facts" of my situation are something that I have to acknowledge; but this acknowledgement in no way commits me to either pleasure or displeasure at these "facts"—nor, for that matter, can it relieve me of all responsibility for whatever expression I may give to whatever pleasure or displeasure I may feel.

So every member of our mythical community finds himself committed as of necessity to the recognition of a range of "facts," to which, given the terms of the common language, all his fellow members must, as of equal necessity, give corresponding recognition. At the same time he has to learn to acknowledge his own desires, his own likes and dislikes, as aspects of himself rather than as features of his surrounding circumstances, which are the "facts" of what other people like or dislike, prefer or demand. (There is, no doubt, an important sense in which his *own* preferences, likes, and dislikes may also confront him as "facts" over which, in the short term at any rate, he may have relatively little control; but then at that higher level of reflection, which, as philosophers such as Henry Frankfurt and Charles Taylor have argued, is a distinguishing characteristic of such language-using creatures as men, he is no way committed by the "mere" fact of their existence to liking or disliking his own relatively lower-order likes or dislikes.) Moreover, he is confronted with the preference, demands, and expectations of others, not only as facts about other assignable individual members of the community; he has also to recognize and adjust to the facts both of collective demand and of standard expectation and "evaluation"—of all those norms of preferential approval, of hierarchical ordering, and of role-determined prescription that structure the community's way of life, which the community transmits to him, as to all its members, through the mediation of its own characteristic institutions.

If our story were told at anything like an adequate length, it would have to include several chapters on the nature and evolution of these institutions—customary, familial, social, religious, and legal.

(In one evident sense, the most fundamental of these "institutions" must necessarily be language and discourse, in whatever forms they may take in our particular community. For the meaningful use of symbols is essentially normative, and the individual participant in language cannot avoid reference to "objectively" inter-subjective norms of appropriate and inappropriate usage by virtue of his very participation in meaningful discourse.) And since we are concerned with a homogeneous community its institutions would have to include the function of regulating and rendering mutually compatible, on behalf of the community as a whole, all potentially conflicting demands of its other institutions; this we may call its "political" institution—though no significance outside our story need be attached (as yet) to the name. It might quite well be, of course, that in our community the religious and political institutions, for example, were in effect one and the same; or the customary and the political, or the legal and the political, and so on. No matter; what is of consequence is that the homogeneity of the community was such that all its members recognized the same institutions as authoritative embodiments of its common purposes, preferences, and expectations; and that, since there was a built-in mechanism assuring the ongoing compatibility of all these institutional assessments and ordinances, individual members never found themselves in the position of being forced (or indeed even able) to choose or to arbitrate between their conflicting claims to rightful authority.

The importance of the roles of these institutions in the self-representation of the community to itself, and in its self-regulation in light of this self-representation, was such that each generation found it at once necessary and natural to pass on to its children a proper awareness of the crucial difference between individual preferences, expectations, and demands and those of the community itself as expressed through its network of institutions. Thus the language of the community evolved distinctive vocabularies by which to refer to or to express either the one or the other. "I want to do X" would be one thing, "I ought to do X" would be another, in reference to the expectation or demand not of this or that individual, but, ultimately, of the community itself. There would be a similar contrast between "Y is good" and "I like Y," the former being clearly understandable by any competent speaker of the language to mean that Y was to receive a high rating when measured by standards the community itself endorsed. And so on. There would even be a difference to be learnt, and to be marked out in language, between, on the one hand, the amounts of goods that particular individuals might be willing to offer in exchange for other goods, and, on the other hand, the amount that the community as a whole might recognize as its proper general exchange "value" determined by its institutions of production and exchange at any given time. (Of course, this latter lesson could hardly be taught or learnt until the community had developed some form of exchange value of any one set of goods for that of any other—that is to say, until the invention of money.)

The language of a community such as ours, must, then, be expected to allow for a threefold distinction. There will be the language of "fact," of recognition and report of all those "objective" features of situations which have simply to be acknowledged whether or not anyone likes them; there will be the language in which individuals, whether singly or in groups, may express or announce their own particular preferences, choices, and demands; and there will be the language that comes to be adapted to the expression or pronouncement of the common preferences, choices, expectations, and commands of the community itself as made known through its authoritative institutions—the language of good and evil, of obligation and permission, or morality and of beauty, of right and wrong, and so forth. This would be, of course, what we of a certain fairly recent European and European-associated culture might call the language of value(s) and evaluation. But we do not have to suppose, in the due order of the telling of our story, that the members of our once-upon-a-time community were from the beginning in the habit of classifying the different aspects of their world under such general headings as "fact," "value," and "individual preference," or the different forms of their language under "statement of fact," "value sentence," and "expression of emotive or prescriptive attitude." Rather we may suppose that as they learnt their earliest lessons of how to cope with their world and its language, they learnt how each type of affirmation was subject to its own type of validation or invalidation—recognition statements from observations made by any competent observer reckoned an equally competent judge; definitions or explications of meaning from linguistic practices common to every full member of the community; statements or expressions of individual preference by reference (where else?) to the preferences of the individual concerned and "value-judgements" from known, or ascertainable, or confidently to be presumed pronouncements of the accredited representatives of the community's authoritative institutions.

It should be noted in passing that to those individuals, whoever they were, who happened at any given time to be in the role of appropriate authority the validation of "value-judgements" would have appeared no different. For the nature of the institutions in the community was such that no individual holding a position of determining authority within them could ever think of himself, *when duly and with full self-awareness acting as such an authority*, as simply making instrumental use of the institution in the exercise of his own particular will. This is not to say that an individual might not at times seek, even consciously, to make this particular use of them; but he could not at the same time suppose himself to be acting as a genuine authority of the institution, but only—at best—as pretending to do so. (Unless, of course, his was a case of more or less self-deceived identification of his own particular interests with those of the community.)

Nor, again, were the institutions of the community thought of as any sorts of essentially independent corporations or pressure groups acting as or on behalf of associations of individual interests in competition with one another within the framework of the state. The community's institutions functioned in practise as the media through which its own communal expectations, preferences, and norms might present themselves as if they were "facts" to all its own members, both individually and when acting together in their subordinate institutional bodies.

One other thing should be noted about the relationship between the community's "values" and its institutions. Everyone, while recognizing that the "truth" or validation of "value-judgements" rested not on individual preference or choice but rather on norms or standards determined through the institutions, recognized also that institutional opinion might differ over time as to just what these norms or standards implied or commanded. Moreover, at any given time competent authorities might have considerable disagreement about the currently correct interpretation of these norms; and although they generally agreed in principle how any such provisional disagreements were to be resolved, the resolution was not always immediate. Appropriate procedures might even be designed for a delay before a properly agreed opinion might properly emerge; and during this time no one, perhaps, even the officers of the institutions, could confidently say just what the opinion would eventually be. Nor, when it did emerge, could it be guaranteed to stand for all future time. Since circumstances and opinions might change, the "facts" of "evaluation" were necessarily open to potential uncertainty and revision, just as what we might now call the "facts" of empirical observation or of scientific theory. The community's fundamental agreement on where the sources of evaluative authority lay, however, held it together in its full homogeneity.

So far, so good. But there came a time in our story when two major disturbances in the life of the community occurred, two major transformations in its very nature. First, for reasons either internal or external (into which we need not enter now), deep divisions began to appear between and within its institutions of validating authority, particularly within the institutions of political authority. These divisions went well beyond the divisions of provisional opinion, which were given time to be sorted out, that we have mentioned. The new and more intractable divisions arose rather with the appearance of rival individuals or groups, each claiming to represent the established authority responsible for the conduct of the procedures of reconciliation, and, by virtue of these claims, thus presented themselves as rival centres of political authority, each of them bound to an insistence on the illegitimacy of the other.

How was an ordinary member of this now questionably homogeneous community to react in the face of such a development? He knew, of course, how to make his own choices—to choose, for example, whether to follow the course of duty or, to the contrary, that of his own desires; but there had, naturally, never been any question of his having to make a choice about the former. But now he was faced with an altogether new sort of individual choice. Here were two rival claimants to the role of chief validating authority of "values," each, according to the other, no better than a group of individual usurpers, each claiming allegiance to itself as standing in the true line of descent for continuing community tradition. Clearly, in principle, there was no further established institution the ordinary member could use for reference to determine the choice between them, no other recourse but to decide for himself where to look for the validation of "values" from now on, and no one, in practice, to support as a validating authority. In other words, he had now to accept for himself the responsibility of deciding or choosing what his own effective "values" were to be, and there were indeed no longer any "facts"—not even the "facts" of what this apparent institution or that might lay down as constituting the appropriate norms or standards—from which he might simply deduce his own choice.

Did this transformation mean that the individual's choice of values was all of a sudden no longer subject to any sort of constraint at all? Some members of the community, either out of a certain despair at the apparent absurdity of their new situation or out of a feeling of exultation and pride in the new-found sovereign autonomy of the individual, even in the matter of his own values, argued that this was indeed the case: that it was at last plain for all to see, if they had the courage to do so, that so-called values rested ultimately on nothing more imposing or mysterious than on an individual's own preferences and demands; and that although it might often be more comfortable to disguise this fact from oneself—or more advantageous to disguise it from others—courage and honesty should lead one to openly acknowledge it. Others, while recognizing, whether with pride or regret, the logical impossibility of deliberately renouncing their evaluative autonomy, now that it had been disclosed to them, insisted that the choice of values, far from being an ordinary choice, had rather to be understood as an ever to be renewed commitment to a whole way of life, one that necessarily *ipso facto* included a settled preference, even a prescription, that the same choice of values should be made by every one else. So, argued some of this latter group, these peculiar implications of the "choice of values," taken together with the basic causal facts concerning standard human desire, constituted in their own way a set of constraints on the content of coherent choice almost as powerful as those of the old institutions themselves. Yet others, more sensitive perhaps to the manifold ways the existing language of values was still rooted in a whole complexity of procedures for determining their validation, other than by reference to the preferences or choices of any individual or group of individuals as such, continued to argue that the standards and norms to which they referred must be regarded as given either by the meanings of the relevant terms, or by long-standing traditional understanding, or by ideal consensus, or by the purposes implicit in the appropriate realms of characteristic human activity, or by some combination of any or all of these.

This first major disturbance to the ordered homogeneity of the community was caused, then, by emerging rival centres of "political" authority, each claiming, against the claims of the others, the sole allegiance of the community in all matters of "value" and hierarchical respect. The second major disturbance to its settled order came with its first serious encounter with the existence of other communities with notably different languages and patterns of life. Our community had not up to then lived in total isolation or in simple ignorance of the fact that it was not the only community in the world; but occasional external transactions with other communities, whether in casual trade or in war, had not hitherto led it really even to consider whether these other communities might have their own particular perspectives on life. In a more serious encounter, the arrival of powerful strangers seeking (implicitly or explicitly) to make the community aware of just what was involved in *their* own very different way of life, made it realize that not only individuals might differ in their personal interests or what they considered was important, but that those differences might also exist between communities. Indeed, these differences seemed to find expression in their languages and in the very different ways in which their vocabularies and syntax seemed to structure the world.

But a simple story cannot easily reveal whether this much more serious encounter with other communities would on its own have given rise to this new realization of the possible diversity of culturally or socially sanctioned values without the parallel development of internal "political" division. However, we may certainly suppose that the two sources of disturbance worked together and on each other. In particular, the idea that different conceptualizations, even different "descriptive" classifications, of the natural and social world might have their "evaluative" as well as their "descriptive" significance in terms of the different interests and types and degrees of importance in one language community or another could only make sense to the extent that the idea also began to make sense that quite different (or rival) sources of authority might equally present themselves as sources of "objective" validation of value-judgements of one sort or another. By the same token, we may also suppose, language could start to make itself visible as itself a sort of institutional source of evaluative authority. For so long as only one language, that of one's own community, was seriously apparent, one could, of course, formulate and on occasion debate orders of interest or importance *within* the terms that it provided; but one had no perspective from which to become aware of them as constituting the terms of such debate itself. With the discovery of other languages and other terms of debate, however, a further dimension of self-recognition of "subjective" self-awareness became available.

There is one further aspect of this double development that should be included in the story. In the golden days of homogeneity, the ordinary individual might experience conflict between the norms and values of his community on the one hand, and what, on the other hand, he himself most wanted to do or most enjoyed; he might find himself disliking what the community deemed to be good, or even refuse to accept its obligations, but he would know with certainty what its norms and values were. (Or at the very least, when there *was* ever any temporary uncertainty over their precise content, he could know with certainty how that uncertainty could and would have to be resolved.) Whether in his community he might be open to adverse judgement, and of what sort, if his failure to fulfil his obligations was due to circumstances beyond his control is a question that this story must leave open. Some, of course, would argue that whatever sort of adverse judgement might be made on someone whose failure to fulfil his obligations in spite of his own best efforts could not be a "moral" judgement. (It remains questionable whether this argument is to be taken as founded on a simple definition of the term *moral*, or as relying on what may itself be seen as a fundamental moral judgement, or as depending on some intricate balance or confusion between the two.) However this may be, and however we understand the term *morality* (which is certainly not to be taken as simply synonymous with the term *value*), it is clear that when the individual member of our community found himself faced with the breakdown of institutional homogeneity and exposed to rival demands for the fulfilment of incompatible and conflicting obligations, he had either himself to assume full responsibility for determining the worth of his own conduct, or to regard himself as being unavoidably guilty and in dereliction of duty *whatever* line of conduct he in fact pursued. For he could not—*ex hypothesi*—act so as to fulfil both of two incompatible obligations at once.

How, then, was he to face this situation? Up to the time of the great disturbances, his values and obligations had always been presented to him as being as independent of his own deciding as the meanings of the words and phrases of his language as he had learnt them in his early childhood. *Within* the institutions of value validation, as we have seen, the possibility always existed of temporary uncertainty or even dispute as to exactly what judgements or practices the relevant norms might be taken to impose; but there had been neither uncertainty nor dispute as to the nature or role of the institutions within which these first-order uncertainties and disputes were to be resolved. *Now* these institutions had somehow doubled themselves as it were. And at first sight the individual might, very naturally, take this to mean that his values and obligations had also, and by the same token, taken on an irreducibly dual and self-contradictory nature.

In a situation such as this, the individual would, certainly, have to choose which values and obligations, if any, to respect and to fulfil. In so doing he would necessarily lay himself open to condemnation by the rival would-be authority whose pronouncements he had chosen to ignore or to flout. If, indeed, he had no recourse but simply to accept that his values and obligations had now somehow doubled themselves in this strangely new and self-contradictory way, he would have likewise to accept that condemnation as being, whether "fairly" or "unfairly," beyond all final institutional appeal.

One view of this state of unavoidable "sin" might be considered as definitive of the human condition, and the guilt attached to it as something only to be expunged by the grace of some altogether superior, ultra-human authority. One cannot, it goes without saying, choose actually to do that which one knows that one cannot do; and faced with incompatible demands, individuals must know that they cannot fulfil both of them. In choosing one of them to satisfy, the individual chooses the values by which he will strive to live, and *in so doing* rejects for all practical purposes the values the claims of which he has refused. It is then only a relatively small step from their rejection "for all practical purposes" to their rejection as "values for oneself." In other words, if the acceptance or endorsement of value-judgements on one's own behaviour *is* to have any practical implications, that individual must, in a situation of conflicting claims, assume his own full share of responsibility for the values by which he is to be judged; and this in turn means that one must be free and able to adopt for oneself a set of values and obligations sufficiently consistent among themselves to be in principle satisfying as a set. If "ought" is to be related in any rational way to programmes of possible action, it must indeed imply "can"; for if one were equally open to condemnation whatever one might choose actually to do, then from any overall evaluative point of view the choice would become empty and arbitrary.

It follows from all this that while an acceptance of the principle that "ought" implies "can" is not, certainly, a sufficient condition of the (individual) autonomy of values, it does figure prominently among its necessary conditions. Where a problem arises from a prima facie incompatibility of obligations or duties, the "can" can be restored only if there is some recognizably acceptable way of resolving the conflict between them, that is to say, by setting them in some hierarchical order of precedence in relation to each other. This implies the existence or construction of some common measure in virtue of which all would have their proper order of priority (the choice between those to which the measure accords an equal ranking may safely be left to be decided by individual preference alone). If the institutions provide no common measure by which to reduce their prima facie competing claims to a coherent order, then the individual himself is left with the responsibility of doing so through his own prescriptive or evaluative choice. (The institution of money may no doubt serve as a model for such a measure of interchangeable values; but what is at stake goes far beyond the values of a market economy to the roots of individual moral responsibility itself.)

Space permitting, we might have tried to follow the course of our community beyond the point of the great disturbances into a number of Borges-like branches of alternative further developments. One such development might have followed the way the pendulum swung back from the first enthusiasms and anxieties of the discovery of the autonomous role of the individual in the formation of values to a renewed insistence on their social or institutional dimension; but then how the very dis-arrangement of institutions brought about by the great disturbances clearly rendered impossible the re-establishment of a basic coherence of values, or any common measure by which all fundamental conflicts between them might be resolved. Individual choice, of whatever nature, according to this version of the story, while a necessary element in the formation of values, was not and could not be sufficient. The role of institutional reference was equally indispensable. But since the institutions had fallen into inextricable conflict with one another, and thus society with itself, the only way forward was a restructuring of society directed towards a reharmonization of its institutions with one another and of individuals with their own value commitments.

There would, of course, be many possible other branches to the story's continuation. However, we must reiterate and re-emphasise that this is just a story, and then only a story in outline. Nevertheless, although the telling has been very compressed and the ending somewhat abrupt, it must, like every good story, strive towards a moral, for which we will take one or two paragraphs more.

The moral, if indeed there is one, may be found in the (still no doubt fictional) supposition that we ourselves live in one of the further branches of the story. Everything is, of course, much more complicated than has been suggested here. We no longer live in one easily identifiable and self-identifying community, but within an overlapping, criss-crossing, highly heterogeneous number of communities with their more or less different languages, which are natural, conceptual, and ideological. But if we take our language of "evaluation," as we now have it in all its contestable variety, to have its roots in the long-ago homogeneity of our fictional ancestors and the modifications their language inevitably underwent as a result of the great disturbances, we may more readily understand the nature of the parameters within which its present usages are contained. There is the parameter of individual responsible decision and the parameter of social "fact" as transmitted through the institutionalized norms of the particular community or sub-community. There are the different ranges and types of evaluation—of approbation, obligation, importance, interest, and so on. There is the meaning of "value words or sentences" and of those of "sortal description"; and there are the forces of the speech acts that we may perform through our use of expressions in one context or another. No doubt, we will probably never achieve a total neutrality of utterance of the whole range of different possible values at once; but equally, there is no particular value from which we cannot in principle distance ourselves within an appropriately given context.

We may hope, however perfectly or imperfectly, to understand all this and much else besides—including the reasons why it is very doubtful whether the search for any overall "definition of value" can have any very direct sense. (Which is not to say that it might not have a great deal of indirect sense.) And we may even aspire to find an argument (of traditionally transcendental status) to show that in the end we shall have always to acknowledge our commitment to a certain range of values at least by virtue of their constitutive contribution to the very institutions of language and communication themselves. But whether such and argument can really be worked out without running into either ideological one-sidedness or self-contradiction, or both, is a question further exploration of which would take us well beyond the specified limits of this chapter.

Bibliography

A story may be presented as a way of stimulating the reader to possible perspectives from which to approach some part of a possible terrain. It does not, evidently, present itself as any sort of "factual" historical report, and the bibliography that follows is not, therefore, one of documentary evidence in support of the "accuracy" of "the record." The books suggested here are rather varied illustrations of one or another aspects of the story—though just how the illustrations may best be construed is left to the reader to explore and to determine for himself.

Hare, Richard M. *The Language of Morals*. Oxford: Oxford University Press, 1952.

———. *Freedom and Reason*. Oxford: Oxford University Press, 1963.

———. *Moral Thinking*. Oxford: Oxford University Press, 1981.

Hollis, Martin, and Steven Lukes. *Rationality and Relativism*. Oxford: Blackwell, 1982.

Lovibond, Sabina. *Realism and Imagination in Ethics*. Oxford: Blackwell, 1983.

MacIntyre, Alasdair. *A Short History of Ethics*. London: Macmillan, 1966.

———. *After Virtue*. London: Duckworth, 1981.

Mackie, John L. *Ethics*. Harmondsworth: Penguin, 1977.

Rawls, John. *A Theory of Justice*. Oxford: Oxford University Press, 1972.

Williams, Bernard. *Morality: An Introduction to Ethics*. New York: Harper & Row, 1972.

———. *Ethics and the Limits of Philosophy*. London: Fontana Press/Collins, 1985.

II

Moral Values in Society

Values and Society

BRYAN WILSON

It could quite plausibly be argued that "value" is the core concept of sociology. This is not to say that, today, all sociologists would accept the proposition that values are the core phenomena of every society. That the sociologist's business is values implies that a self-conscious sociological orientation necessarily differs from narrowly positivist, behaviourist, or materialist interpretations of society. Such approaches take mere external observation, raw empiricism, mechanistic measurement, and/or dogmatic determinism (biological and/or economic) as the implicit methodologies for social science, and observed behaviour (as distinct from social action), instinctivism, and the rationality of interests as its substantive data. Sociologists gradually came to acknowledge that individual behaviour, often prompted by economic or sexual motives, might be, and normally was, conditioned, if not fundamentally shaped, by quite other factors. Those other factors might be culturally transmitted or (especially in advanced societies) personally acquired; whatever their provenance, they represent arbitrary choices or value preferences that are not to be explained by or adduced from instincts, rationality, or materialism, whether invoked singly or in combination. The terms of explanation in sociology came to disavow dogmatic commitment to any rigid model of narrow or proximate determinism, and to specify certain methodological premises necessary to interpret human action. The sociologist was to recognize that his subject-matter—the people whose action he was concerned to record, relate, and explain—was irrevocably value-committed. People espoused values, and social action implied values; the sociologist was, therefore, to accept the need to acknowledge the quality of motivation, and to provide an interpretative comment on what he observed, which took account of subjective meanings (without, of course, simply accepting those meanings as final and sufficient for his own explanation).

At the same time, the sociologist, whilst taking other people's values as part of his data, took it as axiomatic that he should seek this information in a fashion that was itself value-free. Once his problem was defined, and the canons of value-relevance observed, he should seek to be ethically neutral with respect to his subject-matter. Although this principle has been attacked in recent years, it remains the only guarantee of impartiality, fairness, detachment, and objectivity in handling material that might tempt the social analyst to commitment or disavowal. An ethically neutral stance protects sociology from becoming ideology. The sociologist has to treat others' values as his facts. He seeks to be an agent of inquiry, not, either simultaneously or alternately, to be an agent for or against the values that form his subject-matter, with which he attempts to maintain a disinterested engagement.

To acknowledge the significance of values in social action and as a primary objective of sociological inquiry is, however, a different thing from believing that values constitute the distinctive core of society itself. Man is an evaluating animal, and his whole social involvement is predicated on a complex tissue of associated, reinforcing, or, at times, contradictory value assumptions and commitments. Without apprehension of values and their role in determining the individual's social acts there could be no understanding of society or its operation. At the supra-individual level, institutions espouse specific constellations of value, giving or evoking expression to particular established preferences in accord with which men are motivated, relationships are established, or organizations function. Some of these values are clearly articulated in creeds, moral codes, legal systems, charters, declarations, treaties, and the like; others remain inchoate, faintly apprehended, and only rarely or partially articulated.

In pre-literate and traditional societies, values may be premised on ignorance, prejudice, and fear (and residues of all those elements persist, in greater or lesser degree, in more self-conscious, advanced societies), but even value positions that derive from such roots may, none the less, have their functions for a society, either directly in sustaining social identity, consensus, and cohesion, or less directly in the support they afford to other fundamental values. It is not, however, my purpose to evaluate values; to declare some of them warranted and others mistaken—that would be to abandon the sociologist's brief which I have already described. We can recognize the functions of shared values without coming to judgement about the warrant for such values. In so saying, I do not suggest that positive functionality legitimates any beliefs, no matter how absurd; I merely point to the function as something independent of the intrinsic character of values, or of any judgement some external observer might wish to make about them. Thus, a religious body may be committed to certain values that have to be regularly reaffirmed by all members—internal criticism may be stifled on pain of excommunication. Western religions have been, over much of their history, in some measure committed to this position. Such values reinforce the sense of community cohesion and solidarity, and they provide the group with overt expression. The actual beliefs might be regarded as wrong-headed by everyone not a member, but, none the less, there can be no doubt about the function of those values for the life of that community.

Values, even when they are expressed in abstract terms as general orientations, do not at any given time represent a coherent system in any society. There are always divergences; processes of change introduce new values that conflict with older ones; and it is possible for some individuals to hold contradictory values. Each cluster of values can be made into a rallying cry where groups diverge, and values can be encapsulated into slogans expressive of social identity, unity, purpose, or aspiration for particular groups. We can see all this in two distinct examples. Take, for instance, the celebrated study of values by Max Weber, who sought to explain changes in value orientations in Western European societies.[1] The old situation was one in which values were traditional: work was morally approved only if it was directly productive (or spiritual); relationships were essentially personal, including authority relations; and a man's quality was intrinsic to himself, not derivative from role relationships. Europe changed: the new values were the goals of profit, achievement, and success, manifested by instrumental, cumulative, and calculable rational action, free inquiry, initiative, and time-consciousness. These values—hitherto always marginal, and at times even deviant—came increasingly to dominate the social system and to pervade the dispositions of increasing sections of the population. The process of change in values occupied a long, and an even now uncompleted, period of transfer. Older values have been steadily if not yet entirely displaced, since at times such antique values as patriotism and personal loyalty may still be powerfully invoked, sometimes in defiance of calculated rationality. The process of change is analogous to a geological formation in which the superimposed strata of values have come not to lie evenly on those below, but to have undergone with them pressures and tensions resulting in twists, faults, and outcrops, even though the broad sequence of value deposits remains clearly evident.

Or, to take a different example of the diversity of values, consider the persistence of value deviance. Articulate societies extol certain principles and virtues in which primary values are encapsulated and expressed; yet, there are segments of society that never fully embrace those dispositions. They opt out, and may even be given licence to opt out. I refer here not to those deviants who, fully embued with society's values (for example, money-making in contemporary society) find criminal means to achieve them, but to those who espouse society's values in exaggerated form or who stand out as exemplars and models of some romanticized variant of social ideals. Such were the mythic chivalrous knight, the renegade ronin of Japanese society, and, in the West, most conspicuously, the martyred saint. Ideal exemplars they might be, but their practice deviated radically from what anyone might suppose were the value commitments of the generality of men.

Thus, it is apparent that in advanced societies, value dissensus is a readily perceived phenomenon, and this may be said without regard to the conflicts that ensue from divergence of interests (principally economic interests) and differences that arise with respect to the means by which values or interests are to be realized. It need not be averred that value conflict is more of a reality than value consensus; each is necessarily present in all complex societies. Conflict over political, military, religious, educational, moral, and other issues is conspicuous in all contemporary societies, even in those that, and such is Japan, put a premium on harmony. Yet value conflict is often exaggerated by the media, whilst value consensus may often remain uncelebrated and almost concealed. In every society there is a wide area of at least silent acquiescence, to put it no more strongly, in a given spectrum of dispositions and commitments. Such acquiescence is of less moment than conflict, it persists over longer periods of time, and it requires less explicit formulation and less deliberate and less conscious acts of maintenance. But leaving aside the issue of value conflict, let me turn to the matter of value orientations and their function as agencies of social cohesion and/or integration.

The function of values for society has often been regarded by sociologists as the maintenance of social cohesion. The question, "What holds society together?" was answered by reference to shared values, a shared culture in which certain positive dispositions were maintained. In the past, those values sometimes gained symbolic expression in rituals, solemn acts of communion and incorporation that established social boundaries and reaffirmed the individual's dependence on his society as the source of his sense of identity, the place of his belonging, and the object of his responsibilities. The *locus classicus* of this thesis is in the work of Emile Durkheim, explicitly in his study of religion in aboriginal tribal society in Australia.[2] His thesis has been facilely applied by others to complex modern societies, with too little regard for the differences between the two. If we consider that the tribal Arunta numbered no more than a few hundred people, and that American society or Russian society number upwards of two hundred million, we can see that there is some need for sociologists to return to Spencer's problem about the very genus *society*. Such disparity in size is not merely accompanied by increase of complexity, but, it can be maintained, the very organization and internal structure of such specimens call for a completely different analytical framework. Durkheim sought vigorously to maintain that society was a phenomenon *sui generis* that was not to be understood by the reduction of social facts to psychological, much less to biological, levels of analysis: the whole was not only greater than the parts but was intrinsically different from the parts. One might, however, analogously maintain that advanced society is itself *sui generis*, not to be understood from small tribal communities living at a very different level of technical competence in a vastly different environment. Literacy, the harnessing of natural power, technology, automation, and electronics have virtually replaced reliance on the harnessing of purely spiritual power on which primitive peoples relied, and have, with other factors, created a new species of sociation perhaps as different from those earlier forebears as was *Homo sapiens* from some remote link in the evolutionary humanoid chain.

The simplest way of representing this difference may be to say that the so-called society of the small tribe was in fact no more than a community, a collectivity whose members were totally known to one another, and who belonged to a well-bounded, self-conscious group within which they sustained intense and persistent interaction over their entire lifetimes. The contrast with the large-scale, indeterminate, modern society is clear. Individuals are known personally to only a tiny proportion of those with whom they interact: to the rest they are merely role-players. The individual is thus virtually anonymous; his identity is dependent on all sorts of impersonal proofs and authentifications. The boundaries of the society are remote and undetectable in terms not only of kinship but even (excepting perhaps only highly homogeneous and long-insulated cultures like that of Japan) of biological inheritance. Neither ethnicity, nor language, nor shared descent, association with a specific terrain, life habits, culture, moral dispositions, nor shared values—nor even all of these together—identify a society in the modern world. We may safely doubt whether it makes sense to consider the Arunta and the Americans as merely different species of the same genus. Thus it is that I regard the concept of "community"—an ongoing, face-to-face group in which relationships are primary—appropriate to small tribal entities, and the concept "society" more fitting to modern collectivities that are, generally, organized as nation-states, or increasingly now as multination-states. Existing usage does not make it easy to establish this nomenclature, but I shall seek to reinforce the contrast by referring to attributes of the former as "communal," and of the latter as "societal."

It may very well be that the cohesion of the tribal communities Durkheim studied was dependent on shared values. In such tribes, interaction was personal and regular, often dictated by such ascribed factors as sex, age, and kinship relation. Personal comportment was prescribed by, or at least heavily informed by, shared and relatively undisputed values. The moral order, prescribing what was to be done and what was not to be done, was uncontentiously communicated and sustained throughout the whole of such a small, homogeneous grouping in which there was little differentiation with respect to function or personal predilection. As Durkheim himself was well aware, there was a profound difficulty in transmitting moral values in more complex social systems that were marked by the division of labour, the development of role relationships, and the diversity of institutional frame-works, and he devoted himself to the problem of how moral apprehensions might be communicated and shared, and the ways in which value consensus might be sustained.[3]

Value consensus, which may be normal in small tribal communities, is difficult in large-scale societies, despite the development of specialized institutions charged with the transmission and communication of values. Such an agency was formal education, of course, and as long as education remained in the hands of those whose primary orientations were religious, the communication of values remained a central concern of teaching. But even in the relatively early days of formalized education, schools themselves became vehicles for disseminating distinctive religious prescriptions, and hence for communicating some divergences of value orientations. As education has steadily been removed from the specifically religious sphere, the extent to which it even seeks to communicate fundamental values diminishes. And this becomes evident despite conscious attempts—such as that mounted in France under the Third Republic—to undertake a deliberate policy of remoralization (at a time when much of the educational system was being wrested from the control of religious orders).[4] The shift from religion to secularity in schools is but one facet of a wider process of the displacement of tradition by modernity, from what Durkheim would have called altruistic to predominantly egoistic value orientations.[5] Ultimately, the shift is from commitment to arbitrary but substantive values to self-subscribed interests and the techniques by which they may be realized. In the process, individualism comes to encapsulate one pattern of values, as Durkheim observed: one must then ask whether individualism becomes a sufficient value orientation to provide social cohesion, since, in certain respects, it has within it the seeds of its own negation. The question, however, is not whether individualism, with its attendant concerns of achievement, success, prosperity, and eventually hedonism, has become the dominant value system, but rather whether values as such function in modern society, as they are alleged to do in tribal groups, as agencies that hold the society together.

The contemporary value system of major Western societies now heavily subscribes to individualism, a philosophical orientation that implicitly if not explicitly derogates community sentiment and commitment to society (most evidently where that commitment is expressed in some form of nationalism, statism, patriotism, or ethnic allegiance). It is difficult to interpret this as other than a weakening of value consensus. Even were the members of society more or less uniformly to espouse individualism—that is to say, were it to be the substance of consensus—the intrinsic idea content of this value orientation, and the behaviour that it prescribes, must reduce active support for the collectivity and its institutions. The implication is that, if, despite the widespread espousal of a socially prescribed individualistic ethic, society holds together, then it does so less by relying on shared values than by reliance on some other agency.

The very fact that specialized agencies of moral socialization evolved, for instance in the organization of education, indicates the importance of the change in which personal and total moral commitments are transformed into technical procedures and the impersonal functioning that is required by the highly differentiated and role-articulated structure of large-scale social systems. Although education became a specialized agency for inculcating both values and information, as the specialization of society increased, so concern with the transmission of factual and technical information steadily replaced concern with moral socialization. Simultaneously, religion, too, was losing its function as an agency of moral diffusion and as the vehicle for the expression of at least an official value consensus. Today religious commitment manifests not consensus but confusion, and this in several different ways. First, most Western countries have absorbed large numbers of immigrants of divergent religious beliefs and moral practices. Second, there is a sectarian fragmentation within the dominant Western religious tradition (affecting even Catholic and Orthodox communities). Third, within the boundaries of main-line religious bodies, there are polarized attitudes not only to basic doctrines, but to life-styles and traditional morality—from libertarian abandonment of ancient shibboleths to aggressive fundamentalism, and from revolutionism to authoritarianism within the clerical profession. More important than all these variations has been the powerful process of secularization that has critically weakened the capacity of religion to act as society's moral broker or its purveyor of social values.[6]

In modern social systems, morality becomes differentially codified in different social classes and occupational categories, and the increasingly impersonal character of relationships has made technical rules more important than moral apprehensions. Various areas of social life have become steadily "de-moralized," ceased, that is, to be matters in which social value is invested. Dress, which even within the past few decades was still subject to moral stricture, is no longer of much moral concern, and is abandoned to individual preference or the exploitation of the fashion advertisers. Speech has, in large part, lost the discriminatory evaluation once put upon it: modes of address, sensitive choice of terms, and once-required courtesies are steadily eroded. Language becomes matter-of-factly the communication of computers, not the subtle, status-inflected instrument by which the nuances of social value were given expression.[7]

In law, too, similar processes are evident. The basis for legal decisions, which were once the moral sentiments of the community, are increasingly technical, utilitarian, and pragmatic demands of the social system. Strictly moral matters, such as suicide, adultery, divorce, homosexuality, and permitted degrees of marriage, have become subject to less and less regulation—until there is virtually no enforcement of morals because there is no communication of morals. There are no common moral values to enforce. That morality—the social evaluation of behaviour—should become an open issue indicates a shift in what society actually values. Such moral values as the law enshrines are merely teleological prescriptions rather than the deontological value orientations that once encapsulated the inchoate but shared revulsions and preferences of the community.

Thus, education, religion, personal comportment, and law demonstrate the diminishing value consensus—the diminishing value concern—of modern society, at least with respect to substantive values. What, then, of the argument that shared values are responsible for holding society together?

The complex processes implicit in the emergence of contemporary social systems, of which, for a time, local communities were constituent elements, cannot be entered into here. With growing technology and the steady advance of rational procedures, there have been profound shifts in human consciousness, the assumption of matter-of-fact, cause-and-effect thinking, and the need for individuals to behave and think rationally in order to negotiate their way in a rationalized social system. All these have been affected by the evolution of impersonal role structures; the differentiation and specialization of major institutional complexes; the growth of communication (in all senses of that word); the separation of work from home, and leisure from both. New theories of human behaviour have evolved, challenging the very concept of personal moral responsibility and explaining, and often explaining away, morality—a concept resurrected only to charge society, rather than individuals, with immorality. A changing sense of time and destiny has attended this development: men now make society, and make it anew. They plan the future and disregard or derogate the past and its transmitted traditions. The cornerstone of Western morality—the sinfulness and guilt of mankind—is replaced by regular indictment of the system. All these associated processes, and no doubt others, are involved in the transformation of human social organization from the local, communal, and personal to the large-scale social system. These are some facets of change in which the moralized social order gradually gives place to the technically controlled system.

Is it, then, the case that contemporary social systems are devoid of shared value orientations? No simple answer can be given, and much must depend on the level of abstraction at which values are conceived. What the modern social system does is to embrace, at a highly formal and abstract level, certain broad principles. Justice, respect for human life, personal freedom, equality before the law, certain minimal standards of living, educational opportunity—all are values that inform the constitutions and political arrangements of many Western state societies. Yet, there is a sense in which the very politicization of these moral norms, their enshrining in constitutional provisions, is itself a derogation of the ethic of responsibility. By transmuting moral desiderata into political or constitutional provisions, states may tacitly absolve ordinary individuals from the need for further moral commitment. Those aspects of moral concern that can be regulated, quantified, subject to technical criteria of assessment and implementation are embraced in legal or welfare policies; beyond them, individuals may assume indifference to moral norms, because the impersonal, objective, minimal requirements are now "automatically" met. Max Weber rightly divined, in the resistance of that early moralizing agency of Western society, the Roman Catholic church, to the development of impersonal role systems in work and economic relations, that the breakdown of personal bonds implies the breakdown of moral order,[8] hence the breakdown of control for agencies that purvey and communicate values, unless an alternative form of control be found. Then, the resocialization of extensive publics and the internalization of an ethic occurred through Protestantism: self-control in part replaced social control in the maintenance of values, and on this widely diffused self-discipline society depended both for social order and value consensus. But today, social order is sustained by different mechanisms and—where control is needed—there are new, powerful agencies of impersonal control. Beyond that there are wider areas in which pluralism and *laissez-faire* moral attitudes prevail.

The institutionalization of certain moral values, however, may in itself lead to a false impression of consensus. There is a wide and ramifying disagreement about welfare principles, the contours of human freedom, about what constitutes minimum living standards, and the implementation of equal opportunity. Consensus about very generalized but necessarily vague abstractions might be reached (although not always even there) but conflict obtains with surprising predictability regarding the substance of such abstract formulations and the implementation of value commitments. The actual moral codes by which men live in contemporary societies are highly diversified, more pronouncedly so the more heterogeneous, pluralistic, multicultural, multiracial, and multi-religious the society. It is not the shared moral apprehensions or the commitment to agreed values that hold those societies together.

Traditional societies in which the organizational superstructure depended on the generation and maintenance of personal good will, in which social experience and awareness of the real world were so little differentiated that men necessarily entertained a collective consciousness concerning them, relied on value consensus in order to function. Much more of life was directly in the hands of the participants. Values were inextricably implicated in their factual understandings, were, indeed, part of what appeared to be the facticity of the external world. Since relationships were all negotiated among known individuals, shared value commitments and a shared moral sense constituted the framework of social order and social control. Modern societies do not depend—at least not in the short run—on the unanimity of such shared apprehensions. The framework of order is guaranteed by technical procedures, elaborate structures of both a human (bureaucratic) and a technological kind. Common sentiments, the summoning of moral dispositions, and shared commitments to the social good become apparently less relevant to an order in which there are compelling procedures for eliciting support, motivating effort, mobilizing resources, controlling all untoward expression and potential disruption. There is less reliance on socializaton to distinctive values and moral exhortations, and greater expectation that men will be induced to perform their roles by a mixture of rewards and punishments, realized through a wide but interrelated variety of pecuniary, reputational, coercive, and penal devices—moral suasion plays a diminished part.

There was a phase, as we have noted, when advancing societies appeared to be likely to rely increasingly on the subtle forces of socialization and on the internalization of conscience and the education of the emotions. From the Reformation up until the early twentieth century, much effort was expended in gentling the people and the upbuilding of specialized agencies of socialization that promoted moral cohesion (from preaching to professional ethics, promoted through a wide variety of devices, of which Sunday-schools, team games, and the institution of character references were characteristic British examples). This phase has been superseded. As new techniques of social control have been developed, from such functional regulatory devices as traffic control systems, audited accountancy, certified qualifications and registrations, to police files, electronic eyes, and data banks, so there has been less dependence on techniques of socialization and the inculcation of received values. In an impersonal society, men are not held together by common value dispositions so much as by reliance on a network of technological mechanisms in which they are embraced. We are held together by the fiscal system, the examination system, mortgage arrangements, zoning laws, planning controls, exchange controls, market management, health regulations, and a criminal and civil legal code that passes increasingly from concern with morals to concern with technical issues.[9]

Of course, men still sustain values, but these are diversified and differentiated, and so do not establish societal cohesion. Indeed, when appeals are made nowadays in the name of values promoting the collective good, modern man, inured to advertising and its offers of ever-increasing gratifications, is inclined to distrust them. Civic duty, goodwill, patriotism, all of which demand personal moral commitment, are values that many quite consciously reject, and others indifferently ignore. The impossibility in impersonal, modern society of transforming the values associated with loving and caring from kith, kin, and friends to a generalized ethic of concern for (all) others allows such calls for generalized indiscriminate moral commitment to be disregarded as merely another form of official manipulation. Private values cohabit with public cynicism. Public life is sustained by technical organization rather than by value consensus. Although it may still be relatively well integrated, society is no longer cohesive. If society holds together, it does so by virtue of technically coordinated integration, which is far removed from the cohesion of consciousness in those communities that are enmeshed by shared perceptions and evaluations of life and morality. Integration has replaced cohesion.

Modern societies function, perhaps increasingly well, on the basis of technical, mechanical, bureaucratic, and role-related patterns of order. At moments of crisis and tension, leaders still have recourse to so-called overarching ideals to which society is supposedly committed ("patriotic virtue," "the motherland," "our way of life," "the national good," "the British race"). These values have their roots in ancient localism and particularism, and their application to the modern state society is strained and tenuous as their evocation and emotive power diminishes in a rationalized world. Mankind has not yet outgrown—and may never outgrow—the claims of localism and particularistic allegiances, but such claims are not readily transferred to the modern super-state.

Can society flourish without value consensus? Will technical integration suffice to hold society together? Is there no need for shared sentiments of goodwill and the deep-laid sense of common identity that transcend the minimal requirements of conforming to the regulatory frameworks of the system? Particularistic allegiances are not dead (even if they are most conspicuous in distorted form, as in football hooliganism), but are there adequate devices to summon motivation and mobilize goodwill to maintain civic order or to reinforce the politicized moralities of our times? Individualism; extensive personal mobility (social and geographic); the growth—aided by advertising—of hedonism and its attendant invitations to irresponsibility; the increasing articulation of relationships through role performances; the impersonal ownership of wealth; the mechanical techniques of social control; the future orientation that stimulates disdain for the past—all create strains under which modern social systems operate. Modern planning pursues integration in economic, political, legal, and social spheres, and individuals are manipulated as if they were machine parts (take, for example, the Common Market), but can society dispense with those older agencies that called forth the personal dispositions, commitment to order, decency, concern for others, sensitivity in relationships, and works of super-erogation on which, at some point, all sustained human interactions depend? Substantive values have been marginalized in modern society, shifted into peripheral areas of often merely personal concern. In the public sphere, rational techniques effect the replacement of substantive values, end values, by procedural values, concern with means, and the attainment of only proximate goals.

Notes

1. Max Weber, *The Protestant Ethic and the Spirit of Capitalism*, trans. Talcott Parsons (London: Allen & Unwin, 1930).
2. Emile Durkheim, *Elementary Forms of Religious Life*, trans. Joseph Ward Swain (Glencoe: Ill.: Free Press, 1954).
3. See particularly, Emile Durkheim, *Professional Ethics and Civic Morals*, trans. Cornelia Brookfield (London: Routledge & Kegan Paul, 1957).
4. Durkheim's involvement in this attempt to produce a secular morality is reflected in the posthumously published work, *L'Education morale* (Paris: Alcan, 1925) published in English as *Moral Education: A Study in the Theory and Application of the Sociology of Education*, trans. Everett K. Wilson and Hermann Schnurer (New York: Free Press, 1961).
5. Specific use of these concepts is found in Emile Durkheim, *Suicide*, trans. John A. Spaulding and George Simpson (London: Routledge & Kegan Paul, 1952).
6. On secularization, see Karel Dobbelaere, "Secularization: A Multi-Dimensional Concept," *Current Sociology* 29, no. 2 (Summer 1981): entire issue; David Martin, *A General Theory of Secularization* (Oxford: Blackwell, 1978); and Bryan R. Wilson, *Religion in Sociological Perspective* (Oxford: Oxford University Press, 1982); esp. pp. 148–79.
7. These points are placed in a wider context in Bryan R. Wilson, "Morality and the Evolution of the Modern Social System," The Hobhouse Memorial Lecture, 1985, *British Journal of Sociology* XXXVI, 3 (1985): 315–332.
8. Max Weber, *General Economic History*, trans. Frank H. Knight (New York: Collier, 1961), pp. 262–63.
9. For a discussion of changing styles of argumentation behind legal enactments, see Christie Davies, *Permissive Britain* (London: Pitman, 1975).

Bibliography

Aronfreed, Justin. *Conduct and Conscience*. New York: Academic Press, 1968.
Caporale, Rocco, and Grummelli, Antonio, eds. *The Culture of Unbelief*. Berkeley: University of California Press, 1971.
Dahrendorf, Ralf. *Class and Class Conflict in Industrial Society*. London: Routledge & Kegan Paul, 1959.
Martin, Bernice. *A Sociology of Contemporary Cultural Change*. Oxford: Blackwell, 1981.
Martin, David A. *Tracts Against the Times*. London: Lutterworth Press, 1973.
Parsons, Talcott. "On the Concept of Value Commitments." *Sociological Inquiry* 38, no. 2 (1968): 135–60.
Reiss, Albert J., Jr. *Cooley and Sociological Analysis*. Ann Arbor: University of Michigan Press, 1968.
Rieff, Philip. *The Triumph of the Therapeutic*. London: Chatto & Windus, 1966.
Weber, Max. *The Methodology of the Social Sciences*. Translated by Edward A. Shils and Henry A. Finch. New York: Free Press, 1949.
Whiteley, C. H., and Winifred M. Whitely. *The Permissive Morality*. London: Methuen, 1964.

Values and Tradition

EDWARD SHILS

In an essay on "tradition" addressing the subject of "values," I feel it in order and necessary to conjoin these two nouns. The conjunction is a more necessary one than "The Elephant and the Polish Question." They have been associated with each other for polemical purposes by people who regret the way that the world has been going. Those who, at least in principle, dislike egotism, individualism, hedonism, and the belief that human beings should pursue only pecuniary ends and seek to possess, use, and consume material things, contrast these ostensibly tangible ends with the less tangible ideal ends that are implied in the use of the term *value* in criticisms of the contemporary world. In their criticism, they imply, where they do not state explicitly, that the turning away from values is also a rejection of tradition. Tradition was the carrier of values, values were transmitted by traditions. Without values, traditions have nothing to transmit; without traditions of values, values would be inaccessible to new generations.

This rather conservative criticism is not simply an arbitrary construction. There is a connection between values and tradition which I will attempt to elucidate.

I

A "value" may be the object of an act of evaluation, it may be the symbolic configuration of the object of striving, that is, an ideal state or condition that an actor wishes to attain, or it may be an ideal state or condition that is adduced as a criterion or standard in the assessment of an existing or possible state or condition. A value might be a component of an action, an evaluative attitude, or orientation of action. These several meanings of the term *value* are not identical; they are, however, closely related to one another. Throughout this chapter I shall use the term *value* to refer to all of these, the common feature being the status of a symbolic configuration that is neither physical nor psychic. The symbolic configuration to which the term *value* refers has an objective existence—not a physical or neurophysical existence. It has the same objectivity as a proposition of logic or mathematics. Whether already embodied in a physical object or condition, like an existing town or garden, or an existing social pattern, like a particular family or a circle of friends or a university; whether it is an ideal state to be striven for or an ideal that is a standard in judging existing things—like the idea of a university which can serve as the ideal pattern when a particular university is being established; or whether it is an ideal translated into a norm or standard that is applied in assessing a particular social condition like the distribution of income or political authority—it is a symbolic configuration.

It is important to hold fast to the distinction between the object, whether it is a human being, a social arrangement, or a physical object in which the value is embodied or to which it is attributed, and the value itself. The value is not a "psychic state" or "attitude" or "orientation," although it functions as a value insofar as it enters into any one of these. Values are thus constituents of actions and assertions, but they are constituents drawn from the objective realm of symbolic configurations.

Is every object of human desire a value? Is a state of gastric satiation; of dermal pleasure; of sensual gratification; of exhilaration in the destruction, in a state of rage, of a physical object; or in the torture of another human being—a value? Each of these states could incorporate a value if in fact a value as a symbolic configuration has entered into the action that had led to it. Such an evaluative symbolic configuration does not always do so: there is a gradual shading off between a purely physiological abreaction and the presence of an evaluative element.

Is the pleasure of a politician in the exercise of power or in his incumbency in a role or office where power is exercised a value? Is the striving to acquire material objects, or the striving to acquire wealth and to own landed property a value? Is the desire for high social status or for the receipt of deference and submission from others a value? These questions are ordinarily, at least by implication, answered negatively by those who regret the "valuelessness" of the turmoilsome, agitated activities of the modern world. Their judgement would, however, be inconsistent with the implications of the definition given here. Hedonism, "materialism," and individualism are, in my view, designations of a set of attitudes or orientations in which there is definitely an evaluative element: a symbolic configuration has been assimilated into these attitudes and the actions that could realize them. Hedonism and individualism, social snobbery and partisan political activities do contain ideals. They have been at various times elaborated into "philosophies," that is, a set of abstract conceptions regarding the "good life." They serve to legitimate and to guide action. They are as much values as the values contained in the philosophies of asceticism or puritanism or collectivism or socialism; they are as much values as the values contained in egalitarianism or civility.

It is an error to think that only evaluative ideals contained in the world religions are values, that is, to believe that only the ideals and standards of assessments and the objects, conditions, and social arrangements in which such ideals are embodied, derived from world religions, antiquity, or the Middle Ages, are values and that all other ideals and standards of assessment belong in some evaluative vacuum, in some residual category of meaningless strivings. It is quite another matter to decide which of these values are more valuable and which less so.

There are primary values and secondary values. There are fundamental values and derivative values. Primary values are those to which primary importance or decisiveness is attributed by those who hold to them; secondary values are those to which less weight is attached by those who espouse them. In cases of conflict secondary values are treated as dispensable. Fundamental values are those that are pervasive among derivative values either through logical deduction or a sense of fittingness or appropriateness.

Although values have an objective existence, they are frequently ambiguously perceived. Values do not formulate themselves; they have to be formulated by human beings. The capacity for precise formulation is a rare gift and the sense of need for precise formulation is not widely experienced. The vagueness with which values are ordinarily perceived when they are incorporated into decision and action holds in check the tension that might arise if attempts were made to formulate them exactly.

II

Here I would like to assert that there are numerous substantively heterogeneous values. Values do not form a harmonious and logically unified pattern. A system of values, a hierarchy of values is definitely a logical possibility. However, in the nature of values as symbolic configurations the ideals and the standards derived therefrom do not necessarily have to be consistent with one another, they do not necessarily form a hierarchy of values subsumed logically under a central value which is superordinated over derivative and secondary values.

Some values are incompatible with one another. Universal benevolence towards all human beings and affirmation of the equality of all human beings are incompatible with the ideal of solicitude and care for one's family, or solidarity with one's occupational or social class, or devotion to one's national state one's nationality, or one's ethnic group. Devotion to the ideal of the universal diffusion of scientific truth is in conflict with the attribution of very high values to the autonomy and integrity of one's national collectivity.

These conflicts among particular values are not continuous; they arise whenever they are integrated into decisions or attitudes simultaneously. Choices have to be made in such situations when the different actions into which the values are to be incorporated come into conflict with one another in the sense that both actions cannot be realized simultaneously. Not all values are inconsistent with one another and they are not inconsistent with one another under all circumstances.

Ordinarily, human beings do not think of fundamental values; in times of crisis, however, they tend to do so more frequently. On those occasions, they are more apt to become aware of the conflicts of fundamental values and they make their choices in accordance with the exigencies of the situation, which usually entails a renunciation of one or more of the fundamental values for the sake of holding to another. People often do not experience this renunciation as a conflict; it just seems to be the right thing to do.

III

The conflicts of values experienced by individuals are rendered supportable by the vagueness of the values in their incorporation into action; they are not precisely articulated. Calculations of expediency and of principle are seldom made with the precision of an arithmetic operation. Values in their vagueness support diffuse general orientations in action; they are more like affective moods than exact declarations and affirmations of clearly delineated ideals and standards.

Values are acquired through the exemplification and recommendation offered by elders; they are taught in schools both through explicit instruction, and by the overtones in the substance of what is taught—especially in literature and history; they are supported by their exemplification in the conduct and affirmation in the words of coevals. There is undoubtedly no inclusive, comprehensive consensus in any society that is differentiated by occupation and style of life, by region and by linguistic usage. No consensus includes everyone in such a society; no consensus comprehends all the values that are accepted by its members. Yet there is considerable consensus as the occasion arises, regarding many fundamental and primary values.

There is also a similar consensus downward through time. In this manner tradition moves directly from one generation to another in a zigzag-like line. It also moves across generations from the remoter past into periods separated by a sequence of generation. In the former cases, it moves orally as well as in writing and by example and emulation; in the latter it moves by writing, by the presence of monuments, books, works of art, names of places, buildings, and songs. These different modes of the movement of traditions of values are intertwined with one another.

Human action without values, with reference to objetive symbolic configurations does certainly occur, but it is only a relatively narrow band of the variety of human actions. Sometimes values are elaborated and given a novel form by individuals of great originality, of charismatic insight and of extraordinary imagination. But this originality in the creation of new values—of new ideals and standards—is extremely rare. Yet human beings cannot live without values any more than they can live without speech. They can no more create their own values than they can create their own speech. Indeed they must acquire them from others. The body of values, the stock of objective symbolic configurations, is the tradition or the traditions of society.

Human beings accept tradition because they cannot do anything else but accept it. They need tradition because they need what it offers and because they cannot create for themselves what it offers. This does not mean that the values accepted over the course of generations—the traditions—do not change. On the contrary, they are in almost incessant change and in some periods they change more than in others.

The changes in values are often not changes introduced by individuals of great originality. They occur because, for one reason or another, existing values have become unsatisfactory and variants of those values become more attractive. The variants and the distinctively different fundamental values are a part of the variegated stock of values—of ideals and standards—existing at any one time in any differentiated society. There are always some values that are alternative, not always sharply or disjunctively alternative, to those that are the objects of consensus, the objects of the centre of the society.

The changes in values accepted in a society are sometimes called "revolutionary changes," sometimes "total changes" or "fundamental changes." In fact they are none of these. They are part of the stock of values previously accepted by fewer persons that have become accepted by many more; they have thereby become more visible, persuasive, and impose more on other people. They have penetrated into the centre of society and emanated with amplified force from there.

Changes in values are fostered, moreover, by the fact that their acceptance is not wholly univocal. There is frequently some ambivalence, some marginal uncertainty in the affirmation of values. This uncertainty and the ambivalence are kept in check by the reinforcement of the preponderant values by the power of the current consensus and the authoritativeness of the tradition espoused in that consensus.

With the turn to the variant values goes a turn towards variant traditions. Human beings need not only values, they need traditions as sources of values—"ready-made" for them—and as legitimations of their values. Tradition is such a legitimatory power. The fact that values are recommended by a tradition adds to their persuasiveness; the consensus of coevals is not quite enough, despite the appearance to the contrary in present-day Western societies.

Traditions are not ornamental epiphenomena, "afterthoughts," or justifications *post facto* for what one would in any case have done entirely without them. There are certain instances in which tradition plays such a part, but it does not preponderate. Many human beings really "believe in tradition"; they really do think that the traditionality of a value confirms its validity.

There is another variable that affects the stability and change of values, namely, the situation of the centre of society. When internally harmonious, the centre of society—the earthly rulers and powers, the custodians of the symbolic configurations—exhibits the values which are prevalent and reinforces them in the way in which tradition reinforces them. When the different parts of the centre fall out with one another, when they espouse alternative and even clearly conflicting values, the attachment of the rest of society to those values—to those ideals and standards—falters. When the centre of society is ineffectual, lacking force of character and action, the ambivalence in the attachment of the rest of the society becomes more pronounced. The internal heterogeneity of the values hitherto accepted by individuals receives different accents or emphases from those given to them before. When a part of the centre to which authoritativeness is attributed changes its attitude towards the prevailing currents or strands of tradition and attaches itself to an alternative current that carries values declared inimical or hostile to those hitherto prevailing, the hitherto effective authoritativeness of the tradition is impaired.

IV

I wish now to return to the observation made at the beginning of this chapter about the goodness of tradition and values. Are they in themselves sufficient guides to conduct? Has a society said to have discarded them gone badly astray?

Of course, values are indispensable guides to conduct. No human conduct above the level of an animal baseness is possible without them. But having said that, it becomes clear that values, any values, are not enough. There are right values and wrong values, and the only way we can decide which are the right ones and which are the wrong ones is on the basis of more primary, more fundamental values. Even if we penetrate to those further levels, we have no solution awaiting us. The fundamental values are not in harmony with one another. It is not a question of "some people prefer one thing, and others prefer another"; relativism is not at issue. Much more important is the fact that the fundamental values that have been discovered by many powerful minds, and that have passed through long chains of tradition, at each link subjected to the experience of the human race in a number of great civilizations, represent ideals that are not concurrently realizable if they are realizable at all on any significant scale, which is to say, in the conduct of large parts of any large society.

No revelation thus far has resolved this difficulty. Revelations draw some of their effectiveness through their putting completely aside those values that are not in some way affected with sacrality. Excogitating rationality can do no better. Excogitating rationality cannot find a standard or criterion more ultimate than all other standards and which can order those subordinate standards.

Can tradition do more than this? I fear that it cannot do much more, if any more at all. It has the advantage of having arisen out of and having been tried by experience. Although it has that increment of authority which comes with long existence (or persistence), it has, in fact, carried forward in time all these irreconcilable values. If it is not deflected or deformed by ratiocinative rationality with its tendency towards formalized dogmatism or doctrinaire constructions, it allows for flexibility and for the softening of distinctions.

Extreme clarity in the formulation of values can be dangerous to society. It might be an intellectual exercise which merits admiration when excellently done but it is not likely to have any practical benefits. It is unlikely to make action more effective, or, if it does, that effectiveness is short-lived when the costs in terms of other values have to be paid. It is, moreover, likely to further conflict in society between the beneficiaries of the decision to carry out to the full a single fundamental value and those who have to pay the price. Furthermore, many of the beneficiaries of the realization of the single value might become disillusioned with what they have received.

A society in which certain particular values are espoused and incorporated into action and where certain particular traditions are respected will be a better one than societies that cultivate and pursue other values and respect other traditions. It is the respect for certain particular values and certain particular traditions that makes a relatively good society—assuming that the magnitudes of the realization of the values and the observance of the traditions too can be assessed in a plausible manner.

In closing let me say that reasonableness—listening to arguments for values other than our own, weighing respectfully traditions other than our own, and appreciating the value of our own values and traditions—respecting revelation and reason might reduce the agony of this irreconcilability of primary and fundamental values and might reconcile us to the ambiguity of our greatest ideals.

Bibliography

Burke, Edmund. *Reflections on the French Revolution.* London, 1790.
Halbwachs, Maurice. *Les Cadres sociaux de la memoire.* Nouv. ed. Bibliothèque de philosophie contemporaine, 1925.
———. *La Mémoire collective.* 2ième ed. Bibliothèque de sociologie contemporaine, 1968. (Published in English as *The Collective Memory.* Translation by Francis J. and Vita Y. Ditter. New York: Harper & Row - Colophon, 1980.)
Pieper, Josef. *Tradition als Herausforderung.* Munich: Piper Verlag, 1963.
Polanyi, Michael. *Personal Knowledge.* London: 1958.
———. *Science, Faith and Society.* Chicago: University of Chicago Press, 1964.
Shils, Edward. *Tradition.* London: Faber & Faber, 1981.
Toennies, Ferdinand. *Custom: An Essay on Social Codes.* Translated by A. Farrell Borenstein. New York: Free Press of Glencoe, 1961.
von Hayek, Friedrich. "The Three Sources of Human Value," L. T. Hobhouse Memorial Trust Lecture, 44. London, 1978.
Weber, Max. "Science as a Vocation." In *Essays in Sociology.* Translated by H. H. Werth and C. Wright Mills. London: Routledge & Kegan Paul, 1948.

Merit

J. DUNCAN M. DERRETT

> True success seems to be effort and achievement without any reward. It is as bad as true kindness or honest advice or anything else of that kind.
>
> Ivy Compton-Burnett, *Daughters and Sons*

To facilitate an understanding of "merit," an extremely paradoxical entity, I will begin with some cursory remarks on the nature of it. Merit, as the history of the word suggests, is earned, and earned by service; but not all service is meritorious, since to be meritorious service requires a judge of merit, and this judge is not free either to regard all service as meritorious or to construct his own scale whereby he can assess relative merit arbitrarily, still less predictably. In other words, there are inarticulate rules that govern the existence of merit; and there are other rules that govern the degree of overtness permissible to that judge's recognition of merit. These rules, which change in particular but not in principle, are of biological origin, and are therefore necessary to man and hence ubiquitous. One discovery follows: that, although merit is earned, it is not earned in pursuance of any contract or other bilateral arrangement. It is imputed to the earner and can never be created by him. Yet, although merit does not arise out of contract, service is tantamount to an offer to serve that judge, and his ratification of service as meritorious amounts to an acceptance, hence the bilateral quality of merit. The judge opts to recognize the merit (service). The phenomenon of "unrecognized merit" arises where one who is not the judge assumes, in his imagination, that judicial function and believes he would have imputed merit (or would have merit imputed to him) if he, or one like him, were the judge. Logically, merit would exist if someone could recognize it and does not: if one can recognize it, merit must pre-exist the recognition. But this is not so. It is the recognition that turns service into merit.

I

In all ages people have denominated, or not, others as meritorious. Merit cannot be detected in B (even by B himself) until A has proclaimed it. Merit is not a subjectve quality. Value is not self-determined, whatever one may think. This is shown by Shakespeare in *Troilus and Cressida*:

> Troilus: What's aught but as 'tis valued?
> Hector: But value dwells not in particular will,
> It holds his estimate and dignity
> As well wherein 'tis precious of itself
> As in the prizer. 'Tis mad idolatry
> To make the service greater than the god,
> And the will dotes that is attributive
> To what infectiously itself affects,
> Without some image of th'affected merit.[1]

And merit is subject to change apart from the opinion of the seeker after it. Anthony Trollope illustrates this:

> She could tell herself with pride that her conduct towards him had been always such as would become a lady of . . . fine feeling. She knew that she had deserved well of him, and that in all her intercourse with him . . . she had given much and taken little. She was the last woman in the world to let a word on such a matter pass her lips; but not the less was she conscious of her merit towards him.[2]

This quotation befits the arranged marriage system in which a true meeting of minds might not occur. A Western lady who now cherished such an attitude would be classed as "self-righteous" and "condescending." The selfish superiority she revealed would not be admirable but pitiable. For this quality of "a lady" is becoming more and more obsolete, and with it its values. Yet the conception of merit, and of relative evaluation of merit, remains. Our vocabulary often protects many a term from scrutiny, and its concept as well. Let us try to unwind merit, and see what actually happens when an individual who pleases others receives, in any age or clime, their accolade. Merit often seems to demand recognition. Such was the case with Coriolanus. But Shakespeare (as so often) identifies succinctly what may nullify the demand.

> So our virtues
> Lie in th' interpretation of the time,
> And power, unto itself most commendable,
> Hath not a tomb so evident as a chair
> T'extol what it hath done.³

Some performances would be declared meritorious but the performer is subject to reservation; in other words there are qualifications, sometimes hidden, which permit of one's services being recognized. A humble demeanour is helpful. Again, in a conservative society the acquisition of merit by a person from a low class would constitute a problem and Coriolanus may serve as a paradigm. To rate him as highly as he rated himself would upset the established order and throw a shadow over the hierarchy, whose own merits the society did not pause to examine.

II

When X enters into a contract to teach and is paid at the market rate, his teaching cannot be considered meritorious. But if he performs duties beyond his contract accepted by the beneficiaries, any deficiency of payment is a ground for merit in his favour. Pay thus excludes merit.⁴ If he is thanked effusively (that is, if his merit is overtly recognized) his merit balance is diminished. The thanker's need to thank him arises from a sense of humiliation whereby he would otherwise recognize himself, and would be recognized by others, as a debtor. The meritorious person places any non-thanker in a humiliating position. The golden "handshake" is not pay, but it eases the employer's conscience. There are situations in which such "payments" are impossible; then the meritorious person's prestige is impregnable. Where, for example, pious books are written and sold at no profit, the reader who benefits from them suffers a prestige imbalance: the writer is meritorious in relation to his reader, and there is no means of equalizing matters, hence, as we shall see, arises the valuable metaphor of spiritual merit: there is One, or Something, that will equalize matters invisibly. This mightily eases the conscience of non-thankers, non-reciprocators.

The sense of inferiority, as a hurt, is as old as Cain and as Esau. Merit is fugitive and may flow back and forth. It can even be a service to prevent others from feeling inferior. And an excessive subsidy to an artist may diminish his merit if his productions are to be judged meritorious in relation to their quantity as well as their quality. The flattering obituary is an interesting phenomenon, for the deceased cannot be burdened with gratitude for the lies told about him. Its explanation may lie in the newsworthiness of the dead: readers have preconceived notions and expectations that an objective writer would certainly disappoint: therefore "to speak of the dead nothing but good" is not a mere superstition; it serves a journalistic purpose in which, as it so often does, flattery of the reader figures.

Inadequately recognized merit tends to arise where the obvious, potential recognizers, being psychologically threatened (feeling "inferior"), cannot recognize the subject's merit overtly—at least until he dies. Third parties may be aware of a rating that their own "security" admits in this subject's favour, so his merit is not totally unrecognized; he is deprived of overt recognition as a penalty for threatening the recognized judges. Recognition of unreal merit occurs where sycophants (whom leaders need), who are often very near the source of recognition, support the recognizers where they are insecure. That is a service. Again preceptors overpraise the merits of their pupils whose advancement would tend to elevate their preceptor. Not dissimilarly, preachers who would be ashamed to beg for themselves beg most eloquently on behalf of charities with which they have identified themselves, thus enhancing their own prestige. The public is aware of "true merit," that which threatened people cannot recognize, and that which interested parties cannot advertise, at least without incurring detection.

> For who shall go about
> To cozen fortune, and be honourable
> Without the stamp of merit? Let none presume
> To wear an undeserved dignity.
> O that estates, degrees, and offices

Were not deriv'd corruptly, and that clear honour
Were purchas'd by the merit of the wearer.[5]

It is the retired (unless their judgements fail) who are consulted on proposed "recognition." They at once eliminate the majority, the good but unmeritorious, and proceed to put aspirants in a so-called order of merit. Recognition from abroad is very helpful to such judges: foreigners are less easily threatened and less easily hoodwinked.

The thirst for recognition, for rescue from anonymity, is ubiquitous. If people can discover no other means of distinction they will file their teeth into points. If this become a fashion their search for uniqueness is jeopardized. Hence the fashion industry. A sportsman may be knighted, a poet awarded the Order of Merit, institutions of public standing confer honours, memberships and so forth; there is no unitary scheme for recognizing merit. If a tribe possesses only one top hat it may be a claim to chiefship to wear it—and woe betide anyone who monkeys with that hat! A jockey may be "honoured," in spite of his never having been underpaid, because the government wishes to be thought to be interested in achievement in various fields dear to electors. Civil servants, particularly diplomats, obtain knighthoods abundantly, and they will never have been inadequately paid. Selfless devotion beyond the requirements of duty will not be the cause of their honours. The same applies to the armed services. Outstanding achievement is incidental in their cases, but never intentional; thus the Kantian idea of merit resulting from *intention* and *duty* is belied. One is under no obligation to try to become a major-general, and one cannot intend to become one. One can intend to be killed by a train, but not to obtain a merit rating.

The poet who is honoured, though he has been silent for long, is another puzzle. Has he outlived his rivals and ceased to disgrace himself? I once saw an aged poet and a decrepit sculptress receive honorary degrees. Both were honouring the university by accepting what was of no real value, recognizing a status no one had doubted. They had, in fact, lived self-indulgent lives, never having any sense of serving anyone but themselves—their imputed merit coincided with the public's feeling of inadequacy in not having publicly thanked them. It is untrue that merit presupposes *exertion* or *application*: humanity is aware of profiting from intuitive and reflex actions on the part of genius.

State honours may appear quixotic.[6] The MBE may be refused from the hands of those who ought (in the honorand's opinion) to have offered more. It was awarded to the Beatles for a few years' lucrative singing, and to a "tramps' parson" who had lived in total self-denial for a half-century: What is equal in this? The former caused their fellow citizens to gain foreign exchange; the other supported, and therefore sustained, unworthy penury. The ratings are hard to account for. F. Max Müller refused a British knighthood but accepted a Privy Councillorship; to be called *Herr Geheimrat* was an honour he would gladly have accepted in his homeland. The public feels bound to acknowledge a service it wishes to impute to itself; it is a retrospective, and sometimes even a posthumous patronage. This may be the reason why overt recognition is so important; and the meritorious may be justifiably concerned to be correctly recognized, whatever their factual achievement may have been.

Sir Winston Churchill could not be honoured by any amount of "recognition." For his undoubted services no one could remunerate him. Was his exceptionally solemn funeral related to this? Lesser mortals would be humiliated not to have recognized his services, and he was compelled to bear this as an honour. He could not but accept what others thrust upon him to relieve themselves of the humiliation of obligation.

> You shall not be
> The grave of your deserving; Rome must know
> The value of her own. 'Twere a concealment
> Worse than a theft, no less than a traducement,
> To hide your doings, and to silence that
> Which, to the spire and top of praises vouch'd
> Would seem but modest . . .[7]

Thus the truly great have greatness thrust upon them.

It is curious that one can persistently refuse to ascribe merit, although undoubted services have been rendered at a sacrificial rate. No one honours nuns for praying. Nurses are customarily badly paid. This arouses no sense of guilt, except in the "grateful patient." A worker may be refused recognition until he is dead, whereupon praise is smartly accorded, as if the judges felt guilty. Why are people beatified or sanctified long, sometimes very long, after their deaths? Is it because another arrangement (unless the individual's sanctity can be put to direct financial advantage) would be disconcerting to the non-blessed and non-sanctified brothers and sisters? Competition for this kind of recognition is, unlike other insignia of status, regarded as incompatible with the purpose. So beatification and sanctification do not refer to the merits of any living person. Further, the merits of innovative workers, who put subsequent generations into their debt, alarm rather than encourage their contemporaries. All these cases must be capable of explanation.

III

Would it help to compare merit and prestige? Who has prestige? Prestige can be detected even in those to whom no overt recognition of merit is awarded. The best example is "mother," who, until recently, was uniformly respected because her services far outweighed any remuneration offered or even capable of being offered to her. Her case was the paradigm of spiritual merit, that is, a merit not demonstrated tangibly, and therefore in some invisible sense available to her as a kind of compensation for the want of adequate recognition of her merit. Prestige, which is not demanded, or earned, but accorded (more often from below than from above), depends, it appears, on unremunerated services. Prestige is increased in proportion as the services are unremunerated. Competitions to discover beauty queens used to be merely comical: for while in the masculine sphere of activity prestige-worthy people demonstrate their relative ranks by wearing things on their heads in processions; in this feminine sphere, beauty queens do nothing whatever to deserve distinction beyond opting (as women readily do) to be looked at.

If nursing were paid at a rate commensurate with the patients' appreciation it would lose its merit by the same proportion as the nursing profession gained in power. And those who fight real battles are keen that medals should be awarded only for campaigns fought. *So confusion between prestige and overt signs of merit must be avoided.* Secular recognition of the spiritual merit of praying or the organization of praying would be incongruous and objectionable. Merit is measurable against recognition; and prestige, too, exists in a balance with the dramatising of honour. One can even overdraw on one's prestige by making a demand for "payment." That seems to be the reason why prestige-holding people are very particular to appear to be modest, for a cushion of modesty keeps prestige aloft. Merit can be diminished by excessive recognition, and certainly by bogus recognition; and the ancient Jews (a practical people) not only saw "kindness" as an invisible credit (*tovah*) but reached the stage where merit was visualized as a balance like that at the bank. If a miracle was done for one, one's claims to the World to Come were diminished. Odd as this sounds, it corresponds to actual behaviour.

People capriciously honoured are in real danger of humiliation, even those likely to be so honoured. As Michel de Montaigne put it, awards bestowed without a precise regard for merit put the recipient to shame, and (what is worse) are received without gratitude.[8] If the Number 2 jockey is knighted by mistake instead of the Number 1 jockey, he will certainly apologize to Number 1 ("I accepted it for the wife's sake"); the public will respect Number 1 as before, and treat Number 2's "honour" as a joke. "Services to the Turf" are meaningless as such; honours for political services are often merely corrupt; and all ill-accorded honours diminish real merit and would degrade deserved ones if the public took the former seriously. In other words, prestige exists independently of recognition, and this is its principal point of distinction from merit, to which recognition is indispensable. A kind Indian friend who delivered an elephant to my front garden might have done much for his prestige and for mine but he would have earned no merit thereby. But although prestige and merit have this distinction there is an important point of coincidence.

It was at one time meritorious in New Guinea and the Philippines to have "taken (at least) one head." One had proved one's fitness to serve one's society; but more significantly one had established a certain status. Amongst soccer hooligans to have maimed rival supporters, and, still more, some policemen on or near the ground, would be highly meritorious in the eyes of the gang, and status would thereby be gained. Abstaining from evil serves society, but it is never treated as meritorious and is not treated as conferring prestige. No one is publicly honoured for saving himself from crime. Superb performance of a craft or a skill is never honoured. "Hero taxi-cab driver" is an absurd title, and "hero mother" would be absurd except to those who understand motherhood itself to be heroic. The Victoria Cross could serve as a paradigm. How it contrasts with the medal for Long Service and Good Conduct (familiarly known as Undetected

Crime)! Every soldier risks his life, but the VC is awarded sparingly (a case of rarity-value!) to those who have manifested valour, not in their own self-realization, like the poet and the sculptress, still less in self-glorification, like the politician, or in excesses of vanity, like the academic, but in service of others who stood in precise need of that service, while it could, without disgrace, have been withheld. Few VCs claim to have acted *intentionally*, out of a sense of *duty*, and certainly none claims to have acted out of desire for a medal. Their acts, however actually inspired, were beyond the call of duty (and the reach of remuneration), and their prestige relates simply to that. Such acquisitions, and such recognitions of merit, society is happy to dramatize, and it honours itself while staging such dramas, wherein, as it happens, modesty does not have to be dramatized!

Merit, with the apparent exception of spiritual merit, is apropos of society. It is partly explicable by behaviour relative to prestige. Prestige belongs to those (for example, nobles) whose supposed services far outweigh their remuneration (if any), and by analogy to heads of institutions although these do none of the work—to lead is a service out of comparison with other lesser services. A peculiarity of prestige is the need of people of lower ranks to recognize it in those of higher ranks (that is, by uncovering the head, or bending the knee, as our ancestors used to do). Reciprocal recognition, which is *de rigueur*, reinforces the wanted pattern. A prestige that cannot be dramatized is an absurdity. India abolished titles (in 1950) and was soon compelled to develop decorations. People are humiliated by the absence of reciprocity, for that reduces them to the status of outsiders or paupers. It is only before God or *karma* that one can afford to adopt the pose of pauper (see 1 Cor. 16:16: "I urge you to be subject to such men who have devoted themselves to the service of the 'saints' and to every fellow worker and labourer."); for society does not lose if *all* humiliate themselves in unison (although some would like to do so on different tiers).

The non-recognition, or belated recognition, of prestige and the denial of merit are consistent with ignorance, with a conspiracy, or with jealousy, the condition of one who is "threatened," in whatever manner, by the otherwise worthy party. The time-honoured medicine for jealousy is to adopt the worthy person, so that his merits might be imputed to oneself. This is vicarious merit, and it is very valuable for our purposes. Here we have a clue to the nature of our concept, merit:

we are taken back to prehistory, at which level diverse cultures were, in potential, one and they remain at one. We may deny merit to the generality of the good people of our society. Indeed we must do so, or merit ceases to have any meaning.

People were, and remain, allergic to chaotic prestige ratings. Presumption and pretension make all but the saint extremely uneasy (and there have been saints who placed a high value upon their own evident charisma). The boaster may never deviate from truth, yet his boasting (except when ritualized) is absolutely intolerable (except perhaps to his mother). The opposite, self-pity, is resented, though the self-pitier may have every justification. It casts the hearer (the victim of the display) in a prestige rating he does not relish, for pity places the pitied in a lower rank. If he is to be rated above the self-pitier he must patronize him, which he is not prepared to do upon a mere claim (as opposed to a self-humiliating submission). One notices how the "true" objects of pity (having what is called a "proper pride") do all in their power to conceal their title to a low rating. We find that dramatists actually exploit the public's enjoyment of pitying others without responsibility towards them—it is a subtle form of flattery.[9] Now, to what does all this relate?

IV

I submit that it relates to leadership. Only leaders grant or withhold recognition. Leadership permeates society like a stain in a fluid. The lance-corporal does not differ from the general in being a leader, only in the number of people he may lead. Leadership implies trust, into which the trusters invest far more than the trusted. And there is relative and comparative trust. It is important to know whom one trusts. A pyramid of leadership is necessary, and Tolstoy was right in contending that leadership, at whatever rank, is not earned or acquired but conferred. Honours are conferred, recognition is accorded, not for the benefit of the recognized (who may actually be dead), but for that of the led, in whatever rank, including the lowest. Winners of prestigious foot-races do not thank those who lost, nor do the latter commit suicide: they have all painfully ascertained their precise order of merit. Merit is biological and subject to biological rules, and to determine the champion is a leadership exercise of immemorial significance.

No one is honoured for superb performance of a task that the public accepts at no level below the superb. There are no prizes for honesty. But the detection and recognition of leaders of every rank is necessary to an elaborate symbiotic association. So important is this that imputed merit (as with a sovereign) must fill any gaps left by evident want of achievement. Rulers' merits leak over to the advantage of their associates when the latter need to be distinguished above the commonplace citizen. This is an instance of vicarious merit: to strengthen the power base of the leader is a true aspect of leadership. It is said, in India, to be meritorious is to have been born in the right family, of the right caste, and with an uncle in the right job. If all this is attributed to good deeds in previous lives, it can hardly be disproved!

Merit requires recognition, for without it, merit is vanity, fantasy. Both relate to ranking in the leadership of society, which, for its functioning, requires expectations and fulfilments, services and servants, but not any services or any servants whatever. There must be a large commonplace base, such as the producers of basic foodstuffs and primary raw materials, who dare not be signalized; they are cast in the role of "led." Although it is meritorious to have identified oneself correctly relative to the hierarchy, no such worker may ascribe merit to himself in secular terms, for to grade devoted labour as meritorious, at that rank, would make leadership utterly impossible. Liberty, equality, and fraternity must inevitably give way to hierarchy, as night succeeds day. The need to rank people and recognize their merits relative to ranking is universal; hence the apparently insoluble dilemmas of societies made up artificially of disparate components, of which the criteria are irreconcilable. All martyrdoms, defying established secular leadership, must be highly unmeritorious, until, that is to say, conditions change. The criminal who merited condign punishment then becomes the martyr who, fully rehabilitated, helped to establish, with his blood, the ideal commonwealth. Alas, yet other vicissitudes may await him.

Merit is thus a passive condition, the result of grace or favour, as can be perceived from daily experience. Ancient religious usages confirm this. Although fictions, they are the reverse of anomalous. The ancient Jews and the two major Ways of Buddhism attributed merit not to those who performed any actual service in any verifiable sense (least of all to God) but to those who were so placed as to subordinate their life-styles to supersensory considerations. The intricacies of these ideas are irrelevant to our inquiry, but an outline will prove illuminating.

V

Secular leadership tends to offer special problems when it is exercised, over immense periods, by a small clique or caste, or combination of castes. The possibilities of service to the community, through them or otherwise, are restricted. Apparently, it was thus that the notion grew up that merit could exist, and be valuable, although no secular authority could proclaim or dramatize it. Classes that had no prospect of promotion from the lowest level, and to which no merit was attributed, however hard they worked, created in their imaginations a world in which even the humblest citizen could acquire merit superior to any title awarded by the monarch.

The systems of merit developed over many centuries in Judaism, in Christianity, and in Buddhism have been studied intensively, and it would mock both our primary and our secondary sources to pretend that merit was a unitary phenomenon in all of them concurrently. The very names differ. The Hebrew *zekût* means "innocence," "good standing," "standing," "merit"; the Greek *misthos* of early Christianity means spiritual reward for unworldly goodness; the Sanskrit *punya* means "auspiciousness," "supersensory bliss," "righteousness," "merit." There is no semantic coincidence. Yet, for our purposes, the findings and motivations revealed by these concepts *at work* are significant. Leaving intricacies aside, I propose to tackle all together.

Irrespective of secular standing, even the poorest and humblest may acquire (although not by any form of exchange) a supersensory and invisible standing before God, or before the inexorable rule of cause and effect (*karma*), by sacrifice of immediate personal satisfaction, by humiliation before God, or the source of enlightenment, and by subordination to its unworldly or other-worldly requirements. A Jew may obtain *zekût* by abstaining from the pentateuchal crimes and by fulfilling the pentateuchal commandments, however trifling, guided by the traditions of the sages, observing the Law in spirit and to the letter; and his righteousness is manifested to society as a by-product of this, and not least by his charities and his benevolence of all kinds to his fellow men. That he knows the World to Come is his portion if he is true to his pattern, with all his heart, does not diminish his chances of success, but he should work like a servant who does not work solely for his wages.[10]

In Christianity there has been a debate as to the function of reward in Jesus' teaching. All we need to know is that the evangelists reported him as promising reward from the Father to those who preach the Word, and to those who do human kindnesses for Jesus' and the Word's sake, without expecting secular reward, although secular reward is not inconceivable as a by-product. As St. Luke depicts the teaching, it is precisely where no recompense can be expected from man that reward from God can be expected. (Luke 14:12–14 and perhaps 6:32–36) Paul militated against at least one current Jewish notion, namely, that performance of commandments (as input) would ensure merit (as a divine output). Jesus was clear (Mark 10:26–27) that one could not *make merit* (as in fact modern Theravada Buddhists actually believe they do). Where both Judaism and Christianity agreed is precisely at *this* point: all calls to forgo secular benefit in exchange for promises of supersensory bliss depend on the promise made by God to Abraham, Isaac, and Jacob. The promise of the Land (that is, heaven) to the patriarchs in the Bible was the basis of the religious hope. For our purposes, it is enough to note that justification is by faith (Hab. 2:4), and the input by Abraham, and later by Moses, into the promise and the Covenant by which God pledged himself was nothing more than *faith*. No actual performance of commandments, and no sacrifices ever conferred any real benefit on God—as is quite generally admitted.

Similarly in Buddhism the Lesser Vehicle (Theravada) allows merit to be earned, but strictly *not* upon any reciprocal basis (a monk may not be paid for reciting texts).[11] One does acts of charity to monks, who do not thank the householders (just as Jewish beggars allow the passer-by to "earn merit" through them).[12] The monks constitute a laboratory model of selfless living. Merit is earned by other acts spreading worship of the *Dharma*, the teaching of the Buddhas, persons who caused believers to cross over the ocean of ignorance, seeing in true perspective all merely human ambitions and striving. The expenditure of effort and money and the participation in the Buddhist Way are all done out of *faith*, since Gautama Buddha's arguments were directed to the intuition more than to the reason, which works relentlessly on the materials supplied by faith. The Great Vehicle, that is, developed Buddhism, emphasizes the great merit of the legendary, and possibly even actual, Bodhisattvas who, capable of attaining final release from the condition of death and rebirth, voluntarily abstain from so doing until all those who are able to share their merit, offered to them by grace, attain to the same state as themselves. Such sharing of merit, the height of unselfishness, too, depends on faith, not least faith in the Buddhas and Bodhisattvas.

We recognize that Judaism, Christianity, and Buddhism believe in vicarious merit (though Jesus is said to have ridiculed it). (Matt. 25:1–12) The Jews were clear that each descendant of the patriarchs might rely on his ancestors' merit (until that wore out). Pure people, and certainly charismatics, have merit to share. A collective society takes such notions for granted. Merit can, in Buddhism, be deliberately transferred, a commonplace idea. Thus acts of conspicuous consumption, whether in feeding the poor, publishing scriptures or building *stupas* or the like, provide a spiritual counterpart to secular merit. In not one of these religions is any actual service of God, and so forth, performed. Services to man are of a non-contractual kind, and thanks is either excluded or at best not recommended. Non-secular services open to be performed in various ways by everyone are characterized as meritorious, and status affirming. Society shares in the "spiritual" status because it harbours those who act uncompetitively, neglecting the search for secular power. Thus, a leadership in works of unseen significance shadows leadership in secular activities. It is not at all out of the way that those who renounce material wealth out of faith obtain standing thereupon amongst their neighbours. An unconscious compensation is going on. And in the process secular reciprocity is excluded.

VI

Society recognizes it as secularly advantageous that energy should be spent in other-worldly enterprises, even though one must admit that the seekers after merit achieve it. It is a competition that threatens no one. A wakeful suspicion of self and of ambition is helpful to law enforcement agencies! Only the enemies of society will find the righteousness of others a threat to them. (Psalm 37:52)

The equations are probably biological. Even the superstition that merit is *earned*, and is something of which one may be *proud*, a notion devoid of substance (as we have seen), may well be biological in origin. Leadership is necessary to society, and therefore to the race. Leadership has a role in evolution, and presumably merit within that.

We try to tamper with it at our peril. To offer secular recognition to the merely virtuous would tamper with nature. Merit cannot be "created" but is the product of complex relationships that cannot be exploited in calculated action: if this discovery *hurts* or *dismays* we have evidence that it touches the unconscious, the vehicle, itself, of biological truth.

What then are the values in merit, and are these mutable, while merit as a function remains ineluctable? The value of merit is that it enhances the leadership pattern by reinforcing subordination, and enlarging, while, of course, it canalizes ambition. It encourages movement while at the same time proclaiming stability. Merit is valuable as an articulating part of the mechanism of control, and merit in the abstract is not subject to vagaries in society's supposedly meritorious conduct for the time being.

It may be argued that, as manners change and standards are abandoned, merit fades (an ancient Indian idea) and righteousness becomes harder to achieve. Efforts to restore traditional values are often undertaken and surprise is expressed when these fail. The emperor Valerian hoped that the office of censor would be more potent if subjoined to the imperial dignity. Edward Gibbon comments on the fantasy: "It was easier to vanquish the Goths than to eradicate the public vices; yet, even in the first of these enterprises, Decius lost his army and his life."[13] But there is no period in which merit is not recognized, in which it does not play its inevitable role. The fact that what was meritorious in the reign of Victoria would be regarded with indifference today is of no consequence. The manifestation of rank and the dramatization of accepted service, each within the grace and favour of the leader, will continue as long as society endures. It is a separate question whether there must be *some* acts and abstentions that are universally meritorious (for example, obedience), but that intriguing possibility is not the present topic.

Notes

1. *Troilus and Cressida*, II, ii, 53–60. Quoted from G. Blakemore Evans, ed., *The Riverside Shakespeare* (Boston: Houghton Mifflin Co., 1974), p. 461.
2. Anthony Trollope, *The Duke's Children* (London: Chapman & Hall, 1880), p. 75.
3. *Coriolanus*, IV, vii, 49–53. Quoted from G. Blakemore Evans, p. 1429.

4. Babylonian Talmud, Barakot 17b, a saying of Samuel, or according to others, R. Eleazar (construing Is. 46:12): the world is sustained by the meritorious, and yet their merit may hardly feed them. Vicarious merit lends strength to the concept of "sacrificial suffering," which, though relevant to this essay, cannot be "unwound" here. See Raphael Patai, *Man and Temple in Ancient Jewish Myth and Ritual* (London: Nelson, 1947), pp. 199–200.
5. William Shakespeare, *Merchant of Venice*, II, ix, 37–43. For text used see G. Blakemore Evans (above, note 1), pp. 266–267.
6. "Use every man after his desert; and who shall scape whipping? Use them after your own honour and dignity—the less they deserve, the more merit is in your bounty." Shakespeare, *Hamlet*, II, ii, 529–32. Quoted from G. Blakemore Evans, p. 1158.
7. *Coriolanus*, I, ix, 19–25. Quoted from G. Blakemore Evans, p. 1404.
8. Montaigne, *Essais* III, 6, ed. Alexandre Micha (Paris: Garnier-Flammarion, 1969), Vol. 3, p. 118.
9. St. Augustine, William Watts, trans., *Confessions* III, 2 (London: Heinemann, Loeb Classical Library, 1919) Vol. 1, pp. 100–105.
10. Mishnah, *Avot*, I.3 (see Herbert Danby, *The Mishnah*, London: Oxford University Press, 1933, p. 446).
11. Sutta Nipata I.4, 6–7, iii.4, 26. Cited from Robert, Lord Chalmers, *Buddha's Teachings Being the Sutta-Nipata or Discourse-Collection* (Cambridge: Harvard University Press, 1932), pp. 22–23, 112–113. The same ancient collection contains Gautama Buddha's pronouncement on the earning of merit: III.5 (pp. 114–15).
12. Sirach 31:11. Sylvain Levi, ed. and trans., *Mahakarmavibhanga* (Paris: Ernest Leroux, 1932), pp. 62, 67, and 69. See also *Anguttara Nikaya* III.38, cited from Edward M. Hare, trans., *The Book of the Gradual Sayings* (London: Pali Text Society, 1973), Vol. 3, p. 31.
13. Edward Gibbon, *Decline and Fall of the Roman Empire* (London: Oxford University Press, 1920), Vol. 1, pp. 285–86.

Bibliography

Althaus, August W. H. Paul. "Verdienst Christi." In *Die Religion in Geschichte und Gegenwart*, edited by K. Galling, Vol. 6. 3d ed. Tübingen: J. C. B. Mohr, 1962, pp. 1270–1271.

Billerbeck, Paul. "Das Gleichnis von den Arbeitern im Weinberg Mt 20, 1–16 u. die altsynagogale Lohnlehre." In *Kommentar zum Neuen Testament aus Talmud und Midrasch*, by Hermann L. Strack, and Paul Billerbeck. Vol. 4. Munich: C. H. Beck, 1928/69, excursus 20.

Coats, George W. "Self-abasement and insult formulas." *Journal of Biblical Literature* 89, 1970: 14–26.
Conze, Edward. *Buddhism, Its Essence and Development*, 2d ed. Oxford: Cassirer, 1974.
De–la–Noy, Michael. *The Honours System*. London: Allison & Busby, 1985.
Garnet, Paul. *Salvation and Atonement in the Qumran Scrolls*. Tübingen: J. C. B. Mohr, 1977.
Hara, Minaru. "Transfer of Merit." *Adyar Library Bulletin* 31–32 (1967–68): 382–411.
———. "Tapo-dhana." *Acta Asiatica* 10 (1970): 58–76.
Hein, Norvin J. et al. "Verdienst Christi." In *Die Religion in Geschichte und Gegenwart*, edited by K. Galling. Vol. 6. 3d ed. Tübingen: J. C. B. Mohr, 1962 (contains bibliographies).
Holt, John C. "Assisting the dead by venerating the living. Merit transfer in the early Buddhist tradition." *Numen* 28 (1981): 1–28 (bibliography).
Löfberg, Jan. *Spiritual or Human Value?* Lund: CWK Gleerup, 1982.
Marmorstein, Arthur. *The Doctrine of Merits in Old Rabbinic Literature*. New York: Ktav, 1968.
Mayer, Adrian C. "Public service and individual merit in a town in Central India." In *Culture and Morality: Essays in Honour of C. von Furer–Haimendorf*, edited by A. C. Mayer. Delhi: Oxford University Press, 1981.
Pesch, Wilhelm. *Der Lohngedanke in der Lehre Jesu*. Munich: K. Zink, 1955.
Sancipriano, Mario. "Merito e demerito." In *Enciclopedia Filosofica*, edited by C. Giacon et al. Vol. 4, 2d ed. Florence: Sansoni, 1967, pp. 548–9. (Contains a bibliography.)
Sandars, Ed P. *Paul and Palestinian Judaism*. London: SCM, 1977.
Schechter, Solomon. *Some Aspects of Rabbinic Theology*. London: Jew's College, 1909.
Tachibana, Shundo. *The Ethics of Buddhism*. Oxford: Clarendon Press, 1926.
Tambiah, Stanley J. "The ideology of merit and the social correlates of Buddhism in a Thai village." In *Dialectic in Practical Religion*, edited by E. R. Leach. Cambridge: Cambridge University Press, 1968.
Teale, Alfred E. *Kantian Ethics*. London: Oxford University Press, 1951.
Walker, John. *The Queen Has Been Pleased*. London: Secker & Warburg, 1986.

A Comparison Between American, European, and Japanese Values

GORDON HEALD

According to a recent sixteen-country poll conducted in the United States, Europe, Japan, and South Africa, Americans to a greater extent say that given the choice they would rather choose freedom of the individual than equality. Americans also declare themselves to be the most nationally proud of all the countries and they are more willing to fight for their country than anyone else.

Confidence in institutions in the United States is higher than in Europe, except for confidence in the legal system, which was placed comparatively low. And Americans claimed the most pride in their work, surprisingly much more than did the Japanese and West Germans.

Compared to Europe and Japan, on the evidence of this survey, Americans as a society are more religious, with American blacks more than any other group saying that God is extremely important in their lives. Americans are among the highest of all nationalities in their reported satisfaction with life, and after the Irish and British they are the next most ready to claim they are "very happy."

In summary, the United States, according to this survey, is closer to Britain in terms of political and social attitudes than to any other European country, but it is closest to Ireland in terms of religious attitudes.

These are some of the preliminary findings of a major international survey undertaken to compare fundamental values in different countries throughout the world. It focuses on attitudes in such areas as work, life satisfaction, family, political, moral, religious, and spiritual values, and a wide range of social issues.[1]

Initial research for this project revealed a lack of a general theoretical framework for the study of values and the existence of important limitations to the most widely used clarifications. Hence it was decided that original research based on in-depth interviews, group discussions, and survey archive material combined with extracts from other studies (in particular those done in the Universities of Michigan and Chicago) would form the basis of the questionnaire for this survey. It took approximately eighteen months to devise a pilot questionnaire which was then tested in 1980 in 868 personal interviews, each taking an hour and a half, in Germany, Spain, and Britain. The final version of the questionnaire comprises a one-hour, face-to-face, fully precoded interview. In each test country a scientifically selected sample of at least twelve hundred people are interviewed, including a booster sample of two hundred people aged eighteen to twenty-four, so that they can be analyzed in depth.

In thirteen of the sixteen countries the field-work was conducted by Gallup International and in the other three countries by members of the International Research Association group. In Europe about fifteen thousand interviews have been completed and in the United States more than two thousand, including special sub-samples of blacks, Hispanics, and young people. The overall world-wide data collection was co-ordinated by Gallup in London, where the data was processed centrally on an IBM 4331 computer.[2]

The results from 16 questions that have been selected for release from a total of about 150 questions are in tables throughout the rest of the chapter. To facilitate inter-country comparisons the American (US), British (GB), and Irish (IR) results are displayed alongside one another in the tables to illustrate similarity of attitudes in the political, social, and religious dimensions. The Japanese (JP) results follow, together with a total for Europe (EUR) based on a weighted total of ten countries' results (representing a population of 210 million people—Britain, Northern Ireland, Republic of Ireland, France, Germany, Italy, Spain, Denmark, the Netherlands, and Belgium). This is followed by the individual country results for the major countries only, West Germany (WG), France (F), Italy (I), and Spain (SP).

Freedom versus Equality

Given a choice, 72 per cent of Americans would opt for personal freedom rather than equality. Equality, defined as "nobody is underprivileged and that social class differences are not strong," was chosen by only 20 per cent. Britain was very similar to the United States, with 69 per cent choosing personal freedom, compared to 49 per cent in Europe overall. In contrast, and somewhat surprising, was the result that more people in Germany would choose equality rather than freedom, which was also found to be the case in Italy and Spain.

TABLE 1

Q.: *Which of these two statements comes closest to your own opinion?*
(A) I find that both freedom and equality are important. But if I were to make up my mind for one or the other, I would consider personal freedom more important, that is, everyone can live in freedom and develop without hindrance.
(B) Certainly both freedom and equality are important. But if I were to make up my mind for one of the two, I would consider equality more important, that is, that nobody is underprivileged and that social class differences are not so strong.

	US	GB	IR	JP	EUR	WG	F	I	SP
					(per cent)				
1. Agree with freedom	72	69	46	37	49	37	54	43	36
2. Agree with equality	20	23	38	32	35	39	32	45	39
3. Neither (volunteered)	3	4	5	15	9	19	8	5	13
Y. Don't know	5	4	11	16	7	5	7	7	12

Pride in Nationality

Eighty per cent of Americans said they were proud to be American, whereas only 38 per cent of Europeans expressed pride in their nationality. In Europe, national pride was greatest among the Irish (66 per cent), followed by the British (55 per cent). Only 21 per cent of Germans were proud of their nationality, 19 per cent of the Dutch, 33 per cent of the French, and 30 per cent of the Japanese. In many European countries, pride in nationality is regarded as a rather outdated concept, although other questions revealed that respondents in these countries were not particularly "international" in their outlook.

TABLE 2

Q.: How proud are you to be a(n) ———? (e.g. American)

	US	GB	IR	JP	EUR (per cent)	WG	F	I	SP
1. Very proud	80	55	66	30	38	21	33	41	59
2. Quite proud	16	31	25	32	38	38	43	39	34
3. Not very proud	2	8	5	28	12	18	8	11	8
4. Not at all proud	1	3	1	3	7	11	9	6	4
Y. Don't know	2	3	3	7	6	12	7	2	5

Willingness to Fight

Seventy-one per cent of Americans expressed willingness to fight for their country, compared to only 43 per cent in Europe and 22 per cent in Japan. Of all the European nationalities, the British were significantly more willing to fight than the others (62 per cent—and this result, obtained in April 1981, perhaps gives an indication why the British have responded as they did to the conflict in the South Atlantic).

TABLE 3

Q.: Of course we all hope that there will not be another war, but if it were to come to that, would you be willing to fight for your country?

	US	GB	IR	JP	EUR (per cent)	WG	F	I	SP
1. Yes	71	62	49	22	43	35	42	28	53
2. No	20	27	31	40	40	41	46	57	27
Y. Don't know	9	11	20	38	17	24	12	15	20

Confidence in Institutions

Overall, Americans had more confidence in their institutions (except the legal system) than had Europeans. In Europe the police were rated the highest of ten institutions in terms of the percentage placing "a great deal" or "quite a lot" of confidence in them. Britain and Ireland showed the greatest confidence (86 per cent) in the police. The armed forces came second to the police in Europe in general, whereas in the United States they were rated first (81 per cent) with the police coming second.

In the United States the lowest confidence was found in major companies (50 per cent), the press (49 per cent), and labour unions (33 per cent). Europe rated these three institutions in the same way. Japan placed much more confidence in its legal system than did either the United States or Europe.

Overall, the Church was rated midway in both the United States and Europe, but it was rated the lowest in Japan. However, when attention is focused only on institutions in which Americans placed "a great deal" of confidence the churches and organized religion headed the list.

TABLE 4

Confidence in Different Institutions

	US	GB	IR	JP	EUR	WG	F	I	SP
					(per cent)				
The police	76	86	86	67	71	71	64	68	63
The armed forces	81	81	75	37	60	54	53	58	61
The legal system	51	66	57	68	57	67	55	43	48
The education system	65	60	67	51	55	43	55	56	50
The Church	75	48	78	16	52	48	54	60	50
Parliament/Congress	53	40	51	30	43	53	48	31	48
The Civil Service	55	48	54	31	40	35	50	28	38
Major companies	50	48	49	25	39	34	42	33	37
The press	49	29	44	52	32	33	31	46	31
Labour unions	33	26	36	29	32	36	36	28	31

Job Characteristics

In the United States the most important aspects of a job were, in ranked order: (1) pleasant people to work with, (2) good pay, (3) a job that is interesting, (4) a job in which you feel you can achieve something, and (5) good job security. By contrast, Europeans emphasized pay more than Americans did. European rankings were: (1) good pay, (2) pleasant people to work with, (3) good job security, (4) a job that is interesting, and (5) a job that meets one's abilities. Japanese results were in a total contrast with those of the United States and Europe: (1) a job that meets one's abilities, (2) pleasant people to work with, (3) good pay, (4) good job security, and (5) good hours. The two aspects—a job in which they felt they could achieve something and a job that was interesting—were very low priorities to the Japanese, ranking tenth and twelfth, respectively.

TABLE 5

Order of Ranking Job Characteristics

	US	GB	IR	JP	EUR (per cent)	WG	F	I	SP
1. Good pay	2	4	1	3	1	3	1	1	1
2. Pleasant people to work with	1	2	2	2	2	1	2	4	3
3. Good job security	5	3	4	4	3	2	3	2	2
4. A job that is interesting	3	1	3	12	4	4	1	5	7
5. A job that meets one's abilities	6	7	6	1	5	4	6	3	4
6. A job in which you feel you can achieve something	3	5	5	10	6	5	8	6	10
7. An opportunity to use initiative	9	6	8	13	7	5	7	8	11
8. Place to meet people	11	8	10	8	8	7	5	8	10
9. Good hours	10	10	7	5	9	7	9	8	5
10. A responsible job	6	9	8	6	10	6	4	10	11

Pride in Work

One of the most surprising results was that the Americans were the most likely to claim a great deal of pride in their work (84 per cent), followed by the British (79 per cent), and the Irish (71 per cent). In contrast, the European average was 36 per cent, with a surprising 15 per cent in West Germany and 13 per cent in France. Japan did not differ from Europe, with 37 per cent. It could almost be claimed that there appears to be an inverse relationship between these results and national growth rates!

In the pilot study conducted in four countries (Britain, Germany, France, and Spain) in 1981, almost identical results to those of the final study were obtained. Britain greatly exceeded the other three countries in pride in work. The wording and translation of the question into German, French, and Spanish was checked very carefully to make sure differences did not arise from inaccuracies in translating in the final study. Clearly, such consistency in the reproduction of results indicates that this finding has not arisen by mere chance. Given that the results of the other questions have been fairly consistent in the different languages, having made due allowance for factors influencing them, it seems unusual that this question is singled out for an apparent lack of comparatibility.

The fact that it is all English-speaking people who claim such a great deal of pride in work suggests that either there is a problem of concept (rather than translation) in other languages, or that it may be a peculiar Anglo-Saxon cultural value. The results are really brought into focus when we consider South Africa, where among the English-speaking whites, 76 per cent claimed a great deal of pride in work (statistically not significantly different to Great Britain) but among the Africaan-speaking whites it was 60 per cent. Results from Canada again revealed that pride in work was much higher among the English-speaking Canadians (77 per cent—almost identical with Britain) than among French-speaking Canadians (39 per cent) although the differences were less pronounced than in Europe.

TABLE 6

Q.: *How much pride, if any, do you take in the work that you do?*

	US	GB	IR	JP	EUR	WG	F	I	SP
					(per cent)				
1. A great deal	84	79	71	37	36	15	13	29	42
2. Some pride	14	18	21	44	37	38	46	43	41
3. Little pride	2	2	3	9	15	29	16	14	12
4. None	–	1	1	3	9	11	17	12	2
Y. Don't know	–	1	–	7	4	7	7	1	3

Religious Persons

More Italians claimed to be religious (83 per cent) than did any other nationality, closely followed by Americans (81 per cent) and South Africans (80 per cent). Among Africaan-speaking whites this amount rises to 90 per cent. Compare these results with Europe, where 63 per cent claim they are religious, and Japan, where the figure is a low 25 per cent. Except for the Italians, there was little variation in the results across the European countries, with just less than two thirds in each country saying they are religious. Contrast this with weekly church-going, which varied from 82 per cent in Ireland to 3 per cent in Denmark.

TABLE 7

Q.: *Independently of whether or not you go to church, would you say you are:*

	US	GB	IR	JP	EUR (per cent)	WG	F	I	SP
1. A religious person?	81	58	64	25	63	58	51	83	63
2. Not a religious person?	16	36	32	52	24	22	31	9	30
3. A convinced atheist?	1	4	1	11	5	3	10	4	4
Y. Don't know	2	3	3	12	8	16	8	4	4

Importance of God in Life

Respondents were asked to rate, on a scale of 1 to 10, how important God was in their lives. The advantage of this scale, compared to a frequency of church-attendance scale, is that it overcomes the problem of measuring religious commitment among the unchurched. It also facilitates comparisons between Catholics and Protestants where church attendance practices are different.

More than all others, American blacks said that God was extremely important in their lives, with an average score as high as 9.04. They are followed by U.S. Hispanics (8.92), South African whites (8.55), and South African blacks (8.45).

The average rating for the United States on this question was 8.21, exceeded only by South Africa. The European country closest to the United States in terms of religious attitudes was the Republic of Ireland (8.02). Other European countries with comparatively high scores were Northern Ireland (7.49), Italy (6.96), and Spain (6.39). The lowest were France (4.72), Denmark (4.47), and Sweden (3.99); Japan was also very low (4.49).

Belief in God

More Americans and Irish believed in God (95 per cent) than did nationals of any of the other countries. Belief in God was 75 per cent overall in Europe, dropping to 62 per cent in France and 58 per cent

TABLE 8

Importance of God in One's Life (on a scale 1–10)

United States	blacks	9.04
	Hispanics	8.92
	national	8.21
South Africa	whites	8.55
	blacks	8.45
Republic of Ireland		8.02
Northern Ireland		7.49
Italy		6.96
Spain		6.39
Belgium		5.94
Great Britain		5.72
West Germany		5.67
Finland		5.35
The Netherlands		5.33
France		4.72
Japan		4.49
Denmark		4.47
Sweden		3.39

in Denmark. Seventy-one per cent of Americans believed in life after death, compared to 43 per cent in Europe and 40 per cent in Japan. In contrast, only 67 per cent of Americans believed in hell, but this was much more than the 23 per cent in Europe or the 15 per cent in Japan.

TABLE 9

Q.: Which, if any, of the following do you believe in?

	US	GB	IR	JP	EUR (per cent)	WG	F	I	SP
God									
1. Yes	95	76	95	39	75	72	62	84	87
2. No	2	16	3	23	16	16	29	10	8
3. Don't know	3	9	2	38	9	12	9	6	6
Life after Death									
1. Yes	71	45	76	31	43	39	35	47	55
2. No	17	35	14	25	38	40	50	33	26
3. Don't know	13	19	11	43	19	21	14	19	18
Heaven									
1. Yes	84	57	83	20	30	31	27	41	50
2. No	11	32	10	35	47	54	65	44	38
3. Don't know	5	11	7	45	13	15	9	15	12
Hell									
1. Yes	67	27	54	15	23	14	15	31	34
2. No	26	63	35	40	64	73	77	52	52
3. Don't know	7	11	10	46	13	13	8	17	14

The Ten Commandments

Respondents were asked which of the Ten Commandments still applied fully to them today. The American responses were closest to those of Ireland, and the greatest contrast was with those of France. In Japan there was a large percentage of respondents replying, "Don't know," of course because the Ten Commandments are a Judeo-Christian concept with which the Japanese are less familiar. The Commandments are ranked in descending order in terms of the proportion of the population who still believe that they apply fully to them today. The first commandment in the Bible "Have no other gods before me" is ranked eighth by the general population.

TABLE 10

Respondents Who Believe That the Ten Commandments still apply fully to them today

	US	GB	IR	JP	EUR (per cent)	WG	F	I	SP
Thou Shalt									
1. Not kill	93	90	93	65	87	88	80	96	81
2. Not steal	93	87	88	66	82	81	69	93	78
3. Honour thy mother and father	90	83	77	52	77	72	67	91	75
4. Not bear false witness	89	78	86	51	73	73	67	88	56
5. Not covet thy neighbour's goods	88	79	87	51	70	70	62	73	61
6. Not covet thy neighbour's wife	89	79	85	53	65	62	52	64	65
7. Not commit adultery	87	78	85	47	62	64	48	62	58
8. Have no other gods before me	79	48	81	7	48	45	30	68	48
9. Not take the Lord's name in vain	68	34	56	13	47	50	24	66	52
10. Keep the Sabbath holy	57	25	52	14	32	29	20	51	38

Moral Rules

More than half (51 per cent) of Americans believed that there must be moral rules guiding sexual activity rather than leaving it to individual choice. Europeans in general were less emphatic about sexual guide-lines, ranging from a low of 32 per cent in France to a high of 61 per cent in West Germany who favour moral rules.

TABLE 11

Q.: *If someone says that sexual activity cannot entirely be left to individual choice, there have to be moral rules to which everyone adheres, would you tend to agree or disagree?*

	US	GB	IR	JP	EUR	WG	F	I	SP
					(per cent)				
1. Agree, there have to be moral rules	51	40	50	46	43	61	32	42	38
2. Tend to disagree	34	42	27	10	35	18	42	39	34
3. Neither (volunteered)	4	6	4	18	9	9	8	10	17
4. Don't know	8	9	12	17	9	8	16	6	9
X. Not answered	3	3	7	9	3	3	3	2	3

Guide-lines for Good and Evil

Asked whether there were absolutely clear guide-lines about good and evil that apply to everyone whatever the circumstances, only 34 per cent of those surveyed in the United States agreed with this statement, with 59 per cent affirming that there are no absolute guide-lines. In Europe, even fewer (26 per cent) agreed that there were absolute standards. Ireland was highest with 34 per cent in agreement.

TABLE 12

Q.: *Here are two statements people sometimes make when discussing good and evil. Which one comes closest to your own point of view?*
(A) There are absolutely clear guide-lines about what is good and evil. These always apply to everyone, whatever the circumstances.
(B) There can never be clear and absolute guide-lines about what is good and evil. What is good and evil depends entirely upon the circumstances at the time.

	US	GB	IR	JP	EUR	WG	F	I	SP
					(per cent)				
1. Agree with clear guide-lines	34	28	34	13	26	22	21	32	23
2. Agree with not absolute guide-lines	59	64	51	61	60	58	64	58	61
3. Disagree with both	3	4	7	10	7	11	8	3	6
Y. Don't know	3	4	7	16	7	9	8	6	10

Left versus Right

On a scale from 1–10 measuring liberalism versus conservatism in the United States, and left versus right in Europe, South Africa (whites), Ireland, Belgium, and the United States emerged as most conservative or to the right, and Sweden, France, Spain, and Italy were the most liberal or to the left. Clearly, there are relative scales for each country, and the results must be viewed in this context.

TABLE 13

Left versus Right (on a scale of 1–10)

South Africa	whites	6.50
	blacks	5.70
Republic of Ireland		6.20
Northern Ireland		6.14
Belgium		6.10
United States	national	5.94
	blacks	5.84
	Hispanics	6.23
Japan		5.91
Finland		5.81
Denmark		5.77
Great Britain		5.70
West Germany		5.60
The Netherlands		5.51
Sweden		5.39
France		4.93
Spain		4.89
Italy		4.63

Satisfaction with Life

Asked to rate their satisfaction with life overall, on a scale of 1–10, the Danes (8.21) and Swedes (8.02) followed by the Americans (7.72) were the most satisfied. The French, (6.66), Italians (6.62), Spanish (6.60), and Japanese (6.30) were the least satisfied.

TABLE 14

Satisfaction with Life (on a scale of 1–10 average)

Denmark		8.21
Sweden		8.02
United States	national	7.72
	Hispanics	7.67
	blacks	7.46
The Netherlands		7.71
Northern Ireland		7.68
Great Britain		7.67
Finland		7.58
South Africa	whites	7.51
	blacks	5.34
Belgium		7.36
West Germany		7.25
France		6.66
Italy		6.62
Spain		6.60
Japan		6.39

Happiness

Americans generally considered themselves happy, with 32 per cent describing themselves as "very happy" and another 60 per cent claiming to be "quite happy." The Irish (37 per cent) and the British (38 per cent) exceeded the Americans in professing to be "very happy"," but in Europe overall only 21 per cent claimed to be "very happy." The American results are consistent with earlier studies, such as those by the National Opinion Research Center in 1973 and 1978. The Japanese were very low on happiness (15 per cent "very happy") as were the West Germans (10 per cent "very happy").

TABLE 15

Q.: Taking all things together, would you say you are

	US	GB	IR	JP	EUR (per cent)	WG	F	I	SP
1. Very happy?	32	38	39	15	21	10	19	10	20
2. Quite happy?	60	57	55	62	64	69	70	65	58
3. Not very happy?	7	4	5	14	11	12	8	19	18
4. Not at all happy?	1	–	–	1	1	1	1	4	2
Y. Don't know	1	–	–	7	3	8	2	2	2

TABLE 16

Graphical Representation of 16 Countries in Terms of Their Political and Religious Dimensions

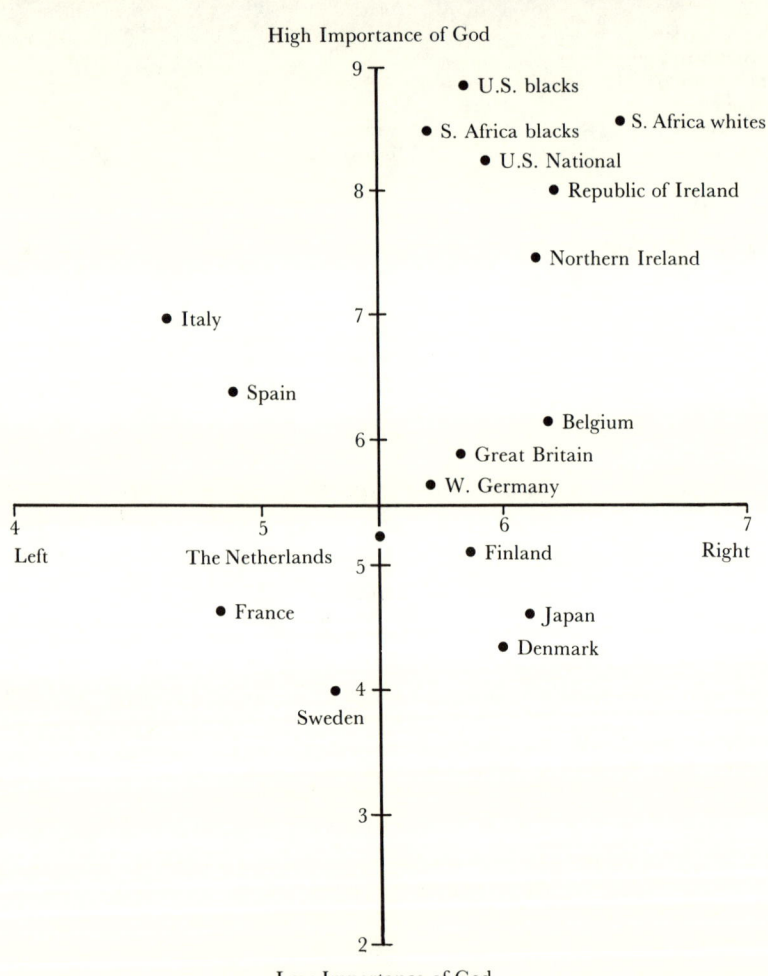

Source: Gordon Heald

Notes

1. The study commenced in 1978 when Professor Jan Kerhofs, professor of Pastoral Sociology at the University of Louvain, Belgium, registered a charitable foundation, the European Value Systems Study Group (EVSSG), to undertake the study, chaired by Professor Ruud de Moor, professor of Social Science at Tilburg University. Its purpose was to analyse and describe the moral and social value systems in Europe today. Also, it would provide a model in order to monitor changes in these moral and social value systems for future studies. An academic steering committee was set up, to be advised by a technical group composed of the principals of four major research agencies involved in the project—Madame H. Riffault, Faits et Opinions, France; Dr. E. Noelle-Neuman, Institute fur Demoskopie Allensbach, Germany; Dr. Juan Linz, Data SA, Spain; and Mr. Gordon Heald, Gallup, England.
2. The survey has been paid for by different sources of funds in each country: industry, government, charitable foundations, voluntary organizations, and church organizations.

    In the United States, the study was organized by the Center of Applied Research in the Apostolate (CARA), an independent Catholic research organization. I am grateful to Dr. Edward M. Sullivan for permission to publish their data, and also to the Leisure Development Centre in Tokyo, for permission to publish the Japanese data.

    CARA was also responsible for the Canadian study, completed in June, 1982. Fr. Gordon Henderson of CARA was responsible for the Mexican study, completed in 1983. Professor J. Stoetzel in Paris has been responsible for producing the overall European report, and in each country academic committees have been set up to oversee individual national reports. The study has been completed in the following European countries: Gt. Britain; Northern Ireland; Republic of Ireland; France; Germany; Italy; Belgium; Spain; The Netherlands; Malta; Denmark; Norway; Sweden; Finland; Iceland; Hungary; the Soviet Union. In the American continent, it has been completed in the United States; Canada; Mexico; Chile; and Argentina. In the rest of the world, the study is now completed in Japan; South Korea, Australia; New Zealand; South Africa.

    Data volumes, entitled *The International Values Data Books*, are to be published in 1987 by Croom Helm (Provident House, Burrell Row, Beckenham, Kent BR3 1AT).

Bibliography

Abrams, Mark, David Gerard & Noel Timms. *Values and Social Change in Britain*. London: Macmillan, 1985.

Fogarty, Michael, L. Ryan & J. Lee. *Irish Values and Attitudes: The Irish Report of the European Value Systems Study*. Dublin: Dominican Publications, 1984.

Harding, Stephen and David Phillips, with Michael Fogarty. *Contrasting Values in Western Europe*. London: Macmillan, 1986.

Stoetzel, J. *Les valeurs du temps present: une enquête européenne*. Paris: Presses universitaires de France, 1983.

III

Values and Institutions

III

Politics and Value

EDMUND IONS

An essay containing the term *politics* sometimes finds it necessary to begin with a definition. Politics is a protean term. Those who write on politics can even disagree on whether the noun takes a plural or a singular verb. (I will treat it as singular.) Again, one needs to distinguish between politics as business, profession, craft, or trade on the one hand, and the academic discipline on the other. Though it goes without saying that questions of value occur constantly in the practical business of politics, the relationship between value and the academic discipline is a complex matter, since we are dealing with a long discourse going all the way from the pre-Socratics through the writings of antiquity and the medieval period to the modern era and the neo-Marxists and neoconservatives of our own time.

I wish to concentrate chiefly, though not exclusively, on the academic study of politics, where there are more than enough questions to occupy the mind. Discussion on the business of politics, or the politician's trade, enters at some points, but a cautionary note may be necessary on the matter of political rhetoric. A discussion of "democratic values" or of "Western values" would seem, prima facie, to be natural candidates for a symposium on value. But a few moments of reflection may persuade us that we would need to distinguish sharply between what aspiring politicians say about these themes, for national or international consumption, and what a symposium may find it profitable to discuss.

The problem, in the available space, is to select one or two *points d'appui* from this long and sometimes tortuous discourse in order to generate discussion on the central theme. The relationship between politics and value is often uneasy, recalcitrant, and sometimes discordant. This partly explains the attempts of one school of thought within the discipline of politics to seek a value-free political "science"—an endeavour that does not succeed, in my view, though the reasons are worth exploring, as I will attempt to do in a concluding section.

One useful point of entry is to raise the familiar but always interesting question, what is politics *about*? Answers are as numerous and various as the political contexts in which the question is put. One eminent American student of politics, the late Harold Lasswell, provided an answer of sorts in the title of one of his works, *Politics: Who Gets What, When, How* (1936). Some may feel that there is an ethnocentric American ring to such a title, with a fugitive whiff of the capitalist ethic to it. That said, Lasswell's title has a certain concreteness about it. At the other extreme we might agree that some fanciful and invented title such as *Politics: The Eternal Verities* is altogether too ethereal, begging far too many questions and pretentious in its claims or implications. Somewhere in the middle ground we might hope to locate a context for discussion that is fairly concrete and not too pretentious.

II

Most students of politics agree that politics is concerned with power in its many forms and manifestations. That is, how power is acquired, why it is sought, how it is used, misused, and abused. Political relationships are almost invariably power relationships in one form or another. Yet clearly it is not only practising politicians who seek power—the quest for power may be found in all walks of life, in every profession, trade, or calling. It seems, then, that power has some utility to a great many people. Does it follow that it is valued? And do people value it for what it promises or for what it can bring about, or is power valued for its own sake?

The answers are as multitudinous as the instances we can bring to mind. The tyrants of history clearly possessed power, and many of them clearly enjoyed, even exulted in it. But equally, historical characters, such as Jesus of Nazareth, or Gandhi, possessed a good deal of power, and by and large, we are not offended by such a reflection. So is power essentially a neutral term, with pejorative overtones reserved for particular instances where we feel it is abused, or is it simply enjoyed for its own sake? With such questions we are moving towards philosophical problems of some complexity, and we might conclude that there is nothing wrong in power, or even the possession of power, provided it is used for good ends. But to assert this is to move towards the linguistic abyss of first defining "good" and then seeking to distinguish between means and ends.

Attempts to define politics therefore soon become involved in problems of language. In democracies we place great value on free elections. But what do we mean by "free" elections? What are the precise terms and conditions that must be present so that they may be said to be "free"? Voting is compulsory in Australia, and it was compulsory in the 1982 elections in El Salvador. The peasants of El Salvador faced punishment if they did not turn out to vote. Were those elections free, or unfree? To put the question is to raise a host of contingent questions on all sides.

At this juncture, the practical politican will be inclined to say that whereas such questions may by explored in the ivory tower, the politician's trade is a practical one. Politics is the art of the possible, and those working in the business must get on with the job. To do the job, a certain amount of power is not so much a desideratum as a *sine qua non*.

From these perspectives (linguistic and philosophical), questioning whether politicians enjoy power, or even place some value on it, is a form of dilettantism. Discussion of this may well occupy an academic symposium, but the practical politician may find it irrelevant as he grapples with the problems of the real world. Indeed, the busy politician might well add a wry note that where academics place the value on discussions about power, which may or may not throw light on its manifestations, the politician values his time too much to engage in such discussions; and who is to decide which order of priorities is more laudable—dare one say more valuable—in the wider scheme of things? Here, I simply raise the question of how we regard one of the defining characteristics of the world of politics, namely, the concept of power, in order to underline the recalcitrant element of value in any such discussion.

III

A second point of entry for discussion could be the perennial debate on liberty versus equality. Here we have two concepts instead of one, which introduces the familiar dilemma that more of the one often entails less of the other. Greater equality for all usually involves less liberty for some. Conversely, the more individual liberty citizens enjoy, the less likely are they to end up equal. We should spare ourselves, I suggest, a digression into the two concepts of liberty adumbrated by Sir Isaiah Berlin some years ago (that is, freedom *from* and freedom *to*). It will be more profitable to admit both definitions. We mean by liberty, that is to say, freedom *from* excessive interference by the state or any of its organs, and also freedom *to* act, speak, think, travel, vote, or not vote as we please.

To pose the familiar dilemma, therefore, which do we favour most—greater liberty, or greater equality? For conservatives and for most liberals, liberty is the preferred choice if a choice has to be made. For socialists, equality would take first place more often than not. Different individuals and different groups allocate different values to one or other of the concepts. Whence the difference? Explanations may go all the way from the psychological (there are conservative types of psyche, it is said, just as there are socialist types of psyche) to the moral and philosophical, to the ideological. Putting aside discussion on personality types, where clinical expertise is required, what principles lie behind these differences of value?

It is easy to assert that a person's value system in these questions derives from different locations in the class system or the economic system. But there are far too many aberrant cases of upper-middle-class socialists and working-class conservatives for any exact correlation to hold. If, in reply, the Marxist directs our attention to such phenomena as false consciousness and *embourgeoisement* in order to defend the central tenets of the theory, we might still ask what it is that distinguishes the aberrant case from the class-conscious norm.

The answers, even within the theory, it seems to me, lie in the direction of the quiddity of the species, which is of course the libertarian argument in another form. People differ. I prefer to stop the argument there, rather than start hares in the fields of ancient controversies on free will and determinism.

On the assumption that people are free to choose, and then exercise choice, is it true to say that some will opt for liberty, others for equality? It is impossible to supply any sort of answer to such a question. As pollsters need to be reminded on occasion, ask a silly question and you get a silly answer. Questions about liberty and equality are neither silly nor trivial, but to pose them in the form of mutually exclusive polarities is unhelpful and often falsifies the real world of day-to-day choices for the individual. We prefer to protect, preserve, and defend our individual liberty, whether the threat or the challenge comes from the state, the town hall, or our neighbours. And we are sometimes deeply affronted by indefensible examples of gross inequality between rich and poor—so much so that we are prepared to act on our beliefs and reactions.

Our answer, then, is to deny the polarity of the either/or, to cast out the Cartesian ghost, and to insist that in politics, polarities are usually unhelpful, often dangerous. We do not value one thing *at the expense* of another; we value both in different degrees at different times, and we order our priorities after an examination of the evidence. The examination may be too brief, and it may even be prejudiced, in the hurly-burly of the modern polis: there are some things about which we feel deeply, others more marginally, and the explanation of our feelings will certainly be accounted for in part by our psychobiographies. But we will also insist that living is very largely a matter of rearranging and reallocating, for shorter or longer periods, our values, and this conviction cannot dispatched by the cynic's retort that what we are really doing is adjusting our prejudices to the demands of felt circumstances.

At this point, I am again conscious that I am intruding somewhat into the preserves of the philosopher. I think this is unavoidable, since the most important questions in politics, it seems to me, lie in the area of polical philosophy. Even the moral precept "Do as you would be done by" has unavoidable political connotations, since what you do to other people is limited by all sorts of political and legal constraints and conditions.

The mention of legal obligation again opens up further territory one must leave to the jurists, but this may be the point to draw attention to a particular difficulty we are bound to encounter when exploring the relationship between value and politics. Whether discussed as a practical trade or as an academic discipline, politics affects and is affected by other arenas of inquiry. These include, most obviously, society's institutions, its totems and taboos, economics, law, literature, and the climate of culture. All are cognate, as we readily perceive. But politics inevitably has a certain catholicity. Among the many definitions of politics, we may note one working definition is that politics is ultimately about how societies allocate fundamental values.

Does this mean that politics is ultimately indistinguishable from religion or morality? There is certainly an affinity, since morality and religion are essential ingredients, though only as instruments, not as ends in themselves. Machiavelli (1469–1527) was the first great thinker to draw attention to the vital distinction. Putting metaphysics to one side for the moment, religion and ethics are means to an end within the polis: politics is its own justification. Morality is not and cannot be part of the process. If a prince wishes to maintain order and to ensure the survival of the state, he must be prepared to act immorally, at times to do evil.

> A Prince, especially a new one, cannot observe all those things for which men are esteemed, being often forced, in order to maintain the state, to act contrary to fidelity, friendship, humanity, and religion.[1]

Machiavelli's great contribution was to assert, in stark, unblinkered fashion, the imperatives of politics. He is not concerned to preach or to moralize; he is concerned to arrive at the actual truth of things—his *verità effettuale*—and in doing so, he separates, with the utmost rigour, politics from ethics. In this way, Machiavelli, not Aristotle, is the founder of the modern study of politics. He is not a philosopher, but an observer who seeks to get at the truth of things—more precisely, the necessary (though not the sufficient) conditions for maintaining authority in the state.

Thomas Hobbes (1588–1679) is the direct heir and lineal descendant of Machiavelli. Whereas Machiavelli's prince—if he would be successful and survive—governs according to rules uncovered by Machiavelli, Hobbes's Leviathan creates the rules and governs according to them. The Leviathan is thus "that Mortall God" who instils obedience and governs according to the prescriptions Hobbes uncovers: "Covenants without the Sword are but Words, and of no strength to secure a man at all." In the same passage Hobbes reminds us that the

> Lawes of Nature (as Justice, Equity, Modesty, Mercy and in summe doing to others as we would be done to) of themselves, without the terror of some Power to cause them to be observed, are contrary to our natural Passions, that carry us to Partiality, Pride, Revenge and the like.[2]

I have selected Machiavelli and Hobbes because they compel us to discuss the realities rather than the pieties of politics. This is not to rule discussion of the pieties out of court, but merely to bring to our attention the crucial distinction between politics and morals, and also between politics and religion. Politics is politics, and although we might well find ourselves having useful discussions on the role of religion and morals within the polis, as we might also discuss the importance of myth and magic in holding society together, we should not delude ourselves, Hobbes and Machiavelli warn us, about the special nature of politics. If we overlook this, we will move into interesting, seductive, but ultimately sentimental arguments about what we wish the world, society, the polis to be like, rather than what they are. This is not cynicism but realism, and our worst enemies are those purblind thinkers and commentators who would have us believe that things are other than they are.

There is an understandable wish among some students of politics to escape from, or at the least to avoid, the discomforting testimony of Machiavelli and Hobbes. Since Hobbes breathes the spirit of the mid-seventeenth century, he is easily—too easily, in my view— identified with a mechanistic view of the universe, and he is sometimes regarded as the first political "scientist." Hobbes regards political truths as similar to the arbitrary truths of geometry so his system is all-pervasive or, in the modern terminology, overarching. His anatomy of the body politic is essentially scientific, therefore, since it is value-free, objective, even predictive.

The intellectual stream flowing from this view of Hobbes to political science in the twentieth century is a fairly complicated one, and there is not the space to pursue it fully here. It involves a parallel stream of ideas belonging more properly to the forebears as well as to the founding fathers of sociology, and we would have to invoke the writings of, among others, Saint-Simon, Auguste Comte, Max Weber, Herbert Spencer, and in our own time, Talcott Parsons to do justice to the theme. But the two streams are congruent to the extent that they converge in the quest for a science of politics on the one hand, and a scicnce of society on the other. I will glance critically at the attempts of one group of political scientists in the mid-twentieth century to make political science value-free.

IV

The main thrust of the intellectual stream came from the United States, and the movement gathered pace in the 1930s and 1940s in a programme calling itself, in its early stages, behaviourism and later, behaviouralism. Since I have criticized this movement elsewhere, here I will condense as efficiently as possible my arguments.[3]

The "behavioural revolution" in political science, as some of its advocates proclaimed in the early, optimistic phase, aimed at a value-free political science which would not be tainted by ethnocentric particularities; its conclusions would be objective, culture-free, and have validity for all political systems. This was the dream and, like most revolutions, the behavioural revolution promised more than it could deliver. At a later stage the claims were muted somewhat, and the behavioural revolution became the "behavioural persuasion."[4] By the early 1960s, leading exponents were declaring that it was a "mood" rather than a doctrinal commitment. The behavioural approach to political studies persists in some centres on both sides of the Atlantic, and perhaps the fairest estimate of its condition is to say that it has now been absorbed into the mainstream of political science, a tendency and an approach practised by some (especially the more numerate members of academia) who continue to hold that their approach is an important advance on traditional approaches to the study of politics.

I am not concerned here to argue the merits of the theological disputes within a particular discipline so much as to assess what we might learn from a sustained attempt to produce a "value-free" political science. The lessons are at the particular and the general level, and it seems to me that we might profit from a résumé of the main ones.

The chief aims of the behaviouralists are to search for regularities of behaviour in political systems by the analysis of pattern variables. Data are quantified and relationships are stated as mathematical propositions. Inquiry proceeds by way of theoretical formulations that yield, in turn, "operational-izable" hypotheses. (The language of behaviouralism is often rebarbative, the jargon pretentious.) Hypotheses are tested against empirical data. According to the level of the inquiry and the degree of generality of the hypotheses, the researcher will speak of "low-level," "middle-level," and "general" theory.

The behaviouralist adopts this approach and this method because he believes that values in politics cannot be established, still less demonstrated, scientifically. If normative questions, and by extension political beliefs, cannot be tested empirically, they can form no part of political science. Moral and ethical questions may be worth pursuing elsewhere, but this would be the task of the philosopher, not the political scientist, whose terms of reference are overt behaviour. The tools of the political scientist are thus multivariate analysis, sample surveys, and in some cases, simulation. The construction of models is also part of the task of the political scientist, and in this way the discipline can be brought nearer to the certainties of mathematics and the natural sciences. I have referred elsewhere to the fallacies and wrong assumptions built into the methods of behaviouralism in political science: the debates and disagreements, for instance, among mathematicians and scientists both in the pure reaches and the applied reaches of those disciplines.[5] I will summarize, again much too briefly, my objections to the behavioural creed.

In the first place, overt political behaviour is only a portion of the world of politics. It may sometimes be the least important, even the most illusory aspect. Political scientists who rely exclusively in their researches on recording responses (which are logically discrete from replies) to surveys and questionnaires at best simplify and at worst falsify more complex explanations of political behaviour. To note this is not to argue for mystification, or to posit some obscure level of belief impervious to inquiry. It is merely to assert that the individual's belief system is a good deal more complicated than the mutually exclusive categories, or the strong-to-weak affirmations of scaled responses can permit. By no means all of our most strongly held beliefs are held "rationally" as the term is normally understood. Bryan Wilson's work on rationality and on magic and millennial movements reminds us of those other reaches of thought and behaviour that may not belong formally to the political order, but that have profound political implications for the warp and woof of society.[6]

The study of politics is not, and never will become in my view, a science in anything but name. Individuals act, think, and behave politically for quite different reasons, and their observable, recorded behaviour does not necessarily provide the best clues to what is going on in their minds. Questionnaires phrased in terms of dichotomous propositions do violence to the individual's underlying attitudes and beliefs. The best evidence for this is individual testimony, including one's own. In the real world, choices rarely come neatly in *either/or* categories. If politicians are forced to compromise—if, indeed, politics is the art of the successful compromise—the same proposition must also be advanced on behalf of the citizen and the voter. Our participation in organized society is always something of a compromise.

The Gauguin tendency is with all of us for some of the time and with some of us much of the time. Organized society has its many advantages but society also exacts its price, in terms of obedience and the acceptance of norms. Like the prisoners in *Fidelio*, we yearn to breathe free, to throw off the shackles and escape from our confinement. We secretly admire the audacious souls who do break free of the bonds, even though we are equally aware that to do so is to court disaster. A Gauguin, a Dylan Thomas, an Isadora Duncan, is an object of envy or admiration only up to a certain degree. Politics and society exact their revenge, and we reflect that, however heady the bout of freedom, it is unwise to "buck the system."

The political order is thus always procrustean. Fierce debates on the merits of parliamentary democracy against the one-party state, of capitalism versus communism, of the virtues of one system against the iniquities of another all tend to obfuscate a more fundamental problem. We are required to choose between one form of government and another, yet our real choices, that is, our preferred choices, lie elsewhere. Our real choice is not between the one-party state and the multiparty state; between parliamentary, Western democracy and Eastern, Peoples' democracies; or between this *ism* and that *ism*. These supposed "choices" derive from the rhetoric. The reality is that we do not regard them as mutually exclusive alternatives any more than the perennial debate between liberty and equality poses genuine alternatives. Certainly we understand the basis for the rhetoric and the necessity for choice. But rhetoric is one thing, reality another, especially the reality of our private universe of beliefs.

What we value most, but we are unable to declare, for reasons of patriotism or the obligations of civic virtue, is to choose not to choose. In many important ways, politics has come to exceed its proper place in the scheme of things. It has gone beyond its purview for complex sets of reasons—historical, technological, economic. The calculus of consent is sustained and imposed by a battery of devices—legal, technical, social; from polling organizations to the party political broadcast; from party manifestoes to distant threats of an East-versus-West Armageddon if we do not choose and are not seen to exercise our choice. The polarities that are supposed to lie at opposite ends of the political spectrum are by no means clear to us, yet the choices continue to be posed in stark and simple terms, for reasons we well understand but do not necessarily endorse.

In this discordant hubbub, the puzzled citizen finds it difficult to assert, still less to order, his preferences along a particular scale. He may feel that there are some things he values above most other things—privacy, for example—but he is equally aware that the right to privacy does not appear in party manifestoes, and even if it did, that he will almost certainly have to settle for less. So political preferences, and the values placed on them individually and collectively, really become a question of swings and roundabouts. What you gain in one direction you lose in another. In one sense, this is no more than a reassertion that politics is about compromise. But it may be that in modern society, those things we are willing to trade, or even trade in for others, do not belong to what we might term our primary set of values; we may feel that too many problems are defined as political problems and that politics begins to exceed its brief.

Notes

1. Niccolo Machiavelli, *The Prince* (London: Everyman, 1958), p. 99.
2. Thomas Hobbes, *Leviathan* (London: Everyman, 1953), p. 87.
3. Edmund Ions, *Against Behaviouralism: A Critique of Behavioural Science* (Oxford: Blackwell, 1977), chs. 13, 16.
4. Heinz Eulau, *The Behavioral Persuasion* (New York: Random House, 1964).
5. Ions, *Against Behaviouralism*, chs. 1, 2, 16.
6. Bryan Wilson, ed., *Rationality* (Oxford: Blackwell, 1970). Wilson's scholarly *oeuvre* on the sociology of religion provides a much more extensive and sustained exploration of the rational/irrational bases of belief systems in Eastern and Western cultures, but see also Michael Oakeshott, *Rationalism in Politics and Other Essays* (London: Methuen, 1962).

Bibliography

Note: The literature on the study of politics is immense, if only by reason of longevity, from the Greek classics to the spate of publications in our own time. The following list is therefore extremely selective, guided by the central theme of the symposium—the study of value.

Aristotle. *The Nicomachean Ethics*. London: Everyman, 1949.

Berlin, Isaiah. *Four Essays on Liberty*. London and Oxford: Oxford University Press, 1969.

Easton, David. *A Systems Analysis of Political Life*. New York: Wiley, 1965.

Merton, Robert K. *Social Theory and Social Structure*. Glencoe, Ill.: Free Press, 1957.

Mills, C. Wright. *Power, Politics and People: The Collected Essays of C. Wright Mills*. New York: Oxford University Press, 1963.

Oakeshott, Michael. *The Social and Political Doctrines of Contemporary Europe*. New York: Basic Books, 1940.

Plamenatz, John P. *Consent, Freedom and Political Obligation*. 2nd ed. London and Oxford: Oxford University Press, 1968.

Sabine, George H. *A History of Political Theory*. Rev. ed. London: Harrap, 1937.

Stretton, Hugh. *The Political Sciences*. London: Routledge & Kegan Paul, 1969.

Wallas, Graham. *Human Nature in Politics*. New York: Appleton-Century-Crofts, 1908.

Sophisters, Economists, and Calculators: on the Notion of Value in Economics

PAUL SEABRIGHT, M. PHIL.

Oscar Wilde's definition of a cynic as "a man who knows the price of everything and the value of nothing" has been so often taken to refer to economists that in contemporary folk wisdom a certain philistinism about value is thought the only common characteristic of a profession notoriously unable to agree on anything else. The complaint is far from new: Edmund Burke lamented the fate of Queen Marie-Antoinette:

> I thought ten thousand swords must have leapt from their scabbards to avenge even a look that threatened her with insult. But the age of chivalry is gone. That of sophisters, economists and calculators has succeeded; and the glory of Europe is extinguished for ever.[1]

Nor is the complaint surprising when to many economists value and price are simply synonymous. The author of a current textbook called *Value*, for example, opens his book with the sentence: "Value, according to the Oxford dictionary, is 'the amount . . . for which a thing can be exchanged': in other words, value is the price which prevails in the market, or equilibrium price."[2] Although economists may claim that they use such a term only in a restricted sense, they have an understandably difficult time persuading laymen that they are not thereby downgrading other conceptions of value. The intellectual division of labour can easily come to resemble verbal apartheid.

In the last twenty-five years there have been increasingly vocal assaults on the alleged supremacy of "economic values" in practical life (and especially in political decision-making). The complaints have taken several, not always clearly distinguished forms. First is the complaint with which we began: that the term *value* in economics means nothing more than price and ignores much else that is of value. Second (and a related complaint), it is sometimes argued that the use of the price mechanism to allocate resources is inappropriate for certain ends that we value. In particular, the market mechanism is often believed to foster self-interest and an attitude of competitiveness at the expense of more communitarian virtues. Third, it has often been claimed that economics focuses attention on values that can be quantified at the expense of those that cannot. And finally, at a more philosophical level, economic method has been accused of presupposing that what is valuable in all the diverse things we esteem can be reduced to some common central component of value. Though this is perhaps not the usual view, I shall suggest that there is more truth, and more cause for concern, in the last complaint than in the previous three.

What, first, of the confusion between value and price made by Wilde's cynic, of the contempt for other values lamented by Burke? Burke's libel is particularly outrageous if applied to two of his contemporaries who must rank among the least narrow and most cultivated men who have ever lived, namely, David Hume and Adam Smith, both of them economists (and much else besides). Adam Smith, who was far from being the unfeeling Friedmanite he tends to be portrayed as today (and who was highly admired by Karl Marx), gave us a clear avowal of the distinction between "the utility of some particular object, and . . . the power of purchasing other goods which possession of that object conveys. The one may be called 'value in use'; the other, 'value in exchange'." Smith went on to point out that

> the things which have the greatest value in use frequently have little or no value in exchange; and, on the contrary, those which have the greatest value in exchange frequently have little or no value in use. Nothing is more useful than water: but it will purchase scarce anything . . . A diamond, on the contrary, has scarce any value in use; but a very great quantity of other goods may frequently be had in exchange for it.[3]

It is precisely this divergence from value in use that makes understanding the determination of value in exchange such a challenging matter. If the two were necessarily the same, economists would have little to write about. So ironically, economic value or price becomes an interesting focus of study only by virtue of being a specialized and particular application of a more general concept of value. (I was about to write "economists forget this to their cost" until I noticed how thoroughly and confusingly economic terms like "cost" have permeated the vocabulary in which we express our more general value-judgements.) The more sensitive economists have been fully aware of this for centuries. Smith's distinction was prefigured in the discussions of the medieval schoolmen about the "just price." It is important, in understanding the evolution of these ideas, to realize that the search for a just price was not the search for a price that corresponded to the "true" worth of a commodity. Many writers pointed out that the just price did not correspond to either usefulness or intrinsic worth. (In true scholastic style, they distinguished further between usefulness and intrinsic worth; a mouse for instance, had no usefulness, but as a creature of God had some intrinsic worth.) Although these writers began from Aristotle's view that "all products exchanged must be somehow comparable . . . there must be one standard by which all commodities are to be measured,"[4] it was not usually claimed that this standard was more than formal, or that it represented "value" in an substantive sense.

Furthermore, the fact that there was a role for the law in enforcing a just price (one recognized as early as the remedy of *laesio enormis* promulgated under Diocletian, whereby a contract exchanging goods for less than half their just price was automatically invalid) shows that the determinants of the just price were not thought to be the same as the determinants of the price in any particular market at any time. Scholars earlier this century used to think that the just price was taken by the schoolmen to be that price at which costs were just covered in the long run.[5] On this view the just price corresponded to what now would be called the long-run competitive equilibrium price, which is clearly different both from the actual price ruling at any particular time and from the utility or value yielded by the article traded. But we now realize that this attributes to the schoolmen an anachronistic understanding of modern economic theory. A better way to represent their view is by reference to the *communis aestimatio*, or the judgement of buyers and sellers as to the price that would best reflect need, scarcity, and cost. In given conditions, there could exist a range of prices that were more or less just. As one commentator has put it, scholastic jurists "were not trying to found a science in which a given set of forces would yield a determinate result";[6] rather, they were trying to shape a process of consensus, of community judgement as to what represented the most appropriate institutional framework for exchanges that were never meant to capture the true intrinsic value of things.

Adam Smith's distinction between use-value and exchange-value was taken up by Karl Marx and formed the foundation of his analysis of the nature of exploitation in the capitalist economy. Marx's theory of value was a complex one; it must suffice here to point out that it would be wrong to see exploitation (in Marx's theory) as proceeding from an unequal exchange in which capitalists forced workers to sell their labour power for less than its true (or "just") exchange-value. Quite the contrary: capitalism was inexorably consistent. Exchange-value was determined by the amount of "socially necessary labour time" required for the production of a given commodity. Labour power was no exception: *its* exchange-value was determined by the time necessary to produce the commodities required to maintain the stock of labour (and was thus equal to the subsistence wage). The surplus value appropriated by the capitalist arose from the use-value of labour, which was that it could create commodities with an exchange-value greater than its own.

The role of justice in Marx's thought is very unclear (he sometimes takes up its cause with passion, sometimes dismisses it as a purely bourgeois concept). But it does seem clear that what injustice there is in exploitation arises not from a distortion of exchange-values through unfair exercise of capitalist power. Rather, it lies in the sale (or "alienation") of productive labour to the capitalist, which is necessary before its use-value can be realized. All production requires the co-operation of labour with capital, and in a system where some people have only their own labour to live on, they must transfer control of this to the owners of capital. This is not a fault of individuals but is inherent in the nature of capitalist production. The result is an appropriation of the use-value of labour solely by the bourgeoisie. A system that functions consistently with regard to exchange-value ends up being highly unjust with regard to its distribution of the true usefulness of things.

Does this amount to an endorsement by Marx of the reproach

against economics with which we began? It is true that Marx inveighed much against "commodity fetishism," or the tendency of producers to imagine that the exchange-value of commodities was a property intrinsic to them. This tendency was due, he wrote, to

> a particular social relation between men that assumes, in their eyes, the imaginary form of a relation between things. To find an analogy we must have recourse to the mist-enveloped regions of the religious world, where the productions of the human brain appear as independent beings endowed with life, and entering into relation both with one another and with the human race.[7]

But this was not a fault Marx attributed to *economists* as such, who (like Smith) had been fairly scrupulous about keeping use-value and exchange-value conceptually distinct. Rather, it was due to the ideology with which capitalism blinded its participants. The fault of economists lay not in confusing economic values with values in a richer sense (which for Marx meant the full flourishing of the human creative potential that was possible only under communism). Rather, it lay in their blindness to the way in which a system of logical and equal exchange in respect of economic value, could systematically and ruthlessly misallocate value more broadly conceived.

If anything, Marx was calling for a wider and more ambitious role for economic theory, one that took account of the way in which economic relations determined the pursuit of a wide range of ends, economic and non-economic, which human beings value. It is unlikely, though, that he would have welcomed the way in which the ambitions of economic theory did expand in the late nineteenth and the twentieth centuries. One might describe the rise of marginal utility theory as a long-overdue attempt to explore the interrelations between value in use and value in exchange. But it took a rather peculiar form. Marginal utility theory explained the price of a good by the utility (or use-value) not of each unit of the good consumed but only by the very last (or marginal) unit. Through the apparatus of demand-and-supply analysis, it determined the prices of goods by the interaction of objective conditions (costs and scarcity) on the supply side with subjective conditions (tastes) on the demand side. Where the supply curve intersected the demand curve lay the equilibrium price. These two curves were derived as follows. The amount of a good supplied at any price is determined, not by the total costs of producing that amount, but by the costs of the very last unit (when this equals the price the producer will cease to supply any more). Likewise, the amount demanded is determined by the utility of the very last unit consumed, not by the utility of the total. The consumer will go on demanding the good until the value to him of the very last penny's worth is no greater than the value of devoting that penny to something else. The result is that at equilibrium the ratio of the marginal costs (the costs of the very last units) of any two commodities is equal to the ratio of their marginal utilities, which in turn is equal to their relative price. And if, for example, consumer tastes change so that their preferences switch towards butter and away from margarine, there will be a movement of productive resources towards butter until the increasing marginal cost of producing butter and the diminishing marginal utility of consuming butter converge on a new (and higher) equilibrium price.

The details of this theory are not here important. What does matter is twofold. First, it describes a precise relationship between a commodity's value in exchange (its equilibrium price) and its value in use. The two values, according to the theory, are not the same. But they are related in that the ratio of exchange-values is equal to the ratio of use-values, *not* of all but only of the very last units of the commodities consumed. Now it is possible to explain the paradox of water, whose price is negligible but whose value is immense. For water is (in temperate climes at least) so plentiful, and we are able to drink so much of it, that the value to us of the very last mouthful we consume is negligible even though we would die if we were deprived of our whole supply. Most of us would gladly be deprived of a glass of water in exchange for a glass of good claret, though we would never choose to drink only claret in preference to drinking only water. Yes it is our preferences regarding the former trade-off that, in equilibrium, determine the relative price of the two liquids.

The second point of importance about marginal utility theory concerns the nature of the explanatory concept itself. What was utility and how was it measured? The first of the marginalists, Hermann Gossen, talked about "enjoyment"; William Jevons took his cue more directly from Bentham and defined utility as the quality possessed by an object of producing pleasure or preventing pain, "provided that the will or inclination of the person immediately concerned is taken to be the sole criterion for the time, of what is or is not useful."[8] Such a concept was not only thought to be well defined, it was also thought susceptible to measurement, so that the laws of economics could in principle be formulated in mathematical terms. Jevons's work *The Theory of Political Economy*, published in 1871, was an explicit attempt to cast in mathematics the laws of economics derived from "the great springs of human action—the feelings of pleasure and pain." Pleasure and pain both came in quantities.

Francis Edgeworth was even more explicit. In his *Mathematical Psychics* of 1881, a book the title of which encapsulates the spirit of the entire enterprise, he wrote: "Let there be granted to the science of pleasure what is granted to the science of energy." He invited his readers

> to imagine an ideally perfect instrument, a psychophysical machine, continually registering the height of pleasure experienced by an individual, exactly according to the verdict of consciousness, or rather diverging therefrom according to a *law of errors*. From moment to moment the hedonimeter varies; the delicate index now flickering with the flutter of the passions, now steadied by intellectual activity, low sunk whole hours in the neighbourhood of zero, or momentarily springing up towards infinity.[9]

In the same book, Edgeworth also stated firmly that "the first principle of economics is that every agent is actuated only by self-interest." In fact, this claim is at least as outrageous as the claim that self-interest—or welfare, as we might now say—consists in nothing more than maximizing the quantity of pleasure and minimizing the quantity of pain, but it was only from the latter that economic theory retreated significantly in the ensuing years. Vilfredo Pareto (and later John Hicks) set about establishing all the predictions of marginal utility theory without appeal to any measurable quantitative utility, merely to the notion of preferences for some goods over others. Under the baleful influence of logical positivism, Lionel Robbins and Paul Samuelson went further still, seeking to cleanse economics of all unverifiable psychological terms (like *preference*) and replacing them with the icy objectivity of observable choices. If someone chose to spend money at the races instead of on improving literature, it could be said that going to the races made him better off (*by definition*, it must be stressed). And Robbins argued that no meaning could be given to comparisons between the welfare of one person and another, since no choice behaviour could ever serve to verify such comparisons. His influence was such that for several decades it was the accepted wisdom that one could never say that a starving peasant was worse off (in any sense) than an affluent professional. It is one of the leading historical ironies of the subject that the periods when it has been most influenced by philosophical fashion (as by utilitarianism in the 1870s and 1880s, and by logical positivism in the 1930s and 1940s) have also been its times of greatest philosophical naïvety. We may borrow a quip from Anthony Quinton and describe the "new welfare economics" spawned by Robbins as the economics profession's answer to the "Charge of the Light Brigade."

Before I turn to an assessment, one final episode is of relevance in this canter through the evolution of the theory of value in economics. The theory of decision-making under uncertainty, pioneered by Frank Ramsey in 1926, rediscovered by John von Neumann and Oscar Morgenstern in the 1940s, and refined in the 1950s and 1960s by L. J. Savage and by Richard Jeffrey, took as its primitive explanatory concept the notion of preference and did not appeal to utility or subjective value in any quantitative sense. But by defining this to include preference over uncertain or risky choices the theory was able to use it to derive both a subjective measure of uncertainty (a probability function) and a utility function that was quantitative (though in a slightly restricted sense that need not trouble us here). It did so by making it true by definition that individuals acted so as to maximize the expected value of their actions, that is, the utility of the result multiplied by the probability of the result's occurring. The expected value was defined as whatever could be said to be maximized by the action. The principle of diminishing marginal utility could then explain why individuals were averse to taking risks—the utility resulting from lucky contingencies was not enough to outweigh the proportionately greater loss of utility from unlucky ones.

The significance of this development lay in its claim to make it unnecessary to measure utility directly, while retaining the theoretical and predictive benefits of a quantitative measure. In this way, the science fiction implausibilities of Edgeworth's hedonimeter could be avoided, along with the naïve psychology that accompanied them. However, at this point economic theory faced a dilemma the horns of which were surgically sharp. On one side was the temptation to abandon the naïve psychology altogether and to make the link between utility and observed behaviour purely definitional. Utility, or the subjective value of an action, could be defined as whatever an individual was pursuing in undertaking it—rather as in physics subatomic particles are not observed directly but are defined as theoretical entities that account for experimental observations. On the other hand, it is by no means evident that utility thus defined corresponds at all closely to the well-being or self-interest of individuals, or indeed to any stable or persistent component of individuals' psychological or moral make-up. To escape emasculation by this dangerous horn, economists have been tempted to insert into the theory substantive claims. Having first made self-interest identical by definition with whatever individuals happen to pursue, we find it seductively easy to claim that this represents their true self-interest as more commonly understood, and to forget that in the process we have moved from a tautology to a crude psychological falsehood. When it is additionally claimed—as it frequently is—that self-interest in this sense is equivalent to the consumption of material goods and services, then all the worst fears of Edmund Burke seem to have been realized.

Does this history warrant the complaint that economics enshrines a philistine conception of value? Does it warrant the four more specific complaints mentioned at the beginning of this chapter? Enough has been said so far to make clear my view that the first complaint, as it stands, is an unfair one. "The price of everything and the value of nothing" is not an apt account of the economist's sphere of interest. Indeed, we owe to medieval and Enlightenment economists the explicit examination of the complex ways in which price or exchange-value was related to other concepts of value while being quite different from them. It is true that use-value has become rather tarnished by association with the development of utility theory. But it is undeniable that, for Smith and for Marx, it could encompass individual and social values over a wide range. A great variety of human purposes and values can have among their consequences that of motivating individuals to enter markets to trade and can be relevant to an explanation of the formation of prices in such a market. And conversely, the most thoughtful economists have always been alive to the influences running in the other direction, to the many ways in which the system of economic exchange expands, restricts, or otherwise alters the opportunities human beings face in pursuit of the diverse ends they value.

The second complaint, that the market is simply an inappropriate mechanism for allocating some kinds of resource, is harder to assess. One reason for this is that markets never have been and never could be the allocative mechanism for all the things, abstract and concrete, that we value. For example, a state of reasonable civil order in which contracts are enforced is an essential precondition for markets to operate in any recognizable way—so the distribution of law enforcement services cannot itself be wholly market-determined (it can, of course, be partially so, as the existence of private armies indicates). Second, there are many reasons in economic theory why some markets cannot operate efficiently; examples include some kinds of insurance market, and markets characterized by so-called externalities, where the actions of some participants directly affect the welfare of others (as in the case of pollution). So it is abundantly clear that the market unaided cannot appropriately distribute everything that we value, just as the market unaided cannot ensure equal or just distributions (unless "just" tautologically means "market-determined," as some right-wing economists believe). The view that the market is sometimes inappropriate is not always, however, directed against such a flimsy target. It sometimes comes more subtly in the form of the claim that there are some things (health care is a frequently cited example) that should not be treated as economic commodities, for that is in some sense to devalue them. The argument is not necessarily metaphorical: Richard Titmuss's book *The Gift Relationship* compares the United States' commercial market in blood for transfusions with the United Kingdom's system of voluntary supply, concluding that the former is economically inefficient and leads to a much greater risk of hepatitis infection. In addition, he argues that "the commercialisation of blood and donor relationships represses the expression of altruism, erodes the sense of community, lowers scientific standards . . . increases the danger of unethical behaviour,"[10] and so on.

Claims of this nature are extremely difficult to judge for several reasons. First, it is not easy to see what makes them apply more to health care than to some other candidates. It is unlikely to be on grounds of the importance of health care to our well-being: food, for instance, is just as important but is obviously subject to the economic realities of scarcity. It is something for which satisfactory alternatives to some degree of market allocation (albeit regulated and assisted) have yet to be found. Second, it is often difficult to distinguish systems of market exchange from those in which exchange is ostensibly communitarian in spirit but nevertheless bound by very elaborate and formal rules of reciprocity, as in the potlatch systems discussed in Marcel Mauss's book *The Gift*. Third, no adequate general reason has been suggested why participation in a market should in itself lead to greater selfishness and a repression of community spirit. As we have seen, people may take part in markets under any number of motivations. It is simply false to say that human behaviour, economic or otherwise, is always self-interested. This is not to say that it is predominantly motivated by honour, altruism, and the love of truth either: malice, jealousy, revenge, snobbery, and hatred are springs of action that can equally ignore the self-interest of the agent. Whatever one believes to be the general balance between self-interest and other motives in accounting for human action, it remains an open question whether (and if so in what direction) participation in markets tilts this balance. Whether it is right to distribute health care by a market mechanism is, as a result, a very uncertain matter. The attitudes of those affected may be as ambiguous as Huckleberry Finn's remark about Uncle Silas, "the innocentest, best old soul I ever see . . . [who] had a little one-horse log church at the back of the plantation, which he built it himself at his own expense . . . and never charged nothing for his preaching, and it was worth it, too."

What of the third complaint, that economics ignores values that cannot be quantified? A context in which this commonly arises is the valuation of human life, particularly in cost-benefit analysis. Two versions of the complaint should be distinguished. First, it is often true that economists performing cost-benefit analysis *leave out* such values on the grounds that they cannot be quantified. This is no more defensible than leaving out any other factor of importance, and it raises no special issues here. Second, economists sometimes attempt to value such intangibles by crude methods that give an air of spurious precision to an inherently imprecise enterprise. There is much force in these complaints, and there is little doubt that the excessive pretensions of utility theory have contributed to economists' tendency to underrate the difficulties of precise valuation. None the less, decisions have to be taken, both individually and in the public sphere. Such decisions have profound effects on, for example, the risks to human life, and so inevitably incorporate assumptions—

perhaps implicit ones—about the value accorded to human life and other intangibles in the context concerned. Such assumptions enter into economic decisions, so it is the job of economists to ensure that they do so explicitly rather than implicitly. Naturally, economists have no expertise, no privileged position from which to pronounce on what the respective valuations should be. But this is as true of values that are quantifiable as of those that are not. The proper task of economists is much less to design the moral architecture of human life than to fix the plumbing. As far as appreciation of the edifice is concerned, a Ph.D. confers no extra insights.

All the same, the complaint about quantification contains an ineradicable element of truth (on my own calculations, 34.8 per cent, plus or minus 7.4 per cent). The way in which economic theory analyses decision-making (on the part both of individuals and, by extension, of societies) involves giving a strong interpretation to the Aristotelian dictum that "there must be one standard by which all commodities are to be measured." Now, of course, if different products trade for money, there is some standard by which they can be compared, namely, their price. So much is a definitional point. But it is going a great deal further to claim that there is some other common component of value, separately identifiable, from which commodities derive their comparability by price. For utilitarians, this has never been disturbing. The central method in utilitarianism is to explain the moral properties of a whole range of diverse actions and situations by reference to the common value of utility. Actions are chosen to maximize utility; once that is achieved there is no residue of value unfulfilled, no foothold for regret. As such, the utilitarian approach stands opposed to pluralism, according to which human goals and values are irreconcilably diverse; the pursuit of some inevitably involves the sacrifice of others, and there is no common property of all these goals that alone represents their true value. Naturally we have to make decisions between them, but to invoke a common utility to explain how we do so is no more illuminating than the explanation in Molière that opium sends people to sleep because of its "dormative faculty."

Economic theory as it stands today has never really outgrown its utilitarian adolescence. It falsely represents individual decision-making as determined entirely by an assessment of future prospects, ignoring the effects of past habits, commitments, and scruples that play a large part in human character. It leaves no room for analysis of the way in which human institutions and cultural practices determine casts of thought (except by "changing the incentives"). By painting human values in monochrome, it ignores the irreconcilability in them, and therefore the degree of sacrifice that choice involves. Economics knows no tragedy. Although rhetorically expressed, this is not just a rhetorical point. For the way in which economists think influences profoundly the way in which they behave, and the advice they offer to others. By representing human values as reducible to a common base, we have been encouraged to think that the choice of policies, for people and for nations, is at root a technical matter. We have thought it a question of discovering (as we might put it) the rates of exchange between different values such as prosperity, equity, job satisfaction, and environmental concern. Disagreements are seen as due to a fogginess in perception, eradicable with time and education. By a process of reinforcement, such an attitude may even contribute to the rancour of disagreement itself, since protagonists convinced that only their opponents' stupidity prevents concord will never easily be dislodged. This has made economists lumberingly ill-equipped to cope with political discourse in a society in which irreconcilability of values, precariously contained within a democracy, is the very stuff of public argument. It is indeed an irony, as I suggested at the outset, that this utilitarian inheritance should be so dominant in a profession that has made disagreement its public trade mark.

Notes

1. Edmund Burke, *Reflections on the Revolution in France* (London, 1st ed.), pp. 112–113.
2. Michael Allingham, *Value* (London: Macmillan, 1983), p. 1.
3. Adam Smith, *The Wealth of Nations* (London: Penguin, 1980), pp. 131–132.
4. Aristotle, *The Nichomachaean Ethics*, translated by J. A. K. Thomson (Harmondsworth: Penguin, 1955), p. 152.
5. For an example, see Rudel Kaulla, *The Theory of the Just Price* (London: John Murray, 1940).
6. James Gordley, "Equality in Exchange," *California Law Review* 69, no. 6 (December 1981): 1587–1656.

7. Karl Marx, *Capital* (London: Lawrence & Wishart, 1954), vol. I, iv, p. 77.
8. William Jevons, *The Theory of Political Economy* (London: Macmillan, 1871).
9. Francis Edgeworth, *Mathematical Psychics* (London: C. Kegan Paul, 1881), p. 101.
10. Richard Titmuss, *The Gift Relationship: From Human Blood to Social Policy* (New York: Random House, 1971).

Bibliography

Debreu, Gerard. *Theory of Value*. New Haven: Cowles Foundation, 1959. (Formidably mathematical, but a classic.)
Hicks, John R. *Value and Capital*. Oxford: Clarendon Press, 1939.
Morishima, Michio. *Marx's Economics*. Cambridge: Cambridge University Press, 1973.
Roll, Epic. *History of Economic Thought*. 4th ed. London: Faber & Faber, 1973.
Samuelson, Paul A. *Economics*. 11th ed. New York: McGraw-Hill, 1980.

Values in the Civil Law

J. K. B. M. NICHOLAS

There is a distinction between procedural values, which set minimum standards of fair decision-making (what lawyers call "natural justice"), and substantive values, which are embodied in the rules of conduct applied in such decisions. This essay will be principally concerned with substantive values; in so far as they reflect moral values, they can be only those minimally necessary for orderly life in society. To attempt more would conflict with the value of individual freedom. This value in turn may conflict with the value of collectivism (as embodied in trade union activity). In other contexts other values may prevail, for example, the economic value of efficient loss-distribution. In some situations a value-governed solution of any kind may be practically unattainable (other than by total judicial discretion, which is the negation of law). In many such situations, particularly commercial ones, certainty, not ideal justice, is the overriding value. But again there are some areas, particularly those of the family and divorce, where a large element of discretion is increasingly prevailing over fixed rules.

To begin with a definition of terms, "civil law" is here taken to mean that part of the law that regulates relations between individuals (to the exclusion of the criminal law, which punishes acts that, although they may be directed against individuals, are penalized because they threaten the good order of society). I also exclude law that governs the relations between individuals and public authorities. My concern is confined to English law, with occasional references to law in the United States. The values I examine are in the main those reflected in the common law, that is, law made by the courts, or in the attitude taken by the courts to enacted law, since obviously enacted law will often reflect the values of the party in power at the time when it was enacted. Conservative trade union statutes exhibit different values from those enacted when a Labour government was in power.

It might seem self-evident that the primary or overriding value of law, whether civil or criminal, must be justice. That great Victorian building in the Strand contains the Royal Courts of Justice, and the judges who sit there are referred to by the title of Mr. Justice, and, farther east, there stands, high over the Central Criminal Court at the Old Bailey, the blindfolded figure of Justice with her scales. And yet it was said in a eulogy of the man who guided my first steps in law, and who was both a good lawyer and an admired tutor, that he always took an early opportunity of bringing his pupils face to face with the vital difference between justice and the law of the land. There is, however, no inconsistency here—merely an exemplification of two senses of the word *justice*. The first sense is a procedural one. Justice means adjudication or the settling of disputes and looks to the procedure by which the adjudication is carried out. The collective name for the courts that sit in the Strand is the Supreme Court of Judicature, and the virtues the statue of Justice at the Old Bailey personifies are those of even-handedness and lack of bias.

The only strictly legal context in which the word *justice* occurs (apart from that of titles such as those I have mentioned) is that of the principles of "natural justice" which the High Court requires subordinate tribunals to observe in exercising their function of adjudication, and which, *a fortiori*, the proceedings of the courts themselves are expected to embody. Those principles of "natural justice" are concerned with the way in which the decision of the adjudicating body is arrived at, not with the substance or content of the decision itself. They are the principles of a fair trial or, as American say, of due process. It would be perfectly possible for there to be one legal system in which iniquitous rules were fairly applied, and another in which rules good in themselves were unfairly applied. An American Supreme Court judge has expressed the view that it might be preferable to live under the former system rather than under the latter (Jackson J. in *Shaughnessy* v. *United States* [1953]).

It is here that we come to the second of the two meanings of justice. When my tutor introduced his pupils to the difference between justice and the law of the land, he was not concerned with the principles of "natural justice" (which are indeed part of the law of the land). He was concerned with substantive, not procedural, justice, with the justice of the rule, not with the fairness of the procedure by which the rule was applied. And he was, of course, concerned to show, not (or not necessarily) that the rule was unjust, but that the values the substantive law embodies are often not those which a non-lawyer would at a first glance expect. The Royal Courts of Justice in the Strand will be called by the bus-conductor, and by most other people, the Law Courts. And this is also right. The rules they apply are the rules of English law. They endeavour to apply them justly, in accordance with "natural justice," but, subject to that, their duty is to apply the rules, not to find the "just solution" to each case.

Accordingly, we deal first with procedural values, and then with substantive values.

Procedural Values

English common law grew out of the proceedings and decisions of the courts, whereas the continental civil law (if an oversimplification be here permitted) derived from the teachings of universities and the writings associated with that teaching. It is, therefore, characteristic of the common law that it places great emphasis on procedural matters. Nor is this in our present context inappropriate. The minimum purpose of law must be to avoid violence by ensuring the peaceful settlement of disputes. Order is a fundamental legal value. And as a *legal* value it must have the characteristic of regularity, that is, of being governed by rules and therefore being predictable. A capricious order is a contradiction in terms. Pure caprice cannot be guarded against by procedural rules, but pure caprice is not in real life a common danger. It is against caprice resulting from bias or neglect that the rules of natural justice are directed. They set minimum standards of fair decision-making. The two central principles are that (a) no one should be judge in his own cause, and (b) both (or all) parties should be heard. From the first of these it follows that the person deciding the case must not have any interest in the outcome, whether that interest be financial or, for example, one of affection or relationship; or, again, that, in a criminal or disciplinary case, he must not have had any part in bringing the charge. From the second it follows that each party must have an opportunity of stating and supporting his own case and of knowing and criticizing the other party's case.

Abundant cases have elaborated these principles in a good deal of detail. Into this we cannot go, but the foregoing summary is perhaps sufficient to indicate what a common lawyer means by natural justice. It is "natural" in the sense that the common lawyer takes it to be inherent in the very nature of the judicial process, though it would be more exact to say that it is inherent in the judicial process as that process is understood in common law systems.

Substantative Values

The non-lawyer may well say that the procedural values we have been so far considering, while they are unexceptionable and unsurprising, are not what he is thinking of when he asks what values the law embodies. He is concerned with the substance of the decision, not the procedure by which it has been reached. Here the lawyer is very much less inclined to be explicit. In part this is because the myth of law, if one may use the word, requires that it be seen as outside and above its transient human instruments, the judges, and too close an examination of the values it embodies may reveal its variability and its dependence on those instruments. The myth carries vastly less conviction now than it did even a generation ago, and no lawyer now is unaware of the large element of choice between different values that necessarily enter into some judicial decisions; but the judge is still reluctant to move too explicitly into an area that, for good constitutional reasons, he thinks to be appropriate to the legislature. The values that are identified in what follows are not therefore authoritatively formulated by the courts in the way that the principles of natural justice are laid down, but they are all invoked, at one time or another, in support of decisions of the courts (which have usually been formally arrived at on more specifically "legal" grounds).

First, however, a distinction should be made between those values a system of law is capable of embodying and those it is not. This is related to, though not identical with, a distinction that is often made between two kinds or levels of morality. Terminology varies, but they may conveniently be called the morality of duty and the morality of aspiration, and, in terms of the Old and the New Testaments, they may be said to be exemplified in the Ten Commandments and the Sermon on the Mount. The distinction is not sharp. There is rather a continuum between the two, at some point on which the pressure of duty gives way to the challenge of excellence, but the broad division is recognizable. In so far as the law embodies a morality, it can be only the morality of duty. The law cannot find a place for mercy, for example, or love. This is not to say that mercy may not be found at work in a legal context. A judge may be moved by mercy in determining what sentence to impose, but this is an area within the legal process that the law does not attempt to regulate. It is significant that where mercy intervenes to give release from or to mitigate a legal penalty, it does so by the exercise of the royal prerogative and is therefore entirely outside the law and beyond the reach of the courts.

The morality of duty calls very largely for abstentions, and this is emphatically true of law. If one leaves aside the area of contract (that is, the area where one has made what the law regards as a binding agreement, an area where obviously one may place oneself under a duty to act), the law only rarely requires one to act, in contrast to a requirement that one abstain from acting; and where there is a duty to act, it is more likely to be sanctioned by the law of tort than by criminal law. In other words, the consequence of failing to act is more likely to be that one is required to compensate someone to whom one's failure to act has caused loss than that one incurs a penalty. Arthur Hugh Clough's "The Latest Decalogue" accurately set out the precept of the law, if not of morality: "Thou shalt not kill, but needst not strive/Officiously to keep alive."

The law says that I may passively watch a child drowning and incur no liability, unless I stand in some special relationship to the child that can be said to require me to do something, for example, I am in charge of the child or have behaved in such a way as to lead others to believe that I am in charge of it. So it has been held that men who stood by as spectators while a woman was subjected to a series of brutal rapes committed no crime (and, though this was not in issue, they certainly committed no tort against her). The reason for this reluctance of the law to impose duties to act lies in its respect for the value of certainty or predictability (to which we shall return). If a man is to be penalized or made to pay damages for a failure to act, the circumstances in which he is required to act must be fairly definable. In the case of the drowning child, the picture in one's mind is of a healthy man beside a placid river. But what if the river is a raging torrent and the man has a very weak heart and is the only support of a large family? Or what if the spectators of the rape are held back by a man with a machine-gun? It would indeed be possible to say that liability for failure to intervene in such cases would be incurred only if intervention would not involve any risk for the rescuer. This leaves a lot to be defined and is open to Bentham's objection that it makes law as a man makes law for his dog—by punishing him after the event. But this is true of all case-law (which was Bentham's target) and the question is therefore one of degree. That such a rule is practicable is shown by the fact that it exists in French law (and in some other systems), although it has there been very restrictively interpreted. That it is rejected in England probably exemplifies, in addition to the value of certainty, another value by which the common law sets store, perhaps to excess, that of individual independence. To this also we shall return.

Within these negative limits, what values does the substantive law embody? For criminal law the primary values are plainly the preservation of order and the protection of life and property by the punishment of acts that endanger or damage them either intentionally or recklessly or even, in a few cases, negligently. (Lawyers are manifestly uncomfortable about the few offences, in relation to such matters as the sale of food, which can be committed without any fault at all.) But our concern is with civil law and here the primary values cannot be so simply or self-confidently stated.

If a person with no knowledge of the law (but with someone to keep him within the procedural principles of natural justice) were told to do justice in a criminal court, he would be much more likely to produce tolerable results than if he were told to do justice in a civil court. If he were presented with a case arising out of an alleged contract, he would no doubt start from the commonly accepted moral principle that one ought to carry out one's promises. But if, in an expansive moment, I promise to give my nephew £10,000 to start him in a business, and then half an hour later change my mind, must I pay? Will it make any difference if, in that half hour, my nephew has bought some equipment for the business? And, if it does make a difference, must I pay him the £10,000 I promised or only the net loss which he suffers from, let us assume, reselling the equipment? English law has traditionally said that if my nephew has promised to do something for me in return for my promise (has "given consideration" for it), I am bound to pay, whereas if he has not, I am free to change my mind, even if he has acted on my promise, for example, by buying equipment. Here the value from which our hypothetical lay judge started was the sanctity of promises; what the law substitutes is the sanctity of bargains (which, in turn of course, poses questions as to what constitutes a bargain). Some, particularly in the United States, would say that my nephew should be compensated for the net loss he has suffered by relying on my promise. The value here is not so much a matter of promises or bargains as of compensating those who foreseeably suffer loss in reliance on my representations.

The values that we have been envisaging so far have been, in some sense, moral values such as might guide an individual in determining his conduct. But by no means are all legal values of this kind. If one turns from the law of contract to the law of tort (that is, the rules that determine the circumstances in which a person is required to compensate another for loss or damage caused to him other than by a failure to perform a contract), one does indeed find that for the most part the law starts from the recognizably moral principle that one ought to make compensation for loss caused to another by one's fault, but one not infrequently finds that this is superseded by other, different principles. The subject my old tutor chose to show the difference between justice and the law of the land was that of vicarious liability, that is, the rules determining the circumstances in which A is liable for damage caused by the fault of another, B (usually an employee), even though A had not authorized B to do the act or, possibly, had even forbidden him to do it, and even though he had exercised all due care in choosing, training, and equipping B. The "justice" that the law here rejects is the principle that one should not be liable unless one is at fault. Various justifications are given—that is, various alternative values are offered. The starting-point of the problem is, of course, that though B is himself liable for his own fault, he is unlikely to have the means to pay compensation. This is not in itself a justification for making A pay, since obviously the same difficulty may arise in other situations where the person at fault is not an employee. But a justification that is sometimes accepted is that the employer, A, usually derives benefits from the activities of B, and since the choice is between leaving the victim uncompensated and imposing liability on A, the latter is preferable. (Of course in any given case A may not benefit or B may in fact be able to pay, but the lawyer will answer this objection in terms of the values of certainty and simplicity.) May I remark in passing that, in somewhat the same way, a person who chooses to indulge in some unusually dangerous activity may be held liable for all the consequences of that activity, regardless of fault.

The "benefit" principle is, however, still a moral principle of the kind that might guide an individual. The most commonly accepted justification of the vicarious liability is, however, of a different sort. It is expressed in the economic terms of loss distribution. The need to compensate the victim should not be looked at in moral terms of paying for one's fault, but it should be seen as one of the statistically inevitable costs of modern business. And it is the employer who is in a position to spread that cost widely, either by passing it on in his prices or by insurance.

The widespread practice of insurance has indeed brought into question the whole moral principle of fault liability. Since the insured person or company does not itself pay for the consequences of its fault (except possibly very indirectly though increased premiums), what is the point of conducting perhaps costly litigation to determine whether or not there was fault? Should not the whole matter of compensation for injuries be taken out of the moral context of fault and treated as simply one of the risks of modern life against which, in one way or another, there is compulsory or state-providing insurance, as there is, for example, for industrial accidents? The question is too large to pursue here, but its relevance lies in pointing to the fact that increasingly, in some areas of the law, problems are seen in terms of economic efficiency, not of moral conduct.

Moreover, even in areas in which, in the main, the values applied are in some sense moral, it may, in some situations, be impossible to do "justice"; and yet the law has to give an answer. To return to the law of contract, there is the problem, familiar to all students, of determining the moment at which negotiations conducted by post can be taken to have crystallized into a contract. When is there a bargain? In the case of negotiations conducted face to face or by telephone, the answer is easy: when they reach agreement on the essentials. But what if I send you an offer through the post to sell you my car for £1,000 and you send an acceptance; but at the time when you post your acceptance, there is aready on its way from me a letter withdrawing my offer? There is no agreement at any time and yet you are assuming that you have bought the car, and I am assuming that you have not. What rule is the law to apply? Was my acceptance effective or not? Here we come to the value of certainty or predictability. There are no convincing reasons for favouring one rule rather than the other. It would be, at least in theory, possible for the law to say that the judge should use his discretion and decide each case on whatever particular merits he can find, but this would leave the outcome of every case uncertain until it had been litigated (or settled out of court), which for businessmen would be intolerable. An arbitrary but certain rule—in English law that the acceptance is effective when posted—is better than no rule at all.

Again, if I take my bicycle in for repair and the repair-man sells it to a buyer who is unaware that the repair-man has no right to sell it, to whom does the bicycle belong, that is, is it I or the buyer who will have to get compensation from the repair-man? This question becomes crucial if, as usually happens, the repair-man is insolvent. There is no "just" rule and yet, as in the previous case, some rule there must be.

For the lawyer, therefore, certainty, is an important value. He mistrusts what he sometimes calls "palm tree justice" (a term derived, when and how I do not know, from the image of the *qadi* dispensing justice on the particular merits of each individual case—an image no doubt unfair to *qadis*). And it is, indeed, universally agreed that an important aspect of justice is that like should be treated alike. What is at issue, of course, is the level of generality at which "like" should be determined. Rules necessarily have a fairly high degree of generality, and when it is said (to take another lawyer's tag) that "hard cases make bad law," the point being made is that the value of certainty or generality will sometimes lead to consequences the *qadi* would not reach.

The lawyer's value of certainty is, however, to some extent linked to another value, which echoes the *laissez-faire* ideas of the nineteenth century. This is the value of individualism and its corollary that the law should confine its intervention to the minimum necessary to enable individualism to flourish. Nor is it surprising that the value of individualism has been strongly emphasized, as can be seen in the early attitude of the courts to the collectivism expressed in the trade union movement. Not only was it in the nineteenth century the dominant philosophy (and it has often been observed that the values the law embodies tend to lag somewhat behind those currently in vogue), but the judges are drawn from a profession itself intensely individualistic.

There has, however, in recent years been a very marked shift away from the values of certainty and individualism towards discretion and paternalism. This has sometimes, indeed, taken place in areas in which the value of certainty is least compelling. For example, a testator can no longer deny his dependants any share in his estate: they can ask a court to order reasonable provision to be made for them. And the courts have a wide discretion to divide up matrimonial property in divorce. But discretion also enters extensively into areas where certainty used to be most powerful. For example, the courts now have power to strike out certain unfair provisions in many types of contract. And recently what might have been thought to be the last stronghold of certainty was breached. It has always been said that certainty is most important where the disposition of property is concerned. And nowadays the disposition of property is intimately connected with the incidence of taxation. In construing tax statutes the courts have traditionally applied the values of certainty and individualism very rigorously. A transaction was not taxable unless it fell clearly within the limits of the relevant statute, even if the sole purpose of the transaction was to avoid payment of tax. Recently, however, the House of Lords has held, in a case involving a complicated series of transactions of this kind, that although each individual transaction fell outside the scope of the tax law, the disposition that resulted from the series was nevertheless taxable because the overall purpose was to avoid tax. Since few transactions of any consequence are entered into without regard to taxation, this new approach seems to enlarge considerably the area of judicial discretion. The value of certainty gives ground to the value of equality (of taxpayers) before the law.

There is, in short, a fundamental tension in the law between the value of certainty or generality and more particular values, between the need for predictability and the desire to adapt each decision to the merits of the individual case. The art of the great judge is to use this tension to creative ends.

Bibliography

Atiyah, Patrick S. *Law and Modern Society*. Oxford: Oxford University Press, 1983.

Dowrick, Frank E. *Justice According to the English Common Lawyers*. London: Butterworth, 1961.

Fuller, Lon L. *The Morality of Law*. Rev. ed. New Haven: Yale University Press, 1969.

Stein, Peter and Shand, John. *Legal Values in Western Society*. Edinburgh: Edinburgh University Press, 1974.

Justice

D. C. M. YARDLEY

> It is not what a lawyer tells me I *may* do; but what humanity, reason, and justice tell me I ought to do.
> —Edmund Burke, *Speech on Conciliation with America*, 22 March 1775.

It is customary for law to be taught, understood, and practised as a series of rules within a framework of justice. The actual practice of law, both in the courts and outside them, in all probability often strays some way from any abstract concept of justice, especially since it is so much tinctured by an adversarial approach. Yet judges still constantly strive to determine cases and jurists seek to explain their views, both by reference to the ideal of justice.

Unfortunately abstract concepts are very difficult to pin down. Jurists have quite often tried to define such fundamental legal concepts as "right," "duty," "privilege," and "power," and judges have sometimes affected to follow their example, though again their efforts have not infrequently appeared to contradict the conceptual structure built up by the theorists. But justice has been so universally regarded as basic to all legal thought that it has largely been taken for granted. Some writers have indeed discussed it, but judges by and large have merely assumed that what they decide is intended to be just unless some possibly obsolescent legal rule happens to impede the search for justice in any particular case. The *Concise Oxford Dictionary* definition of justice is "just conduct; fairness; exercise of authority in maintenance of right." But this does not take us far along the road towards a clear explanation of its meaning. The nature of justice may be readily understood in general, but it is not easily defined.

The meaning of justice may best be approached by an examination of its effect upon the relationships between man and man, and between man and the state. Thus we find that the idea of justice is inherent in most of the rules of civil law and criminal law, of private law (such as family law and the law of contract) and of public law (which includes the law of crime and the rules regulating the limits of the powers of government, both central and local), and even in many of the procedural rules of court. Let us examine the operation of a few of these rules within the British legal system.

In our private law, it is a fundamental requirement before an enforceable contract can be accepted as being in existence that an offer has been made and accepted in the terms in which it was made. Of course, some offers may be illegal for reasons of public policy or because they are criminal, and some agreements may be affected by other rules derived from the laws enacted by Parliament relating to industrial relations, sex discrimination, and so forth. But essentially, a contract's validity and enforceability depends upon the striking of an unequivocal bargain between the offeror and the offeree. Only if there has been a *consensus ad idem* does a contract exist. If there has been some fundamental mistake made by one or both of the parties, or if one party has in some way misrepresented the nature of his part of the bargain, then the court may consider whether the contract has been vitiated thereby. Through this whole scheme runs the basic assumption that there must have been a clear meeting of the minds of both parties before the law will assist either party by enforcing the agreement in the courts: to permit any other solution in law would be to countenance injustice.

In the law of real property the recognition of certain rights over land vested in people other than the owners or occupiers of that land is an important factor. Thus easements, such as rights of way, rights of light, and rights to take water from or discharge it over the land of another, may be enjoyed by the owners or occupiers of an adjacent piece of land. Again, profits, the right to take things of value from property, such as the right of fishery or the right of common pasture, may be similarly enjoyed; and rights in favour of the public (for example, the right to use a public highway) or else of a limited class of the public (for example, the rights of the inhabitants of a village to use the village green for recreation purposes) may also be recognized. The persistence of all these rights, to the apparent detriment of those of the owner of the land upon or over which they are exercised, is clearly related to the demands of comity, common sense, and justice.

A fundamental ingredient found in the law of torts, that is, the law concerning civil wrongs outside the relationship of contract, is reasonableness, especially in connection with the tort of negligence. Where a man has a duty to take care and in failing to discharge this duty injures another, he is liable in damages for his negligence. The test of whether or not he has failed to discharge his duty of care is whether he has done what a reasonable man in his position should have done to guard against injuring the plaintiff. By the use of this test, liability may always be established for physical injury, but it has also in recent years been extended to financial loss caused by a negligent misstatement (rather than an act) when the circumstances show that there was a relationship between two parties wherein there was a duty not only to be honest but also to be careful. Thus in one case, a potato wholesaler who negligently gave a dealer wrong advice about another dealer's credit-worthiness was held liable to the dealer for his loss incurred in reliance upon the advice.[1] The thread of what is reasonable as a solution to the dispute, depending upon what it was reasonable to expect of the parties involved, is closely related to ideas of justice.

A basic assumption of our criminal law is that an accused person should not be found guilty of committing a crime unless he intended to do the thing of which he is charged, or else intended to do something sufficiently close to it in nature. To this rule there is, in practice, a very large exception made by the existence of a whole class of crimes that have become absolute offences in the sense that it is not necessary for the prosecution to prove intent. The crimes included in it are all deemed to be acts or omissions not to be tolerated, whether or not they are intended—for instance, driving a car at a speed above the legal speed limit, or riding a bicycle at night without a real light. But the existence of this large exception does not destroy the essential basis of criminal law which will continue to apply unless there is good reason to the contrary. From among the most serious of crimes let us cite that of murder. The taking of a human life is unlawful and amounts to murder when it is done by an act that is intended or known to be likely to cause death or really serious bodily harm, unless it can be justified on such special grounds as self-defence or the killing of an enemy in time of war. Serious bodily harm is so close in nature to death that intention to cause it is accepted by the courts as sufficient intent to justify a conviction for murder if death actually results.

The practical application of a conscious effort to provide for justice in law is perhaps most clearly seen in the rapidly growing area of administrative law, which governs the relationships between citizens and the administrative organs of the state. In three respects is this seen most clearly: the decisions of the courts that unreasonable behaviour in discharging statutory functions renders such discharge invalid; the reliance of the courts upon the rules of natural justice as basic requirements of administrative action; and the growth of the ombudsman system. Let us briefly examine each of these three areas.

First, unreasonableness. Parliament, under the Constitution of the United Kingdom, unwritten as it is, has undoubted sovereign legal authority in the sense that it can enact anything it wills by an act of Parliament, and that whatever it enacts is of binding force in law unless and until it is changed by another act of Parliament. It follows that Parliament may validly confer upon ministers, local authorities, or indeed any other person or body the power to exercise authority in various fields of activity, and that authority when exercised also has the force of law. But the courts, while constantly stressing their subservience to the legislative will of Parliament, nevertheless maintain their function to interpret statutes and the purported exercise of statutory power; and in this latter capacity they have provided an unbroken stream of authority that power exercised unreasonably is *ultra vires* and thus void.

There have been so many cases apropos of this that it is difficult to choose just one or two for purposes of illustration, but probably the most famous case of all is *Roberts* v. *Hopwood*, decided by the House of Lords in 1925.[2] The Poplar Borough Council just after the First World War was dominated by the Labour party. It was one of the boroughs within the area then covered by the London County Council, although later it became part of a much larger London borough created by the London Government Act 1963. In 1920 the Poplar Council, wishing to set an example as a model socialist employer, introduced a minimum weekly wage for all its employees of £4 for men and women alike. The previous minimum wage had been a little over £3 for men and about £2.10.0 for women. The introduction of equal pay for men and women in any sphere of employment was unusual in the early part of the twentieth century, but apparently no issue was taken on this point at the beginning. However, in 1921 and 1922 there was a marked fall in the cost of living and of wages generally, something that has certainly not been seen since the Second World War, when unemployment has all too frequently gone hand in hand with inflation of prices and of wages. With the fall in the cost of living and wages it was quite normal in many walks of life in the early 1920s for employees to accept a reduction in their wages without demur. But the Poplar Borough Council was determined to stick to its principles as a model employer and accordingly continued to maintain its own £4 minimum wage. Now the council's statutory power was to pay its servants "such salaries and wages as [they] may think fit," which would appear on its face to be a very wide power indeed. But the district auditor, who has to make an annual inspection of local government accounts, disallowed a proportion of the wages actually paid to the employees, amounting to some £5,000 in all, as being an "item of account contrary to law," and he surcharged it upon the councillors responsible, thus making them personally liable to repay the sum. (It may be noted in passing that, by the Local Government Act 1972, s.161, the power of district auditors to surcharge those responsible for unlawful expenditure was removed, and surcharging may now only be effected as a result of a court order.) The House of Lords unanimously upheld the district auditor's order, for it held that Parliament must have intended that in fixing wages the council should have regard to the labour market. By acting without regard to it, and for extraneous reasons which Lord Atkinson colourfully described as "eccentric principles of socialist philanthropy" and "feminist ambition," the council had abused its powers and fixed wage rates that were excessive.

It is unlikely, in these politically sensitive times, that a law lord would today go so far as Lord Atkinson did in his assessment of the motives of the Poplar Borough Council. But even discounting his rather strong language the legal message is clear. The council had acted with improper motives and unreasonably. The test of these motives was provided by the legislation that was being interpreted. Even though the act concerned appeared to confer a subjective power to pay such wages as the council "may think fit," the Lords were taking the view that a council could not think fit unless it actually *thought* fit—that is, considered all relevant factors before coming to a considered decision on the basis of all such evidence before it. It was not enough for a local authority to be high-minded and hope to set a general example for others; it must only act in reasonable accordance with the evidence before it, and, by purposely ignoring such a relevant factor as the level of wages, the council was stepping outside the boundaries of the discretion granted by Parliament and thus acting *ultra vires*.

A more modern case of the first importance is *Padfield* v. *Minister of Agriculture, Fisheries and Food*, reported in 1968.[3] It provided no marked variation from the pattern of earlier case-law, nor did it add substantially to the position already firmly stated by many judges. But it does provide an absolutely clear statement of the court's powers at the highest judicial level, and it is totally uncompromising on the nature of these powers of review. The case concerned the milk-marketing scheme for England and Wales.

The Agricultural Marketing Act 1958 makes various provisions concerning agricultural marketing schemes, and the scheme involved in the *Padfield* case was only one of a number in existence at the time. Under this scheme, milk producers had to sell their milk to the Milk Marketing Board, which fixed the different prices for it in each of the eleven regions into which England and Wales were divided. The board consisted largely of members elected by the producers in the individual regions, so that each region had equal representation on the board. Section 19 of the act made provision for the establishment of a committee of investigation, to be charged with the duty "*if the Minister in any case so directs* [italics added], of considering, and reporting to the Minister on . . . any . . . complaint made to the Minister as to the operation of any scheme which, in the opinion of the Minister, could not be considered by a consumers' committee." The section then went on to provide:

> If a committee of investigation report to the Minister that any provision of a scheme or any act or omission of a board administering a scheme is contrary to the interests of consumers of the regulated products, or is contrary to the interests of any persons affected by the scheme and is not in the public interest, the Minister *if he thinks fit to do so* [italics added] after considering the report (a) may by order make such amendments in the scheme as he considers necessary or expedient for the purpose of

rectifying the matter; (b) may by order revoke the scheme; (c) in the event of the matter being one which is within the power of the board to rectify, may by order direct the board to take such steps to rectify the matter as may be specified in the order.

The two italicized phrases in the quotes are important. At first sight they would seem to give as wide subjective discretionary powers as one could possibly find in an act of Parliament, and this was certainly the view taken in *Padfield* itself by the minister. The differentials in the prices paid to the milk producers reflected the varying costs of transporting milk from the producers to the consumers, but the differentials at the time in question had been fixed several years before, after transport costs had altered. The south-eastern region producers contended that the differential between that region and the far-western region should have been altered in a way that would incidentally have affected other regions. But the constitution of the Milk Marketing Board made it impossible for the south-eastern producers to obtain a majority for their proposals. So they asked the Minister of Agriculture to appoint a committee of investigation under the terms of the act. Of course, had the minister agreed to do so, and had the committee reported in their favour, the minister would then have had power under the act "if he thinks fit" to give mandatory directions to the board; and the south-eastern producers hoped that this chain of results would have followed from their complaint and request.

The minister, however, declined to refer the matter to a committee appointed under the terms of the act. The letters from the ministry explaining his decision not to accede to the request contained references to the wide issues affecting other regions; suggested that the matter should be left to "the normal democratic machinery"; stated that the minister owed no duty to any particular region; that he had to bear in mind that he would be expected to give effect to the committee's report; and that in any case he had an unfettered discretion whether or not to refer the complaint. Thereupon the producers applied to the court for an order of mandamus, and the House of Lords, by a majority of four to one, granted it, directing the minister to consider the complaint according to law. The lords expressly held that Parliament had conferred a discretion upon the minister so that it could be used to promote the policy and objects of the act that were to be determined by the construction of the act, and that this was a matter of law for the court. Although there might be reasons that would justify the minister in refusing to refer a complaint, his discretion was not unlimited. It must be exercised properly and, if it appeared that the effect of his refusal to appoint a committee of investigation was to frustrate the policy of the act, the court was entitled to interfere.

It was argued on behalf of the minister that he was not bound by the act to give any reasons for refusing to accede to the producers' request, but the lords said that as he had chosen to give reasons that were patently bad, it was perfectly within the power of the court to decide that he had not properly directed his mind to the issues before him. Furthermore, even if he had not given any reasons, it would still have been within the power of the court to determine from the context of his refusal whether or not he had properly directed his mind to the issues. Most important of all, the lords decisively rejected the notion that the minister might have an unfettered discretion. Lord Upjohn said that the introduction of the adjective *unfettered* in relation to discretion was an unauthorized gloss upon the statute by the minister, and that, in any case, it would probably not even have made any difference to the essential powers of the court if the word had been inserted into the act by the draftsmen. Those brought up, and properly so, upon the notion that Parliament is the sovereign legislature of this country may be surprised by such an assertion. But what Lord Upjohn was saying in effect was no more than that every act of Parliament must be interpreted by reference to its context, its policy, and its objects. In this sense, no discretion, however apparently widely phrased, can ever be truly unfettered, and the House of Lords did a signal service in *Padfield* in reminding us of this simple but vital truth. It is indeed a recognition at the highest level that justice is the object of law, and that it is in its very nature more important than mere statutory words detached from their proper context.

A parallel use of judicial powers is to be seen in the second area of development relating to the rules of natural justice. These rules are two in number only: that no man is to be condemned unheard, and that no man may be a judge in his own cause. They have been used as basic presumptions of required administrative behaviour which can be obviated only by specific enactment by Parliament to the contrary. The full force of these rules was reestablished in modern times by the decision of the House of Lords in *Ridge* v. *Baldwin*, reported in 1984.[4]

The chief constable of Brighton had been tried and acquitted on a criminal charge of conspiracy to obstruct the course of justice. Two other police officers of his force had been tried with him and were convicted. Donovan, J., in sentencing them, said that the facts admitted in the course of the trial "establish that neither of you had that professional and moral leadership which both of you should have had and were entitled to expect from the Chief Constable of Brighton." Mr. Ridge, the chief constable, had been quite properly suspended from duty when first arrested and charged with conspiracy, but after his acquittal the Brighton Watch Committee, which was then the police authority for Brighton, unanimously dismissed him from office without giving him any prior notice or offering him a hearing. His solicitor then applied for a hearing and was allowed to appear before a later meeting of the committee, but the committee confirmed its decision by a vote of nine to three. Mr. Ridge exercised his statutory right of appeal to the home secretary, but his appeal was dismissed. He was particularly anxious to establish that he had been wrongfully dismissed in order to protect his police pension rights, and so he brought an action seeking a declaration that his dismissal from office was illegal, and also claiming damages for wrongful dismissal. He failed in the High Court, and again in the Court of Appeal, but the House of Lords found in his favour by a majority of four to one. The decision in the High Court had been partly on the basis of an interpretation of the police discipline regulations which are not relevant to the subject of this essay, but also partly on the ground that the power to dismiss the chief constable was administrative, and thus not subject to judicial review. The appellate courts also dealt with the effect of the regulations, but the Court of Appeal came to the conclusion that on general grounds the rules of natural justice must be adhered to before such an officer is dismissed—thus rejecting the view that an administrative decision need not accord with natural justice. However, the Court of Appeal considered that, in view of the trial for conspiracy, the remarks of the trial judge about Mr. Ridge, and the hearing of Mr. Ridge's solicitor after the announcement of the dismissal, there was enough to conclude that Ridge must have known the nature of the charge against him, and had been given adequate opportunity to be heard. The majority in the House of Lords agreed that the rules of natural justice were applicable to the circumstances of Ridge's dismissal, but they drew the opposite inference from the Court of Appeal as to the facts, holding that Ridge had had no adequate opportunity to know what charges he faced before the committee, and that he had thereafter also had no adequate opportunity to put his side of the case to them.

So prominent have the rules of natural justice become since *Ridge v. Baldwin* that they have virtually become the prime test of proper administrative procedure. They are the practical reminders of that somewhat abstract concept, the Rule of Law, and they are the embodiment in administrative practice of just dealing.

Finally it may be worth mentioning the development of ombudsmen. Although the most central theme of administrative law is that of judicial control of power, some areas of administrative power or executive discretion have always remained immune from the possibility of judicial review. A decision made by an administrative officer within his lawful jurisdiction, and neither in breach of natural justice nor in error of law, may well therefore be valid, and of course technically reasonable, but nevertheless harsh, or delayed, or inadequately explained. Again, there are whole areas of executive discretion that have always been held to be immune from any type of judicial review. Examples are the discretion of the Crown to grant or refuse so-called political asylum to refugees, or the powers of local education authorities to make discretionary grants to certain types of students. In such cases the traditional remedy available to anyone who considers himself aggrieved has been to approach an M. P., with a view to getting him to ask a question in the House of Commons of the responsible minister, or to approach a local councillor in the hope that he will take the matter up and prevail upon those responsible to change their minds. Any such approach may well be backed up by letters to the press, or by the agitation of some pressure group, but its success is always bound to be problematical, and doubts would always be likely to remain one way or the other as to the justice of the eventual outcome.

It was in response to this haphazard state of affairs that the movement first grew in the United Kingdom for the establishment of some kind of formal extrajudicial channel for the consideration and possible remedy of complaints. Special impetus to the movement was given by the notorious Crichel Down affair, in which it transpired that certain officials in the Ministry of Agriculture had exercised the powers of the ministry to dispose of its land which was surplus to requirement in a manner that discriminated totally unreasonably against a prospective purchaser whose wife was the daughter of the deceased farmer from whom the land had first been compulsorily acquired for wartime purposes by the Crown. The publication in 1954 of a report commissioned by the minister himself to inquire into any possible maladministration within his ministry concerning this matter[5] was the direct cause of the studies and agitation that led to the first United Kingdom ombudsman legislation, the Parliamentary Commissioner Act 1967. This was followed within the space of only a very few years by several other statutes setting up ombudsmen for different areas of administrative power.

Today, there are seven people in the United Kingdom who occupy posts as ombudsmen in offices created by an act of Parliament, though there is some considerable overlap between them and the various offices held. Thus, the Parliamentary Commissioner for Administration for Great Britain happens at the present time also to hold office as the health service commissioner for England, and as health service commissioner for Wales, and as health service commissioner for Scotland, as well as being an *ex officio* member of the Commission for Local Administration in England and the Commission for Local Administration in Wales. Again, the Parliamentary Commissioner for Administration for Northern Ireland happens also at present to hold office as commissioner for complaints for Northern Ireland. In broad terms, however, the Parliamentary and Health Service commissioners deal with complaints of maladministration in central government departments and their offshoots, while the commissions or commissioners for Local Administration, or the Commissioner for Complaints in Northern Ireland, deal with complaints of maladministration in local government. (Thus I, as chairman of the Commission for Local Administration in England, play my part in the latter field of activity.) All ombudsmen have limitations upon their jurisdiction, and this is not the place to consider any of these in detail, or indeed to deal in any depth with the powers or work of ombudsmen. But wherever they find themselves properly considering complaints they are bound to confine their investigations to the consideration of whether or not there has been maladministration causing injustice, and in this respect they do, it is suggested, provide a useful adjunct to the more normal court process.

There is no statutory definition of maladministration, and this has been deliberate. When the House of Commons was considering the Parliamentary Commissioner Bill, Mr. Richard Crossman, the then Lord President of the Council, stated that the government intended to leave it to the ombudsman himself to work out the meaning of the word, and to decide freely what possible things amounted to maladministration. On 18 October 1966, in explaining this government attitude, he nevertheless gave a guide as to the kind of behaviour he had in mind, and it has since become widely known as the "Crossman catalogue": "bias, neglect, inattention, delay, incompetence, ineptitude, perversity, turpitude, arbitrariness and so on."[6] Perhaps the most significant words are the last three, but, in practice, all United Kingdom ombudsmen have found that the most common cases of maladministration are delay, failure to follow agreed policies or procedures, and failure to have a properly worked out procedure for certain administrative purposes. Ombudsmania is now worldwide, and ombudsmen of various types are to be found in all corners of the world, all of them charged with the duty to obtain just treatment for those who are, in practice, debarred from going to courts for redress in the cases concerned.

Returning to where we started, justice can be seen, from the few examples I have given, as well as from countless others I cannot here cover, to be an ideal towards which any self-respecting legal system will constantly strive, though it may be all too rarely that we can be satisfied that the ideal has been reached. Of course, what is often achieved is a kind of compromise, as is clearly shown in the various ways the concepts of reasonableness or unreasonableness are employed. Yet compromise is no bad thing, especially in a democracy. Even though justice is rarely found in any pure form in our law, it is worthwhile to seek it, and compromise may well achieve a good measure of justice for all the different parties to legal disputes.

Notes

1. W. B. Anderson and Sons Ltd. v. Rhodes (Liverpool) Ltd., 2 All E.R. 850 (1967).
2. Roberts v. Hopwood, A.C. 578 (1925).
3. Padfield v. Minister of Agriculture, Fisheries and Food, A.C. 997 (1968).
4. Ridge v. Baldwin, A.C. 40 (1964).

5. Cmd. Paper, 9176, issued by Command of U.K. Government.
6. H.C. Official Report (5th series), col. 51. (verbatim report of the proceedings of the House of Commons, U.K.).

Bibliography

Allen, Sir Carleton. *Law in the Making*. 7th ed. Oxford: Clarendon Press, 1964.
Dias, Reginald W. M. *Jurisprudence*. 4th ed. London: Butterworth, 1976.
Hart, Herbert L. A. *The Concept of Law*. Oxford: Clarendon Press, 1961.
Smith, John C., and Brian Hogan, *Criminal Law*. 6th ed. London: Stevens, 1983.
Street, Harry. *The Law of Torts*. 7th ed. London: Butterworth, 1983.
Treitel, Guenther H. *The Law of Contract*. 6th ed. London: Stevens, 1983.
Wade, Henry W. R. *Administrative Law*. 5th ed. Oxford: Clarendon Press, 1982.
Yardley, David C. M. *Principles of Administrative Law*. London: Butterworth, 1981.

Investment in Science

J. DUNCAN M. DERRETT

Introduction

When I use the word "science" in this chapter, I mean the mathematical and natural sciences. Like all knowledge, of course, science is preferable to ignorance, since anyone who chooses ignorance must opt either to govern the ignorant, or to be governed by them, in either case without the option of putting a period to his choice. As to the *use* of knowledge, no doubt, there is infinite debate. One of the results of the study of evolution, a theory basic to the concept of man as an evolving species, is to throw doubt on the control man possesses, as a social animal, both of his options and of his power of choice. The notion that we are, potentially, able to direct ourselves without constraining bounds (a fallacy indirectly enhanced by space research on the one hand and the achievements of totalitarian tyrannies on the other) must be checked when one recollects, for example, that in all probability our perceptions of colour derive from that stage of development we once shared with insects (specifically creatures needed for the pollination of plants), and our capacity, nay compulsion, to respond to sound and in particular to rhythm, is no younger than the earthworm. The discoveries of science have not been matched by increasing mastery of the challenges that society, enlarged by science, has posed for itself, which is a problem long familiar within the social

---

The author acknowledges the invaluable help of Drs. Arthur Exell and Bill Adam, but he alone is responsible for the tone and drift of this paper.

sciences. One wonders whether this disparity must be perpetual.

The emperor Darius, who believed that human corpses should be dismembered by vultures, called a conference between Greeks, who believed they should be cremated, and "Indians" who frugally ate their deceased parents. Nothing would induce either of the groups to imitate the practices of the other.[1] The compelling quality of custom and usage was the touch of nature that (then) made the whole world kin and in spite of time, this remains so. Reason could neither make people change their habits nor mitigate their repugnance for the habits of others. The increase in ubiquitous communication has not lessened individual curiosities, only drawn attention to them. Thus, among our inherited limitations is the inability of people accustomed to pursue one profession to visualize problems they share with other professions in terms acceptable to those others—the self-image, and authenticity, of the person, and the profession, is somehow threatened even by such a possibility. "Here I stand . . . I can no other" exemplifies humanity, and by no means at its most contemptible. Each profession is clear as to its own values, and it imagines that the only problem is the choice among them. "The belly will consume any kind of food; but one dish is better than another. . . . Woman will receive any man; but one daughter is better than another," said the sage Ben Sirach. (Ecclus. 36:18, 21) But life is hardly so simple; for in every modern undertaking the major choices, between weal and woe, between, for example, knowledge and ignorance, fall to a plurality of people who must choose jointly although their respective values are not mutually compatible. This is well illustrated by the problem of investment in science.

Now, the lay public imagines that central coordinated planning can be achieved, preferably with the aid of academically advised bureaucrats. It believes that notorious gaps can be filled, redundant schemes scrapped, and investments furnished in compliance with an intelligible order of priorities. In particular, for example, if society has a mind to do so, it can muster joint and individual resources of clinicians, epidemiologists, analytical chemists, experimental biologists, and pathologists, not only to detect and define the causes of man-made non-infectious diseases (created by industry whose interests are often opposed to those of various classes of society), but even to prevent any lamentable epidemics.

But only experts know what is feasible and under what conditions; and many know too much about science to attempt to monitor, let alone evaluate relatively, projects outside their expertise. To monitor, for example, possibly wasteful expenditure by research organizations is still further from the remit of some experts, and good intentions do not always find their way into practice. If the public at large still believes that resources can be distributed among projects on the basis of relative utility, those who actually evaluate applications from would-be researchers become increasingly sceptical of any competence on their part to guide research through use of the public's purse-strings. It is an open question whether scientists should themselves take the initiative to promote expenditure apart from a popular demand for, for example, information technology and automation. Industry makes by far the larger investment, and knows, more or less, what it wants. And one does not forget the public's own subsidy for research through its purchases, directly and indirectly (one thinks of a national health service), of products of research and development. To pin down "value" in a complex situation like this requires somewhat ruthless definitions, ignoring, for purposes of discussion, nuances and marginal aspects that anyone charged with evaluation would instinctively take into account.

Definitions

Sometimes caricatures depict truth. The scientist is often depicted as a rather bumbling, preoccupied fellow who is overtaken by mishaps as embarrassing to himself as they are to his neighbours; the bureaucrat is typically a man who cannot be bothered with detail except to manipulate it, who enjoys frustrating more than facilitating, who drinks tea and discusses promotions. Yet it is incorrect to distinguish the administrator from the scientist in this fashion, for the skills—the ability to work in teams, to enquire in depth, to plan and organize, to structure thought and presentation—that distinguish the scholar from the dabbler and the professional from the amateur, not seldom enable the highly gifted scientist to organize his colleagues without friction, to allocate skills sensitively and precisely, and to search for and to channel funds in profitable directions. It would be ridiculous to complain that professors who have ceased to teach a science to which they have ceased to make contributions through their own research advise the government on the gathering of knowledge. Yet there are recognizable results from the situation that obtains. The chief scientist of a government department, asked whether he was satisfied that decisions relating to the amount of research effort devoted to particular fields were taken rationally, answered that he hoped he might never have been asked that question.[2] And the talent to lead people and to provide them with facilities is different from the talent that produces research itself; just as to report on the performance of one's "subordinates" and on the activities of a project (for example, an "establishment") is quite different from reporting on research. Along with administrative talent go its motivations. Facts are not always so pleasurably, or so easily marshalled as are people. Part-time scientists may operate with full-time administrators, or many double as part-time administrators, but the present "genius at administration" had ceased to be, if ever he was, a genius in science. He may, like C. P. Snow, actually be a crypto-novelist.

Granted the daunting flow of results and the relentless march of knowledge, the sciences, natural-physical and human, are identical with the actual scientists who participate in them. Scientists have four joint and collective functions: to inform, to protect, to assist, and to entertain. Few perform all four concurrently (one can think of a medical mission in Zaïre which undertakes original research into certain diseases and their prevention), but if a person performs none he is no scientist. Thus, scientists have a single characteristic: participation in performance. Watching and criticizing is not science any more than shouting in a stand is football. From someone in the stage of secondary education to the most accomplished specialist, scientists engage in their four functions in varying proportions; and those who do not learn (thus stimulating inquiry) or teach or research, whether they are possibly failed, retired, lapsed, or pseudo-scientist; they are not scientists. It is the scientists' activity that is at issue here, and to know the value of any fragment of science we must apply our minds to what they do. (If administrators waste taxpayers' money or fail to check waste, this has nothing to do with the value of science; it tends simply to deprive scientists of facilities they could put to good use.)

There is a no less significant distinction between those who embody science and those who apply it. One who prescribes drugs other than in an experiment is not acting as a scientist. Operatives in pathological or forensic laboratories, and even public analysts (except in so far as they advance knowledge by developing new tests), are technicians, not scientists. And the same can be said of surgeons who repeat standard operations. Hence teaching hospitals, which do contain scientific physicians and surgeons, are much more expensive than those that do not.

At this point it will be handy to mention that facts do not supply theories; theories find, select, order and rationalize "facts." The lay notion that scientists examine discrete facts and from them deduce their theories is quite untrue. It is much nearer the truth to picture the scientist as the ringmaster who cracks his whip, whereupon the animals sit up. Although it is true that the humanities student has a wider command (an imaginative command) over his "materials" than a scientist has over his data, it is preposterous to suggest that data master or control the scientist—the whole progress of science refutes this. This places the scientists' mental faculties in a category of their own. The verbal distinction between pure and applied science naturally is elusive even for people with scientific qualifications. Administrators and lay observers find only the benefits of applied research and development capable of being quantified or even visualized. Universities tend to lose interest in scientific projects once their marriage to industry has matured; professors' interest flags when their theoretical research passes beyond the practical activities they have, in their early stages, facilitated. We find them actually advertising for sponsors for their departments' special facilities. Pure, fundamental, even "strategic" research goes on, sometimes (and for a period) heavily encouraged by the "customer" (whether he be a state research council or an industrial body), sometimes in spite of him, but its eventual practical value is hypothetical. Yet both pure and applied research is necessary to the definition of scientist. Unless knowledge is continuously expanded by every avenue open to the scientific body it is not science, it is ritual.

Empirical discoveries verifiable by normal methods, are not expected to be repeated. Unless secret, results are published after ruthless monitoring by specialists and remain open to scrutiny for ever. One who invents data to support a theory is exposed, most auspiciously in his own lifetime. Soundly documented experiments will not be repeated unless conditions change, in which case it is not merely repetition. The arts, by contrast, submit to necessary revision and flux. Opinion, the life-blood of humanities, has no scope in science, except as a (rather unhelpful) synonym for untested hypothesis. Duplication is not science, and without progress science withers. This is true irrespective of a society's dependence on foreign technology and products. In other words, the spearhead of research is the natural seeking of infinitely refined curiosity backed with the appropriate resources.[3]

Talent now requires funding. The days are long since past when gentlemen scientists thrust knowledge forward with string and sealing wax. And the omnicompetent and self-fuelled geniuses of the Renaissance can have few counterparts when the idioms of disciplines defy the powers of any one mind. Even the mathematician now requires his libraries. It appears that no matter what is his field—animal behaviour, anthropology, astronomy, zoology, and so forth—the scientist has four pillars of support: (1) his intellect, well-being, and vigour, (2) the commissioning impulse that directly and indirectly selects projects and the people to be involved, (3) the decision-making process that independently approves and costs the project, and (4) the source of funds. (Even though all but the first of these issue from the same place, they are distinct functions: thus an "expert" in "research and development" should not be confused with a "scientific adviser.") To find "value" then in this endeavour we must look into these four supports.

Evaluation occurs independently within each of the four. The scientist consents to operate; the customers rate the project as valuable; the granting bodies envisage the project in viable terms; the ultimate paymaster insists upon accountability, monitoring the earlier decision-making processes, verifying the integrity of the advisers, and referring to the general good, both absolutely and relatively. The source of funds may complain at failure at each stage. Except for the scientist, all these component supports are not manifestations of scientific thinking but of housekeeping, and administrators handle them apart from the enthusiasms of scientists. And if administrators are reluctant to scrap or rethink schemes that were viable when instituted but have become difficult to defend, this obviously hampers new investment.

Research is often stimulated because it has proved effective and valuable elsewhere and to ignore it would be to imperil the nation's welfare. Imitation and exchange, subject to patent laws and the fear of espionage, have a role in research and development. The scientific world is international; a research establishment set up *ad hoc* may turn out to lead a good part of the world in an activity that becomes essential. (And if scientific *dogma* arises anywhere to cripple free inquiry it is so rare that it is as astounding as it is pathetic.) National traditions and cultural specializations are not barriers to human advancement by way of science, and costly international communication powerfully reinforces the morale of the scientist, whose arena of endeavour is far broader than anything dreamed up for him by councils or committees.

Before I deal with "value" and attempt to solve the puzzle created by the scientists' four supports, as it were the four-legged chair in which science sits, what of "science and morality"? Science can be said to have a disvalue if it is immoral. Scientists, no less than technicians, have sometimes lost balance, and their morale has been endangered, by the consideration; "Is my research, or any application of it, likely to advance ends that are immoral?" Innumerable discoveries and applied research have turned out to be inauspicious (for example, industrial pollutants), and this is as much a source of concern to the scientist as it is to the layman. Automation has steadily increased unemployment and diminished skill acquisition by the work-force. But the scientist is not tried—nor should he be—for economic crimes or crimes against humanity. Pursuing orders or assisting in commercial gain, the scientist is both man (with a conscience) and functionary. He may make his choice, as others may. Scientists have been hired by governments to allay the public's fears about processes run by nationalized industries and they have been hired by industry to advertise its products. The moral problem of these "hack scientists" is no greater than that of the "public relations" expert. The scientist may choose environmental studies rather than atomic physics, perhaps to the detriment of his pocket and his dependents' pleasures. And such heroes do exist, working out for themselves the problem of responsibility. Not only the technician (for example, the physician who prescribes a contraceptive pill for a girl aged twelve) but the scientist as well has decisions of conscience to make. The surgeon who decides that he will perform clitorectomies upon Sudanese girls or penal amputations in certain Muslim territories overcomes a moral problem. As a technician he is exactly like other members of society, making choices in which conflicting interests are balanced. The scientist's position seems to be different only in as much as his discoveries can have far-reaching applications.

The specialist in genetic engineering may be aware that science might be used as much to breed an odious superrace as to offer fertility to the infertile (whose infertility may itself be due to scientific advances) and, hopefully, to diminish the births of disabled children which are now all too common. But research must proceed. And if society persuades the scientist to desist from his "immoral" experiments (by cutting off funds) then he will have to stop; but he will take much persuading, since defects in knowledge are tantamount to ignorance, and somewhere, sometime, the gaps will be filled.[4]

The scientist, given facilities and encouragement, advances science. Its profitability is not his affair. If politicians, or their agents, adapt his findings to ambivalent or harmful uses, hastening, for example, or not hastening to adapt to civil ends the discoveries in a defence programme, the decision is not the scientist's; and his research skills must not be hampered by a concern with how they are implemented. Prometheus, it is true, had the option to consign fire to man; but that is myth. Put man and ignorance together and it is the role of the scientific temperament to disperse the latter. Now we can return to the four supports, that "chair."

Value

When a firm finances research in its own laboratories, or commissions research in government research units, for example, to discover how to preserve food to the end best suited to the ultimate consumer's and therefore to the firm's requirements, the value of the research can be computed as accurately as can an advertisement, and in the board room these factors may appear virtually equivalent. A side advantage can arise from the funding of an in-house laboratory wherein additional "accidental" discoveries are made, and the firm, of course, eager to obtain the value of relevant patents, does nothing to discourage unplanned advances. Some firms take this type of endeavour so seriously that they will pay "over the odds" for government research, knowing that ultimately marginal research, whether or not dignified by the term *pure*, redounds to the advantage of consumers. Going further, some will even enter into training programmes with universities, however, not seldom without strings as to the scope of the research to be done.

Advance in science and technology overseas may belatedly awaken a country to an awareness of its limitations. The scientific community may have been small or starved of opportunities, especially in nations that characteristically react to events, resist forward planning, and prize flexibility above rational principles. The country then embarks upon research of unknown potential, stimulated by the state through research advisory bodies in government research units, which can be very numerous and sophisticated. After a period, the firms, which cannot claim yet another subsidy from the public, must begin to pay for research instigated by the state, until the point is gradually reached when the private customer takes over responsibility for most of the funding though not, directly, its direction. A dual system emerges in which research is conducted for customers, private or public, in state research units ultimately maintained by the tax payer through a ministry or in universities which in many territories are themselves basically dependent on the tax payer under a separate budget. The balance between these two methods is so confused that it is almost invisible. Science and engineering advisers exert influence on the body that makes grants to universities. Yet the latter, alert to fundamental advances rather than to application of results, and reluctant merely to follow fashion, may allocate their grants autonomously so as to be found, on inspection, to maintain an under-utilized potential: under-utilized, that is, from the point of view of a customer avid for research and development.

The problem facing administrators operating for governments, for universities and for industries is that whereas applied research can be estimated in some recognizable form, pure research, the particular child of universities, can be made to appear as art for art's sake. The public who can happily fund yet another doctoral thesis on James Joyce or the Son of Man, and is awed by costly aeronautical projects presumed to be useful, when asked to foot a growing bill out of diminishing revenue, is utterly bemused by pure research.

The taxpayer would like to be represented closely in the decision-making, the establishment of priorities, and the assessment of individual projects. But these undertakings are too numerous and complex for him, even for most scientists, to grasp. (For example, the taxpayer is told that commercially competing nations spend more, even per capita, on research, but what is he to make of this information?) It does make sense to him that all scientific undertakings should be commissioned, costed, and paid for (even as a paper transaction) by the "customer," not the "contractor." So to this end research councils, divided for convenience according to science and engineering, agriculture, the natural environment, medicine, and the social sciences (defence stands apart, experts playing a dominant role), exist to receive, initiate, process, and approve applications for research and to channel funds to "contractors," whether these be research establishments or university departments. The taxpayer sets up "cash limits," and the process of selecting, evaluating, and commissioning becomes controversial and competitive in a way hardly known when science was not constrained by this.

Gaps in this process can be filled by charities. Some funds stimulate specific research, a few subsidize general research in a field; and private charities can take the whole responsibility for one or more researchers in a field dear (quite by chance) to the sponsor. Charities and private firms will not feel the effect of government cuts directly: but if universities are impoverished by the removal of a proportion of the income previously devoted to scientific infrastructure and to pure research, the effect will be felt in all areas of scientific activity. As it has been trenchantly put, second-class research is as good as useless, a comment that will give non-scientific researchers food for thought.

Scientific research, subsidized by the nation, as well as some major fields for the application of science, is peculiarly open to the criticism that no *management* can be detected. One is continually overtaken by events. All operatives naturally tend to maximize their own scope of activity, and the value of a particular discovery, for example, genetic engineering, may be found to operate contrary to the value of another, for example, population control—are not sterile people, for example, in parts of Buddhist Asia, public benefactors? Very strange equations may be found to obtain. For another example, extremely expensive operations are made possible whereby a few people receive new hearts and lungs instead of money being channelled or allocated in other ways to many people free of these defects and "better risks" in the long term. Some government-sponsored studies are hardly popular and are not likely to become so. Money is spent on expensive techniques to detect and control cancer; yet the government will not deal drastically with things that are known to cause cancer until it can be shown that the cost of treating people with cancer exceeds the cost of paying a state pension to people who, if causes of cancer were controlled, would otherwise survive! The scientist cannot be concerned with such considerations, as he cannot become involved in complex moral questions, and he is not to be held responsible for the overall management which is so often called in question. He pushes at the frontiers of knowledge irrespective of the possible outcome. He does not expect to control the public purse.

We come at last to the four-legged chair. Can we call the scientist's brain, and his talents, his "resources"? Hardly. He functions by them, as a composer lives by and in his ability to compose. Resources merely provide him with his opportunities. If it be argued that he is a mere servant of society, one may point to the novelist or to the historian, equally servants of society. None of these are "hired hands." If one wants to know whence scientific value comes one could compare asking the man who is satisfied with his suit whether his satisfaction is owed to the tailor, the weaver, dyer, carder, spinner, fuller, shearer, or shepherd: or does it come from someone else? So let us place the four pillars of research round a table like players in a card game. How could the game proceed without all of them? Yet their interests neither overlap nor coincide. Their motivations are distinguishable. We repeat that no research occurs without (1) the scientist, (2) the customer, (3) the arbitrator of claims for funds, and (4) the source of the funds—no one of these four is to be confused with another, for if one person performs two functions (as in careful gifts to medical charities) he wears, as it were, two hats. Are the *funds* the "one thing needful"? A father of a family would answer affirmatively. It seems obvious. The scientist must be remunerated but not necessarily in the light of demand and supply: his standing in society, after all, is vital to his morale. He must be promoted according to achieved, not ascribed merit, and honour must be accorded to discoverers, whether of facts or of techniques, *even if they are joint discoveries*, not to the persons who happen to head their establishments as such. Granted that the public does reward and encourage the scientist, it would seem that the source of reward has all the best cards in that card-game. Not so.

One of the players has Ace, King, Queen, Jack and Ten. And he is the scientist. Which processor of applications, and which supplier of funds could achieve any research? The customer by definition cannot.

None of these is occupied in research, none a scientist. If he claims vicarious merit (common in establishments) this is surely a sociological phenomenon? If administrators are paid more than scientists it may be because they are nearer to the source of higher salaries, and "play games" with it. The scientist's brain is the source of research. He is its focus. His morale is the same as *value in research*. When it is high, research is valuable. The administrator is his servant, his *facilitator*, although he does not remunerate him personally. The fact that when administrators are told this their mouths drop open is a socio-psychological phenomenon; it has nothing to do with our inquiry.

Who Decides?

Decisions as to the relative value of research projects are made, before a step is taken, by research councils and their like, and at a more remote level by governmental bodies, advised by committees. Many decisions, of course, are of real significance for science, and for the community. Others are not. For example, it may be deemed best to carry out research on an international scale, if it proves too expensive for a relatively poor country to undertake, whatever the talents of its scientists. So they may emigrate, if they choose. The value of research is not affected by any decisions of this kind, or even by the reverse, such as "We must make every department computer-conscious."

A product emanates from a coincidence of funds, skills, information, and motivation. Scientists would be motivated even if they were not funded—the concurrence of funds and motivation is a chance factor. No amount of funding can turn inadequately trained and motivated people into requisite high-calibre scientists. But if research beyond the point required by the parameters of the project is nullified, stultified, or frustrated by a cessation of funding, science halts there, and the scientist's motivation is wasted.

Unless the scientist is understood, and his capacity to project undertakings is appreciated, all research schemes are vain. Some contradictory aspects of research and development have surfaced under the pressure of shortage of funds. It was urged that scientists should be introduced to administrative techniques and should acquaint themselves with administrative problems. It was thought that scientists (as opposed to people who once underwent scientific training) should be recruited, if only temporarily, into the administrative cadre, so that there would be more than 10 per cent of the decision-makers and -implementers who knew something about science. But on the other hand it was suggested simultaneously that the scientist should be better disciplined and controlled.

A question repeatedly emerged: Why did scientists not *want* to become administrators? Some did not believe, it was said, that they would be competent; others found their administrative capacity suspect; yet others felt that administrators did not want, except on an *ad hoc* basis, to discuss originality and perhaps feasibility with them. But, as often happens, the true reason was not alluded to. The scientist does not want to become an administrator because then he would betray his talent and vocation. Other attempts to discipline him were hinted at. He was not to indulge in "clandestine" research which would not be costed and charged for. Alas, 10 per cent of funds allowed by administrators for casual and extra-curricular research (the very life-blood of science) refused to be adopted as a credible working limit, and firms and the government can find themselves patrons of discovery that they had not planned and do not know how to further. The patronizing way in which chance discoveries were dismissed by central policy reviewers is interesting. For the administrator never achieves things by chance, but the scientist, the former's would-be marionette, both can and should. It is actually said that such activity must be discounted by long-range planners, for one does not plan (they say) with the aid of a roulette wheel.

Although it is true that scientists should not decide, unaided, what the needs of the nation are, they know what the needs of science are, and each scientist should be subsidized to let his research, no matter in what field, take him where it will. That one scientist would absorb disproportionate resources for the attainment of a hypothetical aim his country could not afford is an exaggerated fear. Some research units already function on just those lines, having no commissioned research; and the gratification (!) of scientists is acknowledged to be one of the duties of a research and development administrator allocating funds amongst laboratories. The self-image of the scientist, his morale, his interaction with his problems, these combine to produce a direction and a level of achievement.

Science should be funded unless the nation believes in being non-scientific, which can actually happen. There are nations that have opted (for the time being) to live, to the extent that it suits them, on the science and technology of others. But that cannot last. If a developed country decides against turning its back on the modern world it must sacrifice some lesser good for a science that will automatically serve it as it deserves. To interfere with this natural process of advance by imposing a framework on what should be spontaneous may be the sort of gardening under which plants wither and the soil becomes sterile.

Final Comment

It may be argued that the conflict between intellectuals and administrators is of venerable age, and that society cannot afford to allow expensive research to be done *either* at the whim of manufacturers *or* to please irresponsible scientists. Correspondingly, some members of the public feel that politicians or at least politics itself is a corrupt medium whereby individuals live parasitically on a supine source of wealth, and therefore the more government the worse. Let me offer an analogy from a scientific field. Machinery is inefficient if it produces effects for which it was not designed. For example, bearings produce heat and have to be cooled. A more efficient machine incurs less energy loss. So with society. Its cogs and bearings need cooling, and decision-making requires interference as often inimical to efficiency as propitious to it. Until society can devise better machinery the present fictions (derived from specialized professions' incongruities) will continue. Every value has a negative component, its cost, and here we have isolated an example.

Notes

1. Herodotus, *The History* III, 38 (trans. George Rawlinson), London: Dent, 1910, vol. i., pp. 229–30.
2. *Select Committee on Science and Technology. Third Report* (see Bibliography below), p. 104.

3. *Advisory Board for the Research Councils. The Support Given by Research Councils for in-House and University Research*, p. 135.
4. Robert, Edwards, *The Times*, 26 June 1984, p. 10, "Embryos: the case for research."

Bibliography

Adam, William B. *A History of the Campden Research Station 1919–1965*. Chipping Campden: Campden Food Preservation Research Association, 1980.

Advisory Board for the Research Councils. *The Science Budget. A Forward Look 1982*. London: HMSO, 1982.

Advisory Board for the Research Councils. *The Support Given by Research Councils for In-House and University Research*. London: HMSO, 1983.

Advisory Board for the Research Councils. *Scientific Opportunities and the Science Budget 1983*. London: HMSO, 1984.

Autton, Norman. *Doctors Talking*. Oxford: Mowbray, 1984.

Dalyell, Tam. *A Science Policy for Britain*. London: Longman, 1983.

Goldsmith, Maurice. *United Kingdom Science Policy*. London: Longman, 1984.

Mason, Sir Ronald. *A Study of Commissioned Research*. London: HMSO, 1983.

Select Committee on Science and Technology. *First-Fifth Report from the Select Committee on Science and Technology* (Sess. 1971–72). London: HMSO, 1972.

United Kingdom. Parliament. *A Framework for Government Research and Development*. Cmnd. 4814. 1971.

United Kingdom. Parliament. *A Framework for Government Research and Development*. Cmnd. 5046. 1972.

United Kingdom. Parliament. *Report of Joint Working Party on the Support of University Scientific Research*. Cmnd. 8567. 1982.

United Kingdom. Parliament. *First and Joint Report: Advisory Council for Applied Research and Development, and Advisory Board for the Research Councils*. Cmnd. 8957. 1983.

IV

Values In Application

VI

Environmental Values

BRENDA ALMOND

Three images provide a focus for thought:

1. A child plays on a beautiful beach in Cumbria. The sun shines. The sea gleams, the childs adorns a lovingly constructed sand-castle with some seaweed washed up by the waves.
2. A woman tends her country garden somewhere in England. The cottage borders on fertile farmland. The summer peace and tranquillity are broken only by the sound of a low-flying small plane passing overhead.
3. An Italian family sit down for their evening meal in a house that has been the fruit of the labour of the parents. There is a possibility that another child has been conceived and the parents are pleased with the prospect.

In each case the tranquillity is temporary, the happiness illusory. For an unseen—indeed an unseeable—menace overlies the scenes. A year later the parents of the child in Cumbria live in fear that the pollution of the shoreline caused by radioactive emissions into the sea from nearby Windscale (now Sellafield) may make their child a leukaemia victim. The woman gardener is paralysed and wheelchair-bound, endeavouring to recover damages for the air-borne poisoning she received in the aerial spraying of crops routinely practised by her farming neighbour. The family in Soveso, Italy, is excluded indefinitely from their house, which is heavily contaminated with dioxin, and the new five-month-old child is handicapped by gross deformities.

It is the generalization of these particular cases that has provided fuel to the fire of the environmentalist movement, and in its philosophical manifestation has raised the question of whether there may not be obligations on the part of humans to respect the natural world. This may be expressed as a demand for a new ecological ethic expressed in terms of values inherent in nature itself—environmental values. Such a transformation of emphasis has sometimes been referred to as a paradigm shift in ethical thought. Up to now, ethics, whether secularly or religiously based, has been human-centered. Aldo Leopold, in his seminal work, *A Sand County Almanac*, traced three stages of ethical thought: an early stage in which ethics is seen as governing relations between individuals, a later stage in which it is seen as governing relations between individuals and society, and a necessary third stage of which he says: "The extension of ethics to this third element in human environment is . . . an evolutionary possibility and an ecological necessity." Of this third type of ethic he writes: "An ethic, ecologically, is a limitation on freedom of action in the struggle for existence," and, in a much quoted definition: "a thing is right when it tends to preserve the integrity, stability and beauty of the biotic community. It is wrong when it tends otherwise."[1]

In the environmental debate certain keywords recur. Words with a favourable connotation are conservation, preservation, wilderness. Words with an unfavourable connotation are pollution, waste, exploitation, and depletion of resources. On the one side is set the notion of sympathy or oneness with nature, whether for practical utilitarian or spiritual and quasi-mystical reasons. On the other, is set the notion of *hubris*—a Greek notion for which significantly there is no satisfactory English synonym and which carries essentially the idea of man claiming the authority and privileges of the gods. In line with this we have the notion of man as dominator, man the species-ist, vandalizing his physical setting and making it unfit for himself as well as for other species which he unthinkingly and for short-term gain ousts. As the authors of *Only One Earth*, an unofficial report commissioned for the United Nations Conference on the Human Environment, wrote:

> There is no doubt indeed that most of our present environmental difficulties originate from man's ecological misbehaviour. Increasingly we consider ourselves not as lodgers on the earth, but as its landlords; we identify progress with the conquest of the external world even if this means destruction of those parts of nature which we assume—often erroneously—to be irrelevant to our welfare.[2]

So where does value lie? And where does the balance of good and evil fall? With those who advance man's prosperity by "making the desert bloom like a rose," or with those peoples, like the former nomadic inhabitants of Israel, the Australian aborigines, or the North American Indians, who have lived on the surface of the planet Earth, leaving their passage and stay unrecorded in the ecology and topography of their land? In answering this question there may be a clash between intuitive and more considered responses. Beauty, nature, and endangered species are evocative words and there may well be an initial presumption in their favour when they are counterposed against man's domination by his own machines, the concrete wasteland at the heart of many modern cities, factory-farming, and pollution of the atmosphere and ocean, carrying with them the threat, perhaps, of the death of the planet and the end of human existence. But not everyone makes this value-judgement or accepts this assessment. We may set on one side vitriolic and blinkered critics like Ayn Rand, who writing of "ecological crusaders—who would pollute any stream by stepping into it," says:

> When man's greatest benefactor, technology, is denounced as an enemy of mankind . . . when the great emancipator, the automobile, is attacked as a public menace, and highways are decried as a violation of the wilderness—when bleary-eyed, limp-limbed young hobos of both sexes chant about the evil of labor-saving devices, and demand that human life be devoted to the grubby hand-planting of truck-gardens, and to garbage disposal—when alleged scientists stretch, fake or suppress scientific evidence in order to panic the ignorant about the interplanetary perils augured by some such omen as the presence of mercury in tuna fish . . . it is time to grasp that we are not dealing with man-lovers, but with killers.[3]

But we must take more seriously philosophical critics of the ecological movement and those who present a considered challenge to the evidence of a planetary threat on which that movement is based. These include those who believe, like H. J. McCloskey, that the "ecological crisis" will be solved by science and technology themselves and that it is to science and technology that we must turn for solutions to the problems they have brought about—problems, for example, of depletion of resources, environmental damage, pollution, overpopulation, harmful pesticides and chemicals, extermination of species, and nuclear risks of peace and war. Solutions are problematic, but the facts themselves, or at least present and past facts, are not substantially in dispute, and it would be as well to indicate briefly what some of these facts are.

The widening of public concern for ecology was triggered by the publication in 1962 of Rachel Carson's *Silent Spring*,[4] but subsequently many international agencies and groups have identified and discussed a whole range of problems precipitated by man's increasing mastery of technology and exploitation of his knowledge without consideration of global and long-term consequences. The Stockholm Conference of 1972 on the human environment organized by the United Nations was based on a sense of urgency concerning world poverty, population increase, depletion of resources, and pollution. It recognized the problem of the disparity between developed and developing countries, which makes the latter understandably averse to any suggestion—even if the affluent nations themselves would find it acceptable—of deindustrialization or "a retreat from the pursuit of material prosperity." This implies acceptance of energy-producing processes which, as things stand, must inevitably bring in their train some environmental pollution, with the generation of nuclear energy by nuclear means presenting the most intractable problems.

Among the undisputed present consequences of industrialized processes is the pollution of rivers, lakes, and oceans by a constant flow of toxic substances, with the Mediterranean providing an example of what happens when the upper limit is reached of what even a massive water region can absorb. (Sixteen countries have now combined in an action plan designed to control the emission of untreated sewage, detergents, pesticides, heavy metals, industrial chemicals, and oil which have been the cause of the Mediterranean's problems.)

Other recognized current problems include various forms of air pollution, both those such as smog caused by automobile emissions in cities, which affect people immediately, and more controversially, those such as chlorofluorocarbons (CFCs) which threaten the ozone layer protecting the atmosphere of the earth. There is also the problem of acid rain, which—apart from its long-term effects on many of the most beautiful forest areas of Europe—has produced dying lakes in Scandinavia and the prospect in Canada that many of its lakes could become fishless over the next decade.

The use of chemicals and pesticides in agriculture and animal husbandry constitutes a third area for concern, for while their use immeasurably increased productivity and the supply of food it has made the ingestion of these chemicals virtually unavoidable in a normal diet. Any catalogue of environmental hazards currently occupying the world's scientific and economic experts must include, too, agricultural problems of desertification and erosion of soil leading to large-scale famine and accentuating the north-south divide. This divide itself is a reminder that other indisputable contemporary facts with environmental implications are the growth of human population and the uneven distribution of economic resources.

But it is the future consequences of these present facts that provoke most controversy. The findings of the Club of Rome as published in *The Limits of Growth*[5] were that time is running out for the human community to face up to and deal with its problems. The authors recount an appropriate French riddle: there is a pond on which a water-lily grows. The plant doubles its size each day and would cover the pond entirely in thirty days if left unchecked. The riddle is posed: If you decide to wait until the plant covers half the pond, which day will you have to deal with it? The answer is that this will be the twenty-ninth day. It is the argument of the Club of Rome that humankind has now reached the twenty-ninth day with respect to most of the environmental threats I have listed. Its findings have been challenged by some, decried as alarmist by others, but in fact the growth of officially sponsored environment-monitoring agencies in the past decade under the United Nations Environment Programme (UNEP) suggests that at the least a responsible attitude is rationally justified.

It is, of course, the question of value that concerns us here rather than straightforward questions of expediency. We may, in other words, endorse Leopold's claim that ethics and aesthetics as well as economics should determine the use we make of the earth. Nevertheless, it would be a mistake to set questions of rational expediency in opposition to questions of value too readily. As H. H. Iltis writes:

> Not until man accepts his dependency on nature and puts himself in place as part of it, not until then does man put men first. This is the greatest paradox of human ecology.[6]

The fate of the human race is bound up, then, with a harmonious solution to its technical planetary problems. Searching for technical solutions alone, though, may not be the best method of approach, and for at least some of these problems technical solutions may be unachievable. As the authors of *The Limits of Growth* point out, this must be so in the case of the arms race, racial tensions, and unemployment.

On the wider range of environmental issues, they write:

> Applying technology to the natural pressures that the environment exerts against any growth process has been so successful in the past that a whole culture has evolved around the principle of fighting against limits rather than learning to live within them. This culture has been reinforced by the apparent immensity of the earth and its resources and by the relative smallness of man and his activities.[7]

Fred Hirsch has added to this assessment the argument that the limits to growth may be social as well as physical and that the pursuit of economic growth, may, paradoxically, result in individuals satisfying less, rather than more, of their aspirations.[8]

The case for adjusting to a reversed assessment in which the finitude of the earth and its resources is recognized and in which there is an acceptance of the natural limits to growth may be argued for, then, on both scientific and economic grounds. And in place of purely technical solutions both expert opinion and common sense suggest a need for a transformation of perspective. Such a changed perspective will involve a new order of values more appropriate for the new order of problems that have been created by the speed at which man's scientific knowledge and technical expertise have overtaken his reflective and moral capacities. Indeed, the situation is one that lends particular point and pertinency to the Genesis story of Adam and Eve, the first parents of the human race. The tree of knowledge in the creation story was the tree of knowledge of good and evil—a foreshadowing of the need of humankind for a moral sense to provide a check to the indiscriminate directions in which the pursuit of knowledge might lead.

But can there be an ecological ethic? Distinguished contributors to the debate like John Passmore[9] have argued that there cannot be and that the moral categories we already employ, those based on attributing value only to human experience and human consciousness, are sufficient to generate all the obligations that may be binding on us as far as nature is concerned. H. J. McCloskey has argued more strongly still that so-called ecological values are actually in conflict with important values implicit within liberal and humanistic ethical traditions, in particular those of individual freedom and autonomy, justice, and respect for human rights. McCloskey argues against the notion that nature is ethically good, pointing out that it can frequently be harsh, savage, and cruel. His view is that environmental concern is a luxury of the wealthy nations at the expense of the poor. Politically, he believes that ecological concern is élitist and dictatorial, and that morally it is based on a narrow and unattractive puritanical asceticism.[10]

These political and social implications will be explored further, but first it must be conceded that a shift in thinking is needed if human beings are to move from a purely human-centred system of morals. Indeed, the first shift needed may be one of language rather than of thought, for a language of values may meet environmentalist needs better than a language of narrowly defined morality, of duties, and of rights. This is not to say that it is impossible to formulate an ethical position that attaches a value to inanimate nature in terms of a traditional terminology of duties. In "Duties Concerning Islands," for example, Mary Midgley lists nineteen categories of beings to whom we might consider duties were owed outside the category of other equal human beings. These include the dead, posterity, the insane, animals, plants, works of art, oneself, and God. This suggests that it does make sense to consider duties not simply as relationships between conscious and thinking equals. It thus makes it possible to claim that Defoe's Robinson Crusoe might have had some kind of duty to his island—a small-scale version of man's duty to the planet Earth—which would have been violated had he considered wantonly destroying his island on departure.[11]

Nevertheless, the question at issue is probably better posed in the language of values rather than in the language of duties. It can then be presented as the question of whether nature, animate and inanimate, has value in itself—intrinsic value. Does a lake or a mountain have value? Or, in the words of another contributor to this debate, concerned to add a legal dimension to the moral one, should trees have standing?[12] The basic question, however, is whether that attribution of value is necessarily and essentially a response of a human being to what is external to him or her, or whether value is in the world—something that human beings may discover, recognize, and become aware of, or may ignore and fail to appreciate.

The answer to this may be a mixture of truism and novelty comparable to the truistic/novel claim that objects depend on us for their perceptual attributes and so, in a sense, for their existence—that *esse* is *percipi*. Berkeley's argument may be construed as the claim that there is no way we can conceive of an object of vision that is not seen or a sound that is unheard, since our imagining has the function of introducing a perceiver into the structure of the thought-experiment.[13] In a precisely parallel way we may argue that we cannot formulate the notion of objects of value outside the experience of human beings—though we can well imagine that there can be such objects to which we do not in fact have physical access—since in imagining them we introduce ourselves as valuers into the imagined situation. So we may attempt to compare the value of two worlds at the outer reaches of the universe, both equally beautiful but one devoid of living creatures capable of sentient awareness. Can this second world, we may ask, have value? If it vanished in some cosmic cataclysm would this matter? It seems clear that in formulating the hypothesis we have removed our imagined worlds, both the first and the second, from the realm of what is truly inaccessible to human valuing. In other words, we do not need an objective sense of value to attach value to inanimate nature, mainly because the contrast in this case between subjective and objective value is unreal. This is not the subjectivist claim that values are in ourselves only—our invention—any more than Berkeley's argument really entailed that the external world was the invention of our perceptual faculties. It is rather the claim that it is through the medium of our moral sense that we must make judgements as to what has worthwhile existence, what counts and what does not.

In this, we are quite capable of placing our own role as observers on the scale of significance it merits. This may well be much lower than a standard human-centred morality or ethics suggests. The philosopher M. R. Cohen wrote of "the unique privilege of being for a brief space a spectator of the great drama of existence in which solar systems are born and destroyed—a drama in which our part as actors is of infinitesimal significance."[14]

Our problem, however, is that we are no longer mere bystanders and inconspicuous observers on the shores of the universe, but have acquired the capacity to destroy at least our own world. And philosophies such as utilitarianism are incapable of providing an argument against destruction because where there are no sentient beings there can be no suffering. Other elements beyond the scope of standard utilitarianism, which it may be necessary to take account of in a full environmental ethic, are suggested by Robert Goodin in a thoughtful article. In particular he argues that special weight ought to be given to irreversibility in our environmental decision-making and that we should beware of opting for gains that are necessarily short-lived.[15] These voluntary limitations and this changed perception of our own species' place in the universe may be summed up under the general heading of humility as the first value in a new environmental ethic.

But a more fundamental ethical perspective is that of holism, which supplies a second element for an ecological ethic, the idea of harmony as an environmental value. There is a child's plaything, a set of Russian dolls. These are wooden dolls of graduated sizes that fit neatly one inside another. The perspectives of the telescope and the microscope show us that we are somewhere in the middle of just such a set of Russian dolls. Just as the parts and cells of our bodies form organic unities of matter that is constantly being replenished by death and regeneration, so, there is cause to believe, our universe itself is such a system. Between these extremes of the galactic and the microscopic, the world in which we live can be regarded as a living and self-renewing whole, and man himself is, in W. H. Harding's words, "a set within a hierarchical system of sets."[16]

One consequence of accepting this, though, is that our judgement of value may not conform to our most immediate taste and interest. As J. B. Callicot observes:

> The natural world as actually constituted is one in which one being lives at the expense of others ... There are desire, pleasure in the satisfaction of desire, acute agony attending injury, frustration and chronic dread of death. But these experiences are the psychological substance of living. To live *is* to be anxious about life, to feel pain and pleasure in a fitting

mixture, and sooner or later to die. That is the way the system works. If nature as a whole is good, then pain and death are also good.[17]

Callicot adds that the aspiration for pleasure without pain is "biologically preposterous." This is consistent with the Routleys' definition of environmental value as "Diversity of systems and creatures, naturalness, integrity of systems, stability of systems, harmony of systems."[18]

Callicot's observation is made in order to point to a potential gulf between those environmentalists concerned to focus on the rights of non-human animals and those, like Leopold, for whom a concern for the environment is not inconsistent with hunting, killing, and eating animals, though for both groups modern methods of raising animals for food—the creation of "animal machines"—will be objectionable. This potential gulf is widened by the claim by the environmentalists that the enforcement of animal rights in an unqualified way would result in some animal species reaching plague proportions, thus damaging the ecosystem in another but equally unacceptable way. But it would be absurd to construe defence of animal rights as a demand for humans to intervene in the role of police to enforce the preservation of individual animal lives against their natural predators. Nevertheless, it is arguable that vegetarianism, with the transfer of land use to the raising of crops that this would involve, is yet another way in which man might interfere with the natural balance of the environment. Here we may distinguish between the morally respectworthy gesture of an individual in personally deciding not to live by the death of other living creatures and the universalized demand for a total change of human dietary habits—particularly if this demand includes the repudiation of fish, consumption of which, overfishing apart, involves no assault at all on the ecology of the earth or the habitats of other non-human creatures. (These observations leave ample space for an animal rights movement concerned with methods of raising animals for food, conditions of slaughter, the preservation of species, and the issue of vivisection.)

The holistic approach to the ecological issue, then, is consistent with varying practical responses. The key ethical concept it involves is, however, clear. It is that of harmony: of creature with creature, of creature with habitat. Harmony carried to its extreme manifestation is identity, so it is understandable that such a view could in the end become a modern form of mysticism or pantheism. The notion of everything that exists composing an organic whole takes us back in the end to the earliest approaches to Western philosophy—the Greek understanding that nothing comes out of nothing; that nothing ever really ceases to exist, but that existence constitutes an endless cycle of transformations of matter. And just as that notion led to the Stoic ethic of acceptance and adaptation—to a recognition of necessity and to a choice of intellectual rather than purely material values—so a parallel awareness in our own and our successors' generations, this time based on more accurate scientific and ecological understanding, could produce a similar reorientation of values and a general rejection of utilitarian and materialistic values, which would bring Western thought closer to the religious and philosophical attitudes of the East and of some primitive peoples.

This phenomenon of progressive and developing awareness is, of course, what is distinctive of the human animal. The insights and discoveries of individuals do not die with them but become part of the collective consciousness. It was this notion of objective knowledge that Karl Popper saw as the basis for an evolutionary epistemology. He used the term *World Three*, meaning by this an entity that is the product of individual human thinkers but that is neither the subjective world of individual mental experience nor the external world of material objects. He saw the human ability to leave behind through culture and pass on through education individual insights, knowledge, and conjectures as the condition and ground of scientific progress.[19] That this collective consciousness should also develop a collective "conscience"—a universal concept of value—would not be an absurd demand, nor would it be an inappropriate goal for human beings to set themselves. Otherwise to follow a metaphor devised by the atomic physicist W. Heisenberg, mankind's position may be compared to that of people travelling in a boat with so much steel in its composition that its compass has ceased to work effectively.[20]

But in practical terms the application of such common human values to ecological problems could be achieved only through international political agencies, capable of monitoring global hazards on a global scale. Here the charges of those who see this as a demand for an "ecological dictatorship" necessarily in conflict with liberal and pluralist values, and inimical to the needs and claims of the poor nations, will need to be taken into account. It is true that environmental problems cross frontiers—but also, equally importantly, that they transcend generations. This is significant when we recollect that liberalism does not make of every man or woman an island, although it is true that it is incompatible with the views of a few being imposed on the many. But this latter consideration applies equally to those who wield technological power: to the manufacturers of chemicals that find their way into the food chain and are involuntarily absorbed by newborn babies in their mother's milk, whether the mother is an inhabitant of a developed or developing nation; to the industrialists whose waste products destroy rivers on which communities have depended; and to governments who opt for energy choices that may create insoluble practical and political problems for future generations. In general those who have become activists in environmental causes have seen themselves and their families as actually or potentially affected in a very personal and direct way by choices made by others over which they have no control. On an issue that is not seen as strictly, narrowly, or purely environmental, the siting of cruise missiles on Greenham Common, one of the women who initiated the continuing protest there described her motivating insight in terms indicating very distinctively environmental concern:

> I was driving on my way through beautiful scenery in Wales where I live and it suddenly occurred to me how this would all be altered in a nuclear war. And it just stopped me dead in my tracks. I couldn't keep driving. I had to stop and I felt really physically very unwell. And I was crying. I sat for about three quarters of an hour before I could continue the journey.[21]

Similarly, Greenpeace activists who place themselves at risk at the point of radioactive or other poisonous discharges are declaring themselves not as "ecological élitists"[22] but as defenders of individual rights. These rights find this form of expression in the face of the powerlessness created by hierarchical social and political structures in which business and military interests, together with the ambitions and misjudgements of politicians, create apparently irresistible vortices into which ordinary peoples are swept willy-nilly without consent or consultation.

What applies to individuals in developed societies applies equally to people in countries still aspiring to material prosperity. While improvements in food supply and distribution are clearly in their interest, they will have gained little if these are achieved at the costs of life and health exposed in the environmental debate.

A search for international agreement, then, on what might be interpreted in the broadest sense as principles for living is not inconsistent with a liberal or individualist perspective, nor with the true interests of both North and South. Liberalism, after all, has never been interpreted as involving a right to kill or maim other individuals at will. So the preservation of the environment as a condition of survival could be the first step in securing wider human agreement on moral norms. Once humanity is in harmony with its environment, it may be in a position to retreat back along the scale of moral evolution described by Leopold, this time on a wider and less fragmented basis. Again, when narrowly geographical boundaries have been transcended in the cause of improving humanity's relationship with nature there can be hope that they may again be transcended to secure a right relationship between individual and society and finally between person and person. In other words, perhaps when humanity has ceased to exploit and torture nature, man will cease to exploit and torture man.

Notes

1. Leopold S. Aldo, *A Sand County Almanac* (New York: Oxford University Press, 1949), pp. 224–25.
2. Barbara Ward and R. Dubos, *Only One Earth: the Care and Maintenance of a Small Planet* (London: Deutsch, 1972) p. 24.
3. Ayn Rand, *The New Left: The Anti-industrial Revolution* (New York: Signet Books, 1975), pp. 172–173.
4. Rachel Carson, *Silent Spring* (Boston: Houghton Mifflin, 1962).
5. Meadows et al., *The Limits to Growth* (London: Pan, 1972).
6. H. H. Iltis, quoted in D. Scherer and T. Attig, *Ethics and the Environment* (Englewood Cliffs· Prentice-Hall, 1983), p. 16.
7. Meadows et al., *Limits*, p. 150.
8. Fred Hirsch, *Social Limits to Growth* (London: Routledge & Kegan Paul, 1977).
9. John Passmore, *Man's Responsibility for Nature* (London: Duckworth, 1974).
10. See H. J. McCloskey, *Ecological Ethics and Politics* (Totowa, N.J.: Rowman and Littlefield, 1983).
11. Mary Midgley, "Duties Concerning Islands," in *Environmental Philosophy*,

ed. R. Elliot and A. Gare (U.K.: Milton Keynes: Open University Press, 1983) pp. 166–181.
12. C. D. Stone, *Should Trees Have Standing? Towards Legal Rights for Natural Objects* (Los Altos, Calif.: William Kaufman, 1974).
13. G. Berkeley, *Three Dialogues* (London: Everyman, 1954).
14. M. R. Cohen, "New Republic" (8) p. 119 (September 1916).
15. R. E. Goodin, "Ethical Principles for Environmental Protection," in Elliot and Gare, *Environmental Philosophy*, pp. 3–20.
16. W. H. Murdy, "Anthropocentrism: a modern version," in Scherer and Attig, *Ethics*, p. 16.
17. J. B. Callicot, "Animal liberation: a triangular affair," in Scherer and Attig, *Ethics*, p. 69.
18. R. Routley and V. Routley, "Human Chauvinism and Environmental Ethics," in *Environmental Philosophy*, ed. Mannison, M. McRobbie, and R. Routley (Canberra: Research School of Social Sciences, Australian National University, 1980), p. 170.
19. Karl Popper, *Objective Knowledge* (London: Routledge & Kegan Paul, 1972).
20. Werner Heisenberg, "Rationality in Science and Society," in *Can We Survive our Future?*, ed. Urban and Glenny (London: Bodley Head, 1971) pp. 84–85. Heisenberg writes: "Every time we are able to make a new gadget, we should ask ourselves before embarking on its manufacture: what purpose and whose purposes is it going to serve? It is not true that everything that can be invented ought to be invented or that everything that is technologically feasible should be manufactured and marketed" (p. 85).
21. H. Weinreich-Haste, "Engagement and Commitment; the role of affect in moral reasoning and moral responsibility," in *Zur Bestimmung der Moral*, ed. W. Edelstein and G. Nunner-Winkler (Cologne: Suhrkamp Verlag, 1987).
22. For the use of the terms *ecological élitist*, *ecological platonist*, and *ecological dictators*, see McCloskey, *Ecological Ethics*, ch. 15.

Bibliography

Carson, Rachel. *Silent Spring*. Boston: Houghton Mifflin, 1962.
Disch, Robert. *The Ecological Conscience*. Englewood Cliffs: Prentice-Hall, 1970.
Eckholm, Erik P. *Down to Earth: Environment and Human Needs*. London: Pluto Press, 1982.

Eliot R. and A. Gare, eds. *Environmental Philosophy.* U.K.: Milton Keynes: Open University Press, 1983.
Ellul, Jacques. *The Technological Society.* New York: Knopf, 1964.
Gabor, Dennis et al. *Beyond the Age of Waste.* London: Pergamon, 1978.
Hardin, G., and J. Baden. *Managing the Commons.* San Francisco: W. H. Freeman and Co. 1977.
Heilbroner, Robert L. *An Inquiry into the Human Prospect.* New York: W. W. Norton, 1974.
Hirsch, Fred. *Social Limits to Growth.* London: Routledge & Kegan Paul, 1977.
Illich, Ivan. *De-Schooling Society.* London: Calder & Boyars, 1971.
Leopold, Aldo Starker. *A Sand County Almanac.* New York: Oxford University Press, 1949.
McCloskey, H. J. *Ecological Ethics and Politics.* Totowa, N. J.: Rowman and Littlefield, 1983.
Marcuse, Herbert. *Counter Revolution and Revolt.* London: Allen Lane, 1972.
Meadows, Donella H. et al. *The Limits to Growth.* London: Pan, 1974.
Midgley, Mary. *Beast and Man.* London: Routledge & Kegan Paul, 1983.
———. *Animals and Why They Matter.* Harmondsworth: Penguin, 1983.
Passmore, John. *Man's Responsibility for Nature.* London: Duckworth, 1974.
Rand, Ayn. *The New Left: The Anti-industrial Revolution.* New York: Signet Books, 1975.
Roszak, Theodore. *Where the Wasteland Ends.* London: Faber & Faber, 1972.
Scherer, Donald, and T. Attig. *Ethics and the Environment.* Englewood Cliffs: Prentice-Hall, 1983.
Singer, Peter. *Practical Ethics.* Cambridge: Cambridge University Press, 1979.
———. *The Expanding Circle.* Oxford: Oxford University Press, 1983.
Stone, C. *Should Trees Have Standing? Towards Legal Rights for Natural Objects.* Los Altos, Calif.: William Kaufman, 1974.
Teilhard de Chardin, Pierre. *The Future of Man.* London: Collins, 1959.
Urban, George R., and M. Glenny eds. *Can We Survive our Future?* London: Bodley Head, 1971.
Ward, Barbara, and R. Dubos. *Only One Earth: The Care and Maintenance of a Small Planet.* London: Deutsch, 1972.

The Value of Invention

JOHN P. HAGGART

> ... that our people be set on works of art and handicraft; that our Realm may subsist more of itself; that idleness be avoided, and the drawing out of our treasures for foreign manufacture stopped.
> Archbishop Morton, Chancellor to Henry VII.

Exploration and inventiveness are basic to human intelligence, and innovation and reasoning have replaced mystery as we move into our present high-technology phase.

Innovation has always been stimulated by problems to be overcome, the search for novelty for its own sake, the personal satisfaction of the innovator, and the hope of financial gain. New mental concepts and ideas have led to the discovery of laws and principles, and industrial development and the development of patent law have engendered the concept of an invention as a property, whose value can be assessed in terms of a reward for the inventor or as a negotiable asset.

Encouragement of the introduction of new industrial techniques and products has always been a factor in our development from an agricultural to an industrial economy, and the improvement of economic and social well-being. In modern times the granting of a patent to an inventor by a state is a recognition, by that state's patent office, that the invention is new and inventive, and in return for a maximum twenty-year monopoly the inventor discloses his invention to the public in a technical description of the best mode of carrying out the invention, thereby adding his contribution to published knowledge. This is the inventor's bargain with the state. However, the state, by the enactment of law, restricts the scope of its encouragement of innovation to what falls within the definitions contained in the law, and in this respect the state is imposing its own set of values on inventiveness.

The concept of an invention as an "intellectual property" is well defined in current United Kingdom and European patent laws in terms that are internationally acceptable. Excluded from this legal concept of an invention are any discovery, scientific theory or mathematical method, aesthetic creations for which the copyright law exists, schemes or plans, and computer programmes (so-called software).

Other forms of "intellectual property" are trade marks, registered designs, industrial copyright, literary and artistic copyright, plant breeders' rights, and so-called technical know-how.

An objective way of assessing an invention is in terms of what can be protected by the patent law. The ultimate worth of an invention is its social value, which is best judged in a historical context, divorced from contemporary issues of assessment of value in terms of a capital sum or a royalty, or of financial reward to the inventor.

An invention of real social worth, which brought only financial problems to its inventor, was the development of movable metal type by Gutenberg in the fifteenth century.[1] He applied goldsmith's skills to his knowledge of wood-block printing and perhaps of movable pottery or metal type used in China, and the inventive step he took was to develop a type-casting method that gave a clear and durable type-face. His Bible, printed in Mainz between 1453 and 1455, ensured his fame but was produced while he was deeply involved in continuing legal wrangling with his main backer.[2]

William Caxton learnt the secret in Cologne and Bruges and brought it to England, no doubt taking advantage of the exemption for "books printed and written" in the trade barrier statute of Richard III which barred foreign merchants and craftsmen. Caxton's publication, under his own distinctive printer's trade mark, of Chaucer's *The Canterbury Tales* was an outstanding contribution to English culture made possible by this invention.[3]

The exploitation of Gutenberg's invention engendered instantly recognizable phenomena: astute financial backers seeking their reward at the expense of the social value of the invention; the creation of an antisocial monopoly by suppressing details of the secret or mystery; and pedantic, moralist reaction to the availability in the home of *Le Morte d'Arthur*, also printed by Caxton, "the whole pleasure of which book standeth in two special points, in open manslaughter and bold bawdry.[4] Modern communicators can point to equivalents, although the values upheld by Malory's knights were a recollection of those of an earlier society. The train of pessimism drawn at the heels of invention had been set in motion.

Was Erasmus himself foolish, when industry began to be a force in England, to rail against "those who are always working to change the face of nature by new and secret devices and search land and sea for some sort of fifth essence"?[5] The inevitable cycle of invention was turning and was encouraged by the practice of the grant of monopolies by the Crown, which were memorialized in letters patent. The careful wording of such grants initiated the practice of defining in a document an industrial property on which a value could be placed. Such grants became debased by abuses in the sale and licensing of monopolies, which became so notorious that Elizabeth I sought to revoke all letters patent of this nature save those grants in respect of new inventions. Here our patent law was born, and the Statute of Monopolies of 1624 sought to harness innovations thought to be beneficial, and to overcome monopolistic abuses, by declaring all monopolies "utterly void and of none effect" with exceptions including:

> letters patent and grants of privilege for the term of one and twenty years or under, heretofore made, of the sole working or making of any manner of new manufacture within this Realm, to the first and true inventor or inventors of such manufacturers, . . . so they be not contrary to the law, nor mischievous to the State, by raising the prices of commodities at home, or hurt of trade, or generally inconvenient . . .

This was the basis of United Kingdom Patent Law until 1978, when our law was then brought into line with European law, in which the definition of an invention is more closely allied to the needs of modern technology. But this definition has not greatly modified our deep-rooted understanding of invention, which stems from the Jacobean definition. Assessment of the novelty and inventiveness of an invention is now mandatory before rights can be granted, and the validity of a monopoly grant has to be tested before the monetary value of the invention can be assessed. The historical concept of invention remains inherent in our thinking as our industrial era turns full cycle, although doubts are being cast on the wisdom of imposing statutory limits on the kinds of invention which can be protected.

The opportunity of acquiring exclusive rights in an invention is thought to stimulate technical progress, mainly in four ways:

1. That it encourages research and invention.
2. That it induces an inventor to disclose his discoveries instead of keeping them as a trade secret.
3. That it offers a reward for the expense of developing inventions to the stage at which they are commercially practicable.
4. That it provides an inducement to invest capital in new lines of production which might not appear profitable if many competing producers embarked on them simultaneously.[6]

The encouragement of research and invention probably holds only in the context of a research organization. The lone inventor is usually motivated by his individual quest, and the patent system offers him the only effective protection against copying which he should seek before he discloses his invention to an entrepreneur or company for development.

In a large organization, development of an invention needs a large team for research and development and assessment of the market. It has always been so. Dr. Johnson commented, "It is pleasing to contemplate a manufacture rising gradually from its first mean state by the successive labours of innumerable minds."[7] Control of the development work must be such that there is a constant reappraisal not only of the effectiveness of the development, for example, for improving the economical operation of an industrial process, but also of the channelling of the development work with a view to providing the information necessary for definition of any inventive step in terms acceptable to the patent system and defensible in the courts. Sometimes these objectives clash, and ebullient inventors resent such curbs. More usually an innovative development in a research programme is itself an invention capable of being protected. This provides some consolation to disgruntled inventors and security for the investment in that development work.

Once an organization is ahead of its competitors, there is a need to keep ahead. This stimulates continued research and the building up of a patent portfolio. Competitors must then look to their future, and their own research is stimulated. The high cost of research slows the pace of invention, but in some industries the battle is on to obtain such valuable rights as are still available before the seam of their branch of technology is worked out.

An inventor does not usually need much inducement to disclose his invention. It is now commonplace that the technical description of an invention which is part of a patent application is printed and published eighteen months after the application is filed. The inventor's achievement is thus publicized and acknowledged. The original purpose of this publication was the inventor's part of the bargain with the state to ensure that there was available to the public a description of the working of the invention that would be available to anyone to use when the monopoly had expired. However, the eighteen-month period of secrecy, now customary, before details of a patent application are published, is a short time in the span of a major development, and publication may give an astute competitor a flying start.

Every week the patent office in London publishes some thousand specifications of patent applications. There are similar publications by the patent offices of all the major industrial countries and by the newly established European Patent Office. The number of published patent specifications now available for study is of the order of twenty-five million spanning the two hundred years of the development of our industrial system. Much of this information is not published elsewhere, but it is drawn into the maelstrom of technical publications, learned journals, and other published media into which innovators, seekers of patent rights, patent office examiners, and patent agents are sinking. The value of patent rights is becoming a relative entity as it becomes increasingly difficult to judge whether an invention is new in absolute terms.

What is certain is that the patent system is the only way we have of ensuring a reward for the cost of development work. This has been borne out in the pharmaceutical industry. Many beneficial drugs could not have been marketed if patent rights had not provided security for the cost of development work and testing. The social significance of pharmaceutical inventions overrides many other considerations. Some countries hold the view that there should be a free market in drugs and other inventions in the medical field. Experience has shown that this may lead to a deterioration in quality, and even to counterfeiting and deception of the public. The tendency is for more of the developed countries to bring drugs within their patent system.

Extensive use of the patent system world-wide brought considerable rewards to Pilkington Brothers P.L.C. of St. Helens, who developed a revolutionary process for making flat glass which has now been adopted by all the world's major glass-makers. Glass, long a mysterious and valuable substance, still holds secrets. For Pilkington a huge investment in the development of the original idea to a commercial scale, followed by two decades of highly skilled technical and design support and an enlightened patenting and licensing policy, has led to the controlled introduction of a new industry, the float glass industry, world-wide, and the return flow of royalty income of tens of millions of pounds per year. But for the strength of the patent system, which protected a valuable invention and its progeny, such a reward for the original determination of the inventors and their employers would not have been possible.

One wonders whether there will be many more such revolutionary industrial developments in these days when much lauded improvements and innovations, for example, in home computers and silicon chips, are really only very small innovatory steps. It is to be hoped that our building of a safe plateau of "new models" and "high technology" on which industry may rest will not preclude those sudden and unexpected leaps forward that could regenerate the regressing industrial cycle.

The inducement to invest capital in new lines of production may be stimulated by competition. In some industries, development work inevitably leads to invention, and equally inevitably competitors in the same field will be meeting the same problems and providing similar solutions. Often, as in the microchip industry, the investment of capital for rapid development work and marketing is the only way to stay in business, and the protection of that investment by the patenting of inventions is somewhat uncertain because the subject-matter often lies on the fringe of the patentable areas staked out by the patent law.

Changes might be desirable in the way in which investment in research and development is protected. But the patent system with its deep historical roots, now bears some strange and undoubtedly expensive fruit. In the United Kingdom the cost of patenting an invention of moderate complexity can be about £700, and a total of £2,600 in official fees are payable to the patent office to keep that patent in force for its full twenty-year term. Increasing complexity of inventions leads to increasing patenting costs. Even greater costs are incurred when patenting in countries where translation of documents is necessary. To embark on an extensive overseas patenting exercise requires the investment of tens of thousands of pounds and must be preceded by extensive and skilled preparatory work to determine, so far as can be, that the worth and future significance of an invention is not diluted as it is moulded and squeezed to meet the requirements of the market and of many different national patent laws.

There is a likelihood, therefore, that only those inventions that are a sudden and surprising leap forward will in future be capable of being protected on an international basis. More new knowledge will be held back as trade secrets and "know-how." Intellectual and monetary inflation are contributing to the demise of the once-sturdy system which, for all its faults, was acting to the public good. Other depreciatory factors are interstate trade barriers; the barriers to the transfer of new technology to third world and iron curtain countries currently being encouraged by a scare-ridden United States executive; and the demands of developing countries for the preferentially priced transfer of new technology to them.

These factors are leading to restrictions both on the freedom to communicate ideas that should be available freely, and on the continual replenishment of the common pool of experience. The encouragement of secrecy for political and commercial reasons is at odds with the natural desire of the inventor for recognition and reward, and there is a gradual debasement of the substructure of invention, patenting, and licensing on which our industrial system has flourished. The requirements of natural security cannot be overlooked, but the patent system has inbuilt safeguards preventing publication and communication of inventions of a defence nature.

In large-scale processes the value of the "know-how" is often equal to or greater than the value of the patented invention. There is therefore a tendency to describe the invention in terms that just satisfy the requirements of the patent law and to retain, as saleable trade secrets, the accumulated technical knowledge of significance not in the public domain. Trade secrets and "know-how" are notoriously difficult to protect. The knowledge of an employee cannot be erased when he leaves to take a job with a competitor.

Industrial espionage is a fact of life in the international scene.

Protection of an organization against unauthorized publication of its "know-how" is fraught with difficulties. Once disclosed, the information is in the public domain and the "know-how" is no longer a saleable commodity. The organization may have some redress if there has been breach of confidentiality or contract. The competitive advantage, which possession of confidential "know-how" imparts, becomes eroded with time as competitors develop competing processes, as employees move between competing organizations, and as the original value of the "know-how" becomes dissipated.

In the past some British companies adopted a superior attitude to countries with industry that was not highly developed, and they relied on a sense of fair play in their commercial relationships with other companies with whom they were exchanging confidential information. This gentlemanly attitude has been rudely shaken by the development of European Economic Community industrial property law which frowns on division of the market. The British sense of fair play has motivated competitors from the United States and Japan to enter the European market and compete with European manufacturers, sometimes on the basis of know-how acquired in a manner that would not have been countenanced by British industrialists.

In the past differing attitudes to property in the Middle and Far East led to blatant copying. This still happens in some Far Eastern countries, although copyright owners are succeeding in the courts in Egypt, Singapore, and Taiwan, where piracy of books has hitherto been notorious. Taiwan is currently introducing new law that proposes terms of imprisonment for copyists and illegal users of well-known trade marks.

Reform of the copyright law world-wide is long overdue, both to ensure stricter adherence to the Berne Convention and to deal with the problems brought about by the explosion of new media for the storage and transfer of information. Many countries are following the lead of the United States in seeking to extend the provisions of the copyright law to provide some protection for computer software. Both the United Kingdom and Japan are leaders in this.

There is also considerable discussion at the moment both in the courts and in reports of the Monopolies Commission, attempting to loosen the hold manufacturers of consumer goods have on those who supply spare parts, particularly automobile spares that have to be made to the design of the original vehicle. The recent *Monopolies*

Commission Report on the Ford Motor Company frowns on Ford's contention that it holds exclusive rights for the provision of spare panels for Ford models. If the monopolists have their way there could be an absence of competition that would operate against the public interest.

There is currently a continual pressure to generate rights that are either unenforceable or against the public interest, and this must not be allowed to obscure the need to provide legitimate protection for important innovations.

Japan has built a new economy on imported technology to some extent, and it is now showing concern about the lack of true innovation in its own research. Tens of thousands of patent applications are filed annually in Japan. It is easy to misinterpret such numbers, which are not a measure of the quality of individual inventions and which without the vigilance of the Japanese Patent Office would build up to a mass of unenforceable rights to subject-matter that should rightly be in the common pool of knowledge. Western values are more selective both in the boardroom and in the operation of the patent system.

There is a tendency for the media to glamorize innovations. The BBC's "Inventor's World" programme and the "Technology and Innovation" columns in the daily and weekly newspapers are often quite irrelevant to the mainstream of commercial innovation and often deal with subject-matter that is either trivial, uncommercial, or years out of date.

Successful exploitation of inventions necessarily involves initial secrecy. The ever-increasing cost of financing the current systems for the protection of intellectual property, in the absence of public funding which is currently frowned on by our Government, encourages a retrogression into secretiveness and a more closed society in which the value of an invention may be assessed in terms of the rapidity with which it can be brought to the market-place for a quick profit, rather than its long-term social value. Notable inventions of significance and of social and economic value are resilient, however, and continue to survive.

There is a dichotomy between the need to protect innovation so far as that is possible, and to safeguard intellectual freedom to exchange ideas by ensuring that "the purely functional should not be protected against copying; indeed unless it attracts patent protection as being inventive it should not be protected at all," thereby maintaining "a substantially common pool of experience from which all can freely take."[8]

The Prime Minister held a conference in 1983 to seek to harness innovators. There were many calls for better technological education. This perhaps brought down to earth some of those who were dazzled by "high-technology innovation." The importance of market-led innovation was stressed, along with the need to educate innovative recruits in an industrial rather than an academic environment. The overstressing of academic virtues for their own sake has undoubtedly led to the diversion of innovative effort away from the need to create markets and to feed those markets by commercially oriented innovation. The Japanese are better at market-led innovation than we are.

However, a recent Cabinet Green Paper misguidedly states, "The ability to claim ownership of ideas is a vital step in securing a profit on them."[9] This suggests that we should emulate the Japanese experience by swamping ourselves with patents for minor innovations.

We must avoid the creation of a monopolist system that places a price on every interchange of ideas both on an academic level and in the "common pool of experience." But an awareness must be maintained of the danger of inadvertent disclosure. The scrutiny of proposed publications for patentable subject-matter is commonplace in industrial organizations, although it may not be so in our academic institutions where the acquisition of merit through publication is sometimes the only goal.

Jefferson wrote, in the course of his early work in setting up the United States Patent Office:

> If nature has made any one thing less susceptible than all others of exclusive property, it is the action of the thinking power, called an idea, which an individual may exclusively possess as long as he keeps it to himself; but the moment it is divulged, it forces itself into the possession of everyone and the receiver cannot dispossess himself of it.[10]

It would be absurd to seek to build our future simply on the marketing of ideas.

In the eighteenth and nineteenth centuries Britain was the great innovator. These days we read of our industrial decline. Rather, we have come full cycle through an era and must continue to propel the advance of innovation into areas where the nineteenth-century concept of invention is no longer sufficiently flexible. Recent advances in computer technology and biogenetic processes, for example, require totally new thinking. Not only must our concept of industrial property rights be reformed, but the educators must reform so that, as in the United States and Japan, scientists and technologists are educated in industrial strategies and languages, from an early age, in order to facilitate cross-border exchanges.

To obtain value from the development of inventions of merit, it is important to generate a level of inventiveness sufficient to pass the test applied by patent offices and courts, so that enforceable rights are granted to innovators who have the ability to undertake detailed technology exchange, and have licensing skill. This would encourage the world-wide spread of innovation. All mankind must be allowed to derive advantage from inventions of value.

We must guard against the generation of unenforceable rights and the squandering of resources on the protection of petty improvements, and avoid reversion to the foolishness of those ridiculed by Erasmus who "show wonderful ingenuity in always thinking up something whereby to deceive themselves afresh. They go on enjoying their self-deception until they have spent every penny and can't even afford to set up a small furnace."

Notes

1. Fernand Braudel, *The Structures of Everyday Life* (London: Collins, 1981), pp. 399–401.
2. Julius Victor Scholderer, *Johann Gutenberg, The Inventor of Printing* (London: British Museum, 1963).
3. Julius Victor Scholderer, *William Caxton* (London: The British Library, 1976).
4. Roger Ascham, quoted by G. M. Trevelyan, *Illustrated English Social History* (London: Longmans, Green & Co., 1949), p. 76.
5. Desiderius Erasmus, *Praise of Folly*, trans. Betty Radice (Harmondsworth: Penguin, 1971), p. 124.
6. Committee to Examine the Patent System and Patent Law, *The British Patent System, Report of the Committee to Examine the Patent System and Patent Law* (London: HMSO, Cmnd. 4407, 1970), p. 10.
7. Samuel Johnson, *The Rambler 9*, Prose and Poetry (London: Rupert Hart-Davis, 1963), p. 177.

8. *Reform of the Law Relating to Copyright, Designs and Performer's Protection* (London: HMSO, Cmnd. 8302, 1981), pp. 5, 6.
9. *Intellectual Property Rights and Innovation* (London: HMSO, Cmnd. 9117, 1983), p. 1.
10. Thomas Jefferson, *The Portable Thomas Jefferson* (New York: Viking Press, 1975), p. 530.

Values in Education

JOHN WILSON

This chapter is in two parts. The first deals with the notion of value in general, which, I shall argue, is largely empty or unintelligible in itself: it has to be cashed out in terms of particular human goals and enterprises. The second section deals with educational values; these are partly inherent in the concept of education and partly dependent on what is worth learning, either for human beings at particular places and times, or for human beings always and everywhere.

"Value"

In the heading to this section I put the term *value* in quotation marks because it is not normally used (except in grandiose philosophical discussion) by itself, but more often in combination with other words or concepts, stated or implied, of particular goals or interests. Thus we are reasonably clear about what is meant by "property values" on the open market or the value of a painting or jewel. Professional "valuers" are expert in determining such things. We may also be clear when talking about the value or importance of, for example, a proper grounding in classical Latin for a full understanding of romance languages such as Italian or Spanish. But if someone were to ask what Value (with a capital V) was, or what was truly valuable, we might well be baffled. I value, or count as important, all sorts of very different things in life: getting enough food, being healthy, not being assaulted, being free to speak my mind, my children, playing tennis, sunsets, memories of my childhood, and so on. I value these in different ways and for different reasons. It might even be impossible to answer the question, "Which do you value most?" for how am I to weigh, for instance, food and air against philosophy and children?

There is a parallel with other broad notions, including that marked by "truth." If asked in a general way about truth (or Truth), one of the things we should certainly want to say is that there are a number of different *kinds* of truth or true propositions. I believe that $2 + 2 = 4$, that not all swans are white, that some paintings are better than others, that my children love me, that Caesar crossed the Rubicon, that inflation can be dangerous, that lying is wrong, that one ought not to worship Hitler, that "educate" implies "teach." What makes these truths different is that they are backed by different kinds of reasons, evidence, or tests for truth—we verify and falsify them in different ways. Sometimes we need to attend solely to logic, sometimes to observe and experiment, sometimes to use our imagination; we consult different kinds of facts and different kinds of experts.[1]

This does not imply that terms like *value* and *truth* have no *meaning*; it implies only that they have no content *apart from* particular contexts, enterprises, goals, structures, or forms of thought and life. To repeat: when we say, as we very commonly do, "That's right," "That's good," "True enough," and so on, we always have some background in mind: we are trying to work out a sum in arithmetic, or cook a satisfactory dish, or find out who did the murder, or whatever. We can of course attempt to give some kind of translation or paraphrase of such words. Thus "true" might be taken to mean "what is in correspondence with reality, as opposed to our own desires and feelings." But this does not establish what actually is true; it establishes only what we mean by "true."

Words like *value* (*good, important, worthwhile*) have a special difficulty of their own, which does not apply to *true*. A very great deal has been written by philosophers about this,[2] but I will try at least to clarify one important point. On the one hand, we may raise questions about what different people do in "fact" value or think good or count as important. Here we should be acting as sociologists or psychologists, simply noting the facts. We should have to consider not just what people commonly value—freedom from pain, their children, interesting work, justice, and so on—or just minority tastes—Shakespeare, philosophy, and so on—but also cases where what is valued seems arbitrary or hard to understand. Thus what Hitler or de Sade valued, or why obsessional people think it important to go through certain rituals, or why some misers enjoy hoarding but not using their money, or why in some cultures a person might prefer to die rather than be taken prisoner are not immediately transparent to us: we cannot always see what *sort* of good they are pursuing, what kind of interests make these things valuable to them. On the other hand, we may inquire in a quite different way into what people *ought to* value, or what is really or truly valuable, or what a reasonable (sane, unprejudiced, right-thinking) person would value. To use Aristotle's distinction, we can inquire into "apparent goods," what things appear as valuable to people, or into "real goods," what things really are valuable (whether or not people see them to be so).

The point I want to make here is a methodological one. In the very wide range of human interests, there are some about which we are reasonably clear; very roughly, those that might be called "utilitarian." Most people, for reasons we can fully understand (even if not articulate fully), want to remain alive, be healthy, have enough to eat, enjoy their families in peace, and so on. But in other cases—and these are the ones that cause most of our troubles—we are not so clear. We may consider common phenomena like falling in love, or following some kind of religion, or trying to maintain one's dignity or sense of identity or purity; or we may consider deviant cases like the miser and the sadist mentioned earlier. Characteristically people elevate their feelings, in such cases, into some kind of *doctrine*: they will talk about God, or Arab destiny, or their honour, or something of that kind (even de Sade elevated his desires into a kind of philosophy). But the truth is, as I see it, that we shall get nowhere with our second inquiry—the inquiry into what is truly to be valued—unless we have a much clearer notion of what such people are really after. Just *what is it* to want to "preserve one's integrity" or gain "a sense of identity"? Just *why* do we fall in love with people in the way we do? Just what *sort* of satisfaction does the sadist or the miser achieve?

Pursuing these matters is the task of a certain kind of psychology (or perhaps a task for all of us, if we will only use our insight, common sense, and ability to describe such phenomena with linguistic exactitude). We need to discover just what the basic human feelings and desires are that generate these symptoms and rationalizations. We know, or ought to know, how to handle utilitarian matters: how to make the trains run on time and get food properly distributed. But when we start arguing about value in non-utilitarian fields—in religion, the arts, literature, even morality and education—much, perhaps most, of what we say is coloured by certain attitudes (largely unconscious), which makes rational progress difficult or impossible. We are already *parti pris*, because there are certain things we unconsciously fear or desire, certain deep-rooted fantasies that unconsciously control our views. Thus—to take a notorious example—it seems to me unlikely that we shall make much progress in religion unless we have a better idea of just what religion is *about*, of what psychological *work* it does. Until then we shall merely repeat fruitless arguments at the level of rationalization, without the honesty and understanding to get at what we really feel. I do not deny that trying to face the basic facts here is difficult, but it is the only way forward.

This in turn involves trying to establish a context of communication in which our feelings have a genuine chance of coming to the surface and being inspected and understood. We have, of course, psychological vested interests in trying to avoid this; and we defend ourselves against it in various ways. Unsophisticated people, indeed even sophisticated people, lose their tempers, or break off discussion, or join demonstrations, or go to war, or retire into some sect or group that reinforces their fantasies: those more accustomed to the conventions of academic discussion write books and articles at one another, or engage in well-mannered but sterile academic argument—sterile, because the locus of the argument is not where it ought to be, that is, about the kinds of feelings that underlie the words. What happened to the Nazis, and what happens to people falling in love, is a common phenomenon: we cannot write it off as beyond reason or pathological, and then give up. We need to find some context, some set of rules and procedures, that will enable genuine communication to take place with such people—which includes all of us. This applies to almost any important question about educational values, to which I shall now turn.

Educational Values

I shall rely here partly on what I have written more fully elsewhere,[3] but I will try to bring out the distinctions between different kinds of values more clearly, without repeating my defence of these distinctions.

We have first to recognize that certain human enterprises are *given*, so long as we wish to remain alive and human. Because people are people, they will have bodies and will want to preserve them in good condition; this necessitates good health and enough food, so the enterprises we mark by "medicine" and "agriculture" ("economics," and so on) are inalienable. In the same way, so long as we wish to keep the human race going, or even if we wish to live well as adults, we shall want our children or ourselves to *learn* certain things. Education (or any other counterpart in any other language) marks, roughly, the enterprise that takes the learning of human beings seriously and attempts to promote serious learning above the level of nature. It goes beyond (and may sometimes go against) what is marked by such terms as *training*, *instruction*, and *indoctrination* in that we educate *people as such*: we are concerned with individuals, not just with producing fillers of social roles or people who will do and believe what we tell them. Education includes making people viable in their particular places, times, and societies, but is not exhausted by this goal. So long as we have a concern for people *qua* people and not just as members of particular societies or social groups as potential Christians or Communists or boiler-makers or English gentleman or whatever), education is an enterprise we cannot opt out of. I think there are (rather complex) conceptual reasons why human beings could not grow up to be people unless they were treated as people for at least some of the time; but in any case it is hardly conceivable that parents would be content to see their children solely as role-fillers or members of particular groups—they will always care about their personal welfare, and hence want them educated.

Certain practices, procedures, virtues, and values *go along with* the idea of education and derive from the twin conceptual truths that education involves (a) learning and (b) people. There are, fairly obviously, a set of virtues involved in learning almost anything—that is, what can be stated without our having to decide in advance about what is most worth learning, amongst others, such things as determination, conscientiousness, enthusiasm, willingness to accept criticism, and so on. Certain practices are also necessary: the establishment of some form of discipline to make learning possible, and some form of examination or assessment to ensure that the learning has taken place. I have enlarged on these elsewhere;[4] here I want to stress that things may go more badly wrong because these logically necessary features of education are disregarded than because we make bad decisions of extra-educational value. Absence of discipline or the desire to indoctrinate are anti-educational, *whatever* one's view may be about the content of education, because they do not fit logically with the nature of the enterprise. Things go wrong, most of the time, because people are not sufficiently attached to education as an enterprise but prefer to do other things instead—social engineering, the promotion of some political or religious ideology, whatever. By far the most important thing for the realization of educational values, in my judgement, is that teachers and educators—and governmental authorities—should fully grasp the concept of education itself and appreciate all the many values that this concept carries with it.

To take an obvious example,[5] the reason education in controversial areas—morality, politics, religion—has made little progress in practice is, quite simply, because educators have not been willing to face, let alone answer, the question, "What is it to be *educated* (not given a specific set of answers, or left in a vacuum) in the fields marked by morality (religion, politics)?" Even to face that question squarely would show us that we need some general criteria of reason into which pupils can be initiated in these various fields, criteria that are not the peculiar possessions of any class, creed, or culture, but that (once we are clear about them) can be used to prevent our pupils from falling into a vacuum of total relativism. This is the sticking-point that prevents these subjects from getting off the ground; for, of course, we prefer our attachments to our own creeds and values, or an equally misguided attachment to a timid relativism—our attachment to education and its values is much weaker.

It may be worth adding here that the same point applies to other enterprises. Science and the practice and appreciation of the arts, to take but two examples, could perhaps be shown to be a necessarily desirable pair of enterprises for all human beings; but both are liable to be invaded by values external to themselves—in these days, political or (in a broad sense) ideological values. Soviet authorities who exercised sanctions against biologists with anti-environmentalist views did, *pro tanto*, make the practice of science difficult or impossible: they replaced it by politics. British public opinion that exercised sanctions against the playing of German music when Britain was at war with Germany thereby made the appreciation of music less viable: nationalism was preferred to aesthetics. Enterprises are always liable to invasion in this sort of way; and perhaps the most helpful thing that can be done in the area of values is to construct a careful list of those enterprises that seem either inalienable or of particular importance for human beings, and describe their virtues and values fully, so that they can then be protected against such invasion—or, at least, so that we can know when we are invading and corrupting them (as, on certain, one hopes rare, occasions, we may have to do).

Indeed it is clear that the same operation that I have tried to conduct with the enterprise of education—that is, the proper delimitation of this enterprise, together with some account of its attendant virtues (and vices), practices, procedures, and other things that logically go along with it—has also to be conducted with other enterprises if *any* enterprise is to feel safe and stay within its proper bounds. We shall not be able to prevent the invasion of, for example, politics or religion from corrupting, for example, medicine or music unless and until we have a clear and well-based idea of the limits of politics and religion, as well as the limits of medicine and music. Here the crucial questions, or some crucial questions, are of the form "What are we going to *exclude* from the realm of the political (ideological, religious, and so forth)?" "What are the *limits* to political reasons, political goods, political goals?"

Some maintain, or appear to maintain, that these questions are unanswerable on the grounds (so far as I can understand them) that the concepts marked by politics, education, and so forth are contestable, so that the limits of various enterprises cannot be immutably drawn. There is much to be argued here; but it seems clear to me (and I have argued this more fully elsewhere[6]) that, however concepts may be marked at different times and in different languages, there are in fact a number of *different* human interests that cannot reasonably be confounded. Mental health is one thing, political deviance another: one objection to imprisoning political trouble-makers on the grounds that they are mentally ill is simply that the categories *are* different. Again, it is surely *one* thing to object to playing Wagner on the (no doubt reasonable) grounds that it may remind people too painfully of their experiences in concentration camps, *another* thing to object on the grounds that Wagner's music is boring or aesthetically poor. Our interests in health, learning, political order, the arts, and so on are not constructed by ourselves; they are given, because we are human and landed with inexpellable human interests. I do not of course deny that it is a task of some philosophical or taxonomic difficulty to sort out these categories, nor that this sorting will not always tell us which categories are most important (sometimes education should yield to politics). But at least it would give us an agreed set of enterprises to work with, and we should be clear when one had to yield to another.

So much, then, for those values that are conceptually connected to the notion of education, and for the elucidation of which conceptual argument is our proper tool. We then face a number of questions of which perhaps the most important is the question of what is most worth learning, what the content of education should be. Here conceptual argument alone will not entirely settle the matter, if only for the obvious reason that the answer must partly depend on contingent facts about who is doing the learning, in what kind of society and at what historical period.

Even at this point, however, it is very important not to jump straight into some particular set of values or ideology of one's own. This for two reasons. First, there is the practical point that we are going to have to negotiate our answers and values with other people, not only those who hold different opinions about what is valuable in the adult world, but more particularly with the pupils, so that we shall benefit if we can reach as much common agreement as possible. Second, and in my judgement more important, there is the more theoretical point that any value or ideological commitment to the importance of certain kinds of learning must be based on reason if we are to have any reason for promoting it (this is a tautology); so that, if we are to remain in the camp of reason, our prime allegiance must be to the anterior principles and procedures of reason rather than to our particular commitments. We need, therefore, to proceed very slowly and cautiously in this matter, spending a good deal of time in making categories and looking at various kinds of arguments for various options, before determining a particular curricular content.

Here, one distinction is surely useful. We can argue for items of content (1) on the grounds that any human being anywhere at any time needs to learn something, just because he is human and that thing is worth learning for him, and/or (2) on the grounds that particular people need to learn it for particular reasons that apply to their position in space and time. Thus we might think (1) that everyone needs to learn how to make friends, communicate with other people, enjoy good music, or understand the principles of rational discussion; (2) that in 1939 a lot of British young people needed to learn how to fight and fly Spitfires and so on, just because they were engaged in a (just) war. Other distinctions between different kinds of arguments ought also to be made: for instance, between learning something (a) for its own sake, without any thought of its being useful for the attaining of some other end, and (b) in order to gain some other end; or between learning something (a) for the benefit of the individual, or (b) for the benefit of that individual's society or the world at large. No serious curricular theory, or theory about what is valuable to learn, can be constructed without paying attention to these and other distinctions; but for the sake of brevity I shall attend only to points (1) and (2).

By and large, (1) will include things that may (incidentally) be "useful" to the individual and/or his society, but it will chiefly consist of things for which "useful" is too trivial a word. For instance, it is obviously of the highest importance that people should engage in learning that will, as it were, make sense of their lives, or give them some kind of psychological security and identity. We might hope that learning to appreciate literature and the arts, and to think properly in various forms of thought (mathematics, history, science, philosophy), would go along with this. Such learning is too important to be described as "useful," in the way that it may be useful to be able to speak French if one is in France, or to know how to operate a computer in certain jobs. (2), on the other hand, will often incorporate items of items of a more utilitarian kind: we need to learn how to keep our bodies healthy, to master those skills that will make us employable, to understand the norms of our society well enough to enable us to survive in it.

Clearly we cannot pronounce that (1) is more (or less) important than (2). Without (1), we should hardly be recognizable as human beings at all, or have any sort of human life worth living; without (2), we should not have mastered the practical, utilitarian world well enough even to survive, let alone maintain a level of material prosperity that enabled us to extend the benefits of (1). At certain times (during a war or plague, for instance) we may be able to spend very little time on (1) and have as our work to keep our heads above water;

at other times we find space, time, and money to educate ourselves in a fuller way. Nevertheless, there are reasons for thinking that (2) is often stressed more than it should be. One is, of course, that governments are, in modern industrialized societies at least, wholly or chiefly concerned with economics, with the utilitarian goods that come under (2), and less interested in (1)—and governments exercise great control over the educational system. Another is that individuals find it easier to concentrate on what is useful or immediately advantageous, on the particular and the material, than upon the more impalpable kinds of learning in (1): everyone will pay lip-service to the view that friendship, morality, the arts, and so on are important, but more time is actually spent on what will be profitable in terms of money and status. I argue, therefore, that we need to spend a good deal more time on the values in (1)—that is (to repeat), on what is necessarily desirable for all people *qua* people to learn.

In considering (1), we have of course to allow for individual differences in pupils. Not much is gained by demonstrating the desirability of learning about, for example, Proust or Kant, if a large percentage of pupils are simply not able to learn anything much about them despite our best efforts. Nevertheless, we must not use this point as an excuse for giving up, still less as an excuse for retreating into a kind of relativism according to which there is nothing objective to be said about what is valuable for people *qua* people. Granted that people are in many ways different; granted that we do not want to impose values on them by force or brainwashing; granted that any values people may come to adopt must, if they are to be significant to them, be learned and understood and properly appropriated by the individuals themselves; granted also (what many modern philosophers, for example, Isaiah Berlin,[7] are keen to say) that not all values may be fitted neatly together without loss in some ideally good life; granted all this, nevertheless there are still important points to be made.

By far the most important of these points, in my judgement, is that we have to equip pupils with the tools, procedures, abilities, and virtues to work out their own values reasonably. Any serious moral (or religious, or political, or emotional) education must proceed on the twin principles (a) that there are such things as better or worse answers, more or less wise decisions, about what is valuable in life; and (b) that to a considerable extent each person has to come to see these answers and make these decisions for himself—they cannot be handed him on a plate, so to speak. Hence, our efforts must be concentrated not on providing lists of right answers, but on elucidating more clearly the bits of equipment, the intellectual and emotional tools, that the pupil needs in order to find his answers for himself. I have tried elsewhere to list these bits of equipment;[8] a great deal of empirical work needs to be done if we are to understand how in practice we can actually bestow them on pupils. This equipment includes, for instance, the concept of human beings as moral equals, an understanding of the emotions, the determination and alertness to think seriously and act on decisions, and many other attributes. Similar lists could and should be made for other areas of inquiry—not only the methodologically uncertain areas of religion, politics, mental health, and so on, but the more well-defined areas of existing curricular subjects: science, history, mathematics, and many others. Despite constant talk by modern educationalists about "skills," there is no adequate taxonomy (that I know of) in any area.

We need, in any case, a great deal of analytic thinking to establish the value of various items of learning in (1). This is a task for philosophers in conjunction with educators: it has nothing to do with "society," "relevance," "the modern world," or any other of the catch-phrases so often imported when discussing the curriculum. Such thinking would result, I believe, in at least one practical suggestion: the teaching of philosophy itself in all schools—something that is certainly not done in any organized and coherent way even within individual countries. For educators, though they must make provisional or *ad hoc* decisions about what is valuable for pupils to learn, are not always obliged to sign up for particular answers to this question that are beyond criticism, and a large part of their task must be to promote precisely those forms of inquiry that bear on the question itself. Of these forms, philosophy is certainly one.

So far as (2) is concerned, the question seems one not so much for educators as for those representatives of society who are best placed to pronounce on what items of learning happen to be necessary at particular places and times—governments, economists, industrialists, and so forth. Whether or not, or for what contexts, pupils will need to understand (for example) the working of computers is not, strictly speaking, an educational question: it is a question about the future shape of society and the nature of employment. For this reason alone it is important to preserve, both in theory and in school practice, the distinction between (1) and (2); and unless it is preserved, both will suffer. At present we operate in a far too *ad hoc* way, adding and subtracting curricular items in accordance with fashion and local pressures, rather than on any clear set of distinctions and arguments for the value of this or that item.

Postscript

Some twenty years' experience in the field of moral education persuades me to add a practical point. There is a great deal, indeed more than enough, concern about value and education; indeed about "value" more generally. Such concern is apt to express itself in various ways: in the holding of conferences, the writing of books and articles, or the founding of particular ideologically based groups that try to promote some partisan commitment of their own. As an initial step, there may be some value (use) in such expressions; but (apart from the fact that they have been going on for many centuries) they rapidly lose momentum unless they are given a practical shape.

It follows, I am sure, from what I have tried to say—or indeed from any serious consideration of the matter—that real progress, both in theory and in practice, needs sterner and more efficient methods. Only a properly financed team of people, however small, with a clear brief to engage in and make sense of one area of "value," is likely to influence our schools or society in any significant way. This is, chiefly, because the difficulties of communication between academics themselves, and between them and the practical world, are such that no amount of conferences or published writings will accomplish this. To create adequate conditions of communication and of practical progress we have to designate a small number of people and pay them to do the work efficiently. For the work requires not only a commitment to scholarship but a commitment to putting the results of scholarly inquiry into practical or educational shape, in a form which will actually be viable in schools or in society at large. Forming such a team is a task with high priority for any person of good will who wants to do more than engage in high-minded conversation. We suffer at present from a fatal division between two worlds: the world of academic scholarship, on the one hand, and the world outside in which adults and children fight, suffer, despair, and are lost in a sea of chaos. Only an effective moral education, in a broad sense of "moral," can help them keep afloat; and an effective moral education demands some such structure as I have just described.

The absence of any such structure is, again, due to our failure to believe strongly or sincerely enough in the importance of education as such. Money and other resources can be easily found to promote some partisan cause or ideological outlook—indeed, as we all know, some very bizarre religions and ideals are heavily subsidized. What is lacking is the desire, and hence the resources, to promote the general ideas of rationality and sanity in education—the objective that pupils should be taught to think *for themselves*, but also to think *reasonably*, about value. To most ears that sounds too vague, too far removed from our own ideological commitments and personal preferences, to be worth supporting. But until we find the resources to give a proper shape to this task, the world will continue to be the plaything of various competing sects and gangs, leaving our young people in a dazing supermarket of values and ideals where (for lack of any proper education) they can only buy on impulse.

It is striking and regrettable fact, but one that has to be faced, that university departments (schools, faculties, and so forth) of education are not capable of providing a proper context for this task. This is partly because they lack funds; but chiefly because they have been corrupted, as educational systems in general have been corrupted, by extra-educational values—usually by political or social pressures of various kinds. Particularly in time of recession, but in any case for the foreseeable future, these institutions tend to be utilitarian and (so to speak) pseudo-practical in their approach. They are, to some extent understandably, but far too much, concerned with the latest political and economic demands, with ideological climates of opinion in society, with training students as functionaries within the existing system; and hence they have little time for consideration of the wider, and ultimately more important, areas of educational inquiry, in which value education must figure as one of the most important. The same, I am sure, is true in respect of other kinds of education. Because they are orientated towards the system as it is, there is an immense divorce between the thinking and practice that goes on about, for example, literature or science or almost any other subject in university departments of education on the one hand, and the thinking that goes on under these headings in the rest of the university. The values, the presuppositions, even the quality and interests of the faculty members are entirely different.

For this reason only private enterprise, in a broad sense, is likely to make any serious impact in the region of value and education, in much the same way, to make the point by a rather depressing parallel, as many parents (not only the rich) have despaired of trying to change the state system of education in the United Kingdom and opted to send their children to private schools. It is sad, but inevitable, that progress here depends on finance; but there seems little hope of reorganizing or restaffing those institutions that now engage in the study of education radically enough to do the job unless money is allocated to them, under fairly stringent controls, for that particular purpose. That a local authority should be prepared to finance a school adviser on microchips, but be unwilling to finance one on religious education, is a characteristic symptom. In the non-academic world, there is a strong current of feeling that appreciates the importance of questions of value and is prepared to count such matters as of at least equal importance with more utilitarian and pragmatic concerns. But that current of feeling, admirable in itself, needs urgently to take on a practical shape.

I am suggesting, then, something in essence quite simple: that private foundations and funding bodies that are concerned with values—and there are a great many of these in one form or another—need to take the initiative; they cannot hope to rely on what governments or official institutions of education are likely to do. In particular they have to realize

> that only a non-partisan, value-neutral kind or research and development is satisfactory; for if we are to understand each other's values, we cannot *start* from (although we may reach) the presumption that this or that set of values is correct;
>
> that only a properly financed team of first-rate scholars is likely to be able to make much progress in this thorny areas; and
>
> that the research and development done by such a team must be in the area of education; in the hope that, even if we ourselves cannot get all that far, we shall at least be able to show our children how to make progress.

My colleagues and I of the Warborough Trust have said a good deal about this elsewhere,[9] and this is not the place to repeat it. Many problems—some practical, others theoretical—remain to be faced; but these problems cannot be properly tackled except on the kind of practical and theoretical basis that I have briefly discussed in this chapter.

Notes

1. Paul H. Hirst and Richard S. Peters, *The Logic of Education* (London: Routledge & Kegan Paul, 1970).
2. See particularly Richard M. Hare, *Moral Thinking* (Oxford: Oxford University Press, 1981).
3. John Wilson, *Preface to the Philosophy of Education* (London: Routledge & Kegan Paul, 1979); and Harold Loukes, John Wilson and Barbara Cowell, *Education: An Introduction* (Oxford: Martin Robertson, 1983).
4. John Wilson, *Philosophy and Practical Education* (London: Routledge & Kegan Paul, 1977).
5. Loukes, Wilson, and Cowell, *Education*, pp. 73 ff.
6. John Wilson, "Concepts, Contestability and the Philosophy of Education," *Journal of Philosophy of Education* 15, no. 1 (1981): pp. 3–16.
7. Isaiah Berlin, *Against the Current* (Oxford: Oxford University Press, 1979).
8. John Wilson, *The Assessment of Morality* (Slough: N.F.E.R., 1973).
9. John Wilson et al., *Introduction to Moral Education* (Harmondsworth: Penguin, 1968).

Bibliography

Berlin, Isaiah. *Against the Current*. Oxford: Oxford University Press, 1979.
Hare, Richard, M. *Moral Thinking*. Oxford: Oxford University Press, 1981.
Hirst, Paul, H. and Richard S. Peters. *The Logic of Education*. London: Routledge & Kegan Paul, 1970.
Loukes, Harold, John Wilson and Barbara Cowell. *Education: An Introduction*. Oxford: Martin Robertson, 1983.
Wilson, John. *The Assessment of Morality*. Slough: N.F.E.R., 1973.
———. *Philosophy and Practical Education*. London: Routledge & Kegan Paul, 1977.
———. *Preface to the Philosophy of Education*. London: Routledge & Kegan Paul, 1979.

———. "Concepts, Contestability and the Philosophy of Education," *Journal of Philosophy of Education* 15, no. 1 (1981): 3–16.

Wilson, John et al. *Introduction to Moral Education*. Harmondsworth: Penguin, 1968.

Values and the Novel

BERNARD RICHARDS

This chapter studies three main questions: How do values manifest themselves in the novel? What kinds of values are presented in the novel? and What kinds of values is the novel most effective at presenting? It then concludes by asking a final question: What indispensable contribution does the novel have to make in propagating values?

Values fall into two main categories: the very basic values (some of which we may feel to be God-given and capable of operating irrespective of human existence) and secondary or functional values ("procedural values" as they have been labelled by some contributors to this volume) that make a practical contribution in securing the survival of the basic values. One might regard the value of the human race and the necessity for its survival as basic values, and principles of honesty, reliability, consistency, and perseverance as secondary values. We often describe people as "narrow" when they erect secondary values, some of which may be of not more than utilitarian use, into primary ones and follow them relentlessly. Temperance and self-control may be desirable values, but it is hard to see them as absolutes when we remember that Christ surrendered himself to righteous anger on occasions (although one is never quite sure that Christ's anger was the same as ordinary human anger). Even the stiff Knight of Temperance in Book II of Spenser's *Faerie Queene* gives way to vengeful anger, albeit in a good cause. In discussing the two types of value and their relation to the novel, I want to suggest that the novel is very effective at dealing with both primary and secondary values, but that it opens itself to dangers when it tries to deal with secondary values too explicitly.

The novel is a rich and complex art form; it is rich and complex for the same sorts of reasons that the English language is rich—it has a wide and varied ancestry. On the one hand, it descends from the moral fable and the *exemplum* (taking on board as it developed in the eighteenth century the value-transmitting devices of poetry and drama); on the other hand, it descends from the essay, the journal, the epistle, and the memoir. At any point in the history of the novel, one or another of these ancestors can surface—rather as a family trait can crop up after a gap in a generation. The moral fable tradition relates to the novel's desire to make general and universal statements, whereas the journal and epistle relate to a quite different tradition of particularity, individuality, and relativism. The essay is in between, since one part of the essay tradition relates to the literary tradition of making general and universal statements, but the other, associated with Montaigne and Swift, for example, relates to the local conditions of place and personality that affect the way a man thinks and writes. The history of the novel is the history of the development of a literary form that has gradually tried to shed its burden (if it is a burden) of general and universal statement (or at the least implication) in order to take up particularity and specificity. But even to this day, it has not *quite* managed to shed the burden entirely.

Not all fictions are novels (and I shall try to make the case for the special features that make novels a small subdivision of the wider realms of fiction), but it is worth remembering that there is bound to be shared ground between novelistic and philosophic thought since philosophers always have recourse to fictions sooner or later. To invent an example to illustrate an argument is to write a brief fiction, and to use grammatical forms such as "as if it were the case" is to share in fictional creativity. The difference, however, between the philosophical example and the novel is that the former operates within very limited parameters and is immediately applicable in a wide number of abstract cases, whereas the novelistic episode (or indeed the novel itself) has first and foremost particular application (with all the attendant special circumstances) to the characters involved, and then, perhaps, relevance to real people outside the book and to abstract considerations. The novel invites one to attend to those details and special case pleadings that the philosophical example has to dispense with at the very outset.

Let me try to answer my first question, How do values manifest themselves in the novel? One's immediate sense is that they appear in the language itself, for it is very difficult to keep value words out of a novel; they appear in the dialogue and in the narrative (although naturalistic novelists have tried to restrict themselves to neutral terms in the narratives). Values also appear in the action, and here analysis becomes trickier. Novels have been written in which there are neat systems of punishment and reward. As Miss Prism says, "The good ended happily, and the bad unhappily. That is what Fiction means." The phrase used to describe this activity is "poetic justice"—there is a kind of rightness in what happens to the characters that satisfies one's sense of shape and pattern both in the moral world and in the imaginative world—with the important caveat that the imaginative worlds of these fictions are ones in which moral judgements match plots. In Dante's Hell, poetic justice operates in the grand manner: crimes on earth (some of which remained unpunished while the characters were alive) are punished in Hell with an appropriateness so apt, so symbolic, so physically matching with the crime that the imaginative connections between the physical and ethical world are indeed poetic. In some ways poetic justice is an unfortunate phrase, since it is danger of violating the respect one has for poetry, but in the bridge it forms between the ethical and physical world, which at times has the force associated with metaphor, to establish general truth it is obviously a useful phrase. Of course, Dante is standing on firm ground, because his poetic justice operates in eternity, although admittedly it is an eternity he concocts in the privacy of his own tortured mind. Poetic justice is less acceptable when it operates in *this* world, because in *our* world we take it that it is not a norm; certainly it is not a norm in the secular view of this century, and I do not think it was invariably a norm under the aegis of Christian world views. A possible exception to this might be Christians who emphasized the providentiality of God very strongly—and his providentiality often looks like the divine version of poetic justice. When poetic justice happens in our world, we point to it in amazement—as if it is the exception that justifies the rule, as if it is a point at which life uncharacteristically impinges on fiction.

Admittedly life sometimes throws up cases of poetic justice where a moral failing leads to an action and a result picturesquely in accord with the failing. Proper names, too, can exhibit this same picturesque accord in real life. There is at least one dentist in this country called "Dentith." The argument goes: if life throws up these oddities (and in a world governed by chance, and in which very little is said to contain *essential* meaning, they *are* oddities) then fiction should also be allowed to do so. But to this day a large section of the novel-reading public remains unhappy with violations of both particular and general probabilities in the novel. Life *has* coincidences, but we always feel them to be remarkable and improbable, as if violating norm and expectation. We are reluctant to allow coincidences in novels—at least more than a due number. Hardy's early reviewers worried about excessive coincidence, and for some reason the charge is tiresomely reiterated. (Actually I do not think Hardy is excessively guilty of using the device.) In other words we have *still* not shaken off the idea, inherited from the eighteenth century and beyond, that the novel should address itself to some general norm, that it should contain something like proportional representation. So that in a given plot some villains should be punished either by a process of law, which may not be particularly poetic given the prosaicness of the law, or by a picturesquely appropriate punishment, and some should go scot-free; some virtuous characters should be rewarded and others should be unrewarded, or even unjustly punished. Sometimes the votaries of "norms" do not merely consider a single novel by an author; they look at his whole canon and tot up the score there. Here again, Hardy causes distress and annoyance, since by the law of averages fewer of the characters in his novels taken as a whole should come to such sticky ends. This approach to norms is still active among critics, and certainly the public at large. Many of the letters to the *Radio Times* about films and plays use the proportional representation line of argument. This shows that the idea of fiction as a generic and exemplary form is far from dead. One also sees in the *Radio Times* letters of another sort that appeal not to realist norms but to idealist norms. These correspondents take the line that sin should always be punished and virtue always rewarded, not because this corresponds to what happens in real life, but because it would be desirable if it did, and they hope that fictions will help to promote that eventual outcome. This may seem a very silly line of argument, especially since many of the so-called punishments administered to people in their lives are meted out not by the comparatively rational forces of human decision but by chance and nature, and so far as *this* world is concerned there has never been a just correspondence between vice and punishment and virtue and reward—as many orthodox theologians have held. Indeed the intellectual force maintaining the idea of heaven, hell and Last Judgement has arisen from the recognition that since there is so little justice on earth one desperately requires that it should exist *somewhere*. Idealist norms may then seem silly, but they have informed literature of all kinds for a very long time, and it is only in the last hundred years or so that they have been attacked with any vigour.

As the novel developed it became increasingly clear that it was best at dealing with particular cases, and that the dominance of what I call secondary values damaged the effectiveness of the medium. Suddenly, in the mid-nineteenth century, a bogey word sprang up: *didacticism*. On the face of it, *didactic* seems a harmless enough word, since all literary works teach *something*. In discussion of novels, however, didacticism came to be associated with a teaching that was narrow and unsubtle. It came to be associated with novelists interested in presenting arguments rather than in presenting human experience, action, and visions of life. The Victorian attacks on didacticism are outlined very well by Kenneth Graham.[1] In 1865 the *Westminster Review*, castigating the pretentiousness of Bulwer Lytton, said: " . . . a novel ceases to be a novel when it aims at philosophical teaching. It is not the vehicle for conveying knowledge. Its business is to amuse, and give us that insight into human affairs which is obtained by the observation of character."[2] In the same year Edward Dowden disapproved of the novelist "who would entice us into listening to his homily under pretence of amusing us; we see the sulphur in that treacle, pah! and will none of it."[3] Often the complaints were not that novels embodied moral lessons but that they embodied them very crudely. I tend to agree with that position. One could be very radical and say that novels should *only* be entertaining and amusing, but then, it is hard to imagine how one could read anything as long as a novel and not pick *something* up of an informative or ideological kind on the way. One could also be very radical by saying that novels should be very aesthetic, and offer us the delights of pure form, and appeal *only* to that mysterious faculty called "the aesthetic emotion." This seems to me a dead end: even with a painter who deals in forms, such as Cézanne, to confine one's reactions to the pure form elements is somewhat jejune, and it is next to impossible to confine a reading of a novel to the aesthetic realms. Life keeps breaking in. We can never quite forget that the language of fiction impinges at some point on the language of our everyday transactions.

Pure amusement and pure aestheticism then are dead ends; one is forced to engage in the question of what kinds of teaching the novel is good at, and what are the rhetorical forms this teaching takes.

The first thing that is apparent on opening a novel is that values are attached to characters, in what they say and do and even in their appearances. In this way there is potentially something very insidious about the novel, which is why evangelical churchmen in the eighteenth and nineteenth centuries were so hostile to it (as they had been hostile to the drama before that). An attractive character espousing wrong principles could, if one were not very vigilant, make even vices seem attractive and not detachable from the general impression of his being. The novel can present values lived through and acted through; it can explore them in social contexts and in the interior contexts of the mind with a freedom and a flexibility for which there is no other literary correlative—especially if the novelist is an omniscient novelist. Even when a novelist decides not to be omniscient, but restrict himself to the kind of analysis a historian or journalist might employ (and both Henry James and Joseph Conrad thought they would impose such self-denying ordinances on themselves), he still has access to more information than a historian or journalist can ever have. Real autobiographies and fictional autobiographies are often rhetorically indistinguishable, but the fictional autobiography has access to a kind of anecdotal inventiveness, and hence a kind of poetic justice, not possible in any extended sense in the real autobiography.

Much more powerful than maintained and explicit values in a novel are implicit values, and here the novel does have a unique contribution to make, a contribution summed up very well by Anthony Quinton in his Chichele Lecture of 1982 called "The Inner Life":

> The emotional life of civilized human beings has an intellectual complexity which no colourful sequence, however artfully organized, can properly convey. For that we have to go to the great bourgeois analysts of the inner life, Proust and Henry James. In them we find people it would be worth getting to know and through whom, by getting to know them vicariously in imagination, we are enlightened about ourselves . . . Today the species [of the unique human individual] . . . is endangered and if the [human] species survives it may be at the expense of the individual. The great analytically introspective novels of the last century

testify both to the existence of the individualizing inner life and to its value.[4]

Novels are written in a very wide spectrum of ideological principles, and not all of them press the case for individual development and the inner quality of life very strongly, but the best of them do make very strong pleas for these values, if only by the degree of attention accorded. Sometimes the intensity of experience leaves traditional moral categories some way behind (this is usually the case in Lawrence novels), but at other times this intensity can in fact underwrite those categories. Henry James did not write *The Wings of the Dove* in order to show the evils of exploiting the emotional resources of other human beings (his novel is in any case much more complex and filled with incidental richness than that). But since we follow the experience of indulging such behaviour through and *see* it destroy the relationship between the exploiters (Kate Croy and Merton Densher), we have a much deeper awareness of the cost of such exploitation than we could otherwise gain by *any* other means (except actually living through a similar experience ourselves—and most of us have neither the intensity nor the perception to do that).

Philosophical and moral writing might *tell* us about exploitation, but novelistic writing can *demonstrate* it. If philosophical writing goes in for demonstration then it infringes the boundaries of fiction. This it is fully entitled to do, but it always does it less effectively than does the novel proper, since really to generate interest and a sense of life more space is needed. To generate the sense of life is to draw the reader into the world of the novel which he will take seriously. He may not learn lessons in moral strategy from the book, but he will learn what it is to be an experiencing human being, and it may be that our civilization is more dependent than we imagine on the widening effects of fiction.

Novels activate imaginations that might otherwise lie dormant. Imagination in one sense is dangerous—the sense Dr. Johnson had in mind when he talked about the dangerous prevalence of the imagination; but in the Coleridgean sense of extending our knowledge of other beings, it is highly necessary for the conduct of civilized life. Precepts are never very powerful because they are too isolated. To see where precepts go we need narrative, and this is where the novel offers us models for the construction of a picture of self. In previous eras, when novels did not exist, human beings had to envisage themselves in some other way (many of these ways being connected, somehow, to the rhetorics of artifice). For individualistic Western societies, the novel is very bound up with these maps of self-definition, so much so that one is hesitant to give either priority. For our society, individuality and opportunity for self-development probably constitute what I call principal values. Perhaps, without even knowing it, many novelists have placed a value of this kind very centrally in their works. In Henry James, the villains time and time again are those figures who hamper or damage the flowering of another human personality. I mentioned earlier that novels are, strictly speaking, a branch of fiction rather than the whole of fiction. It will be now apparent why this is so: because fictions embrace a wide range of invented circumstances, some of which would not necessarily involve human beings at all, whereas the novel is, *par excellence*, the means to depict the history of a human reaction to an invented circumstance. The novel has been very good at analysing the past; it is, especially nowadays, a tool for anticipating the future: "What would happen if?"

I have been assuming, up till now, that the way experience gets into novels is not very problematical. In fact, however, it is highly problematical, and the ultimate treatment of experiences in the novel (including moral and ethical experiences) would be very involved. One can get a sense of the scope needed for this by considering the length of Wayne C. Booth's *Rhetoric of Fiction*, for instance. In most novels direct speech accounts for relatively little of the total content. Most of any given novel is taken up with narration (of thoughts and events) and in many cases narrative comment. This comment can be very value-laden indeed, and when Victorian reviewers objected to "preaching" in the novel what they often had in mind was interference in narrative flow as the narrator inserted his opinionated comments. Sometimes this "narrator" was a separate and coherent being, organized and planned by the author with as strict an attention to detail and integrity as the characters themselves, but in other cases to use the word *narrator* is to be excessively generous, since the figure telling the story is the undisguised author, as loose and rambling in the novel as he would be in any other context. Charles Kingsley infiltrates himself into his novels with no sign whatever of any kind of artistic conscience. George Eliot stops the flow of her narrative a good deal to drop in moral and analytical comments, but at least they help to build up a coherent picture of a sibylline figure who is dignified and serious. These comments have a way of attaching the novel to the real world—by suggesting that the particular situations in the novel help to build up a picture of the real world, and that general principles, learnt in the real world, can be used to throw light onto particular situations in the novel.

The principle continues with another serious novelist of our century, D. H. Lawrence. In *The Plumed Serpent* and *Lady Chatterley's Lover* he repeatedly stops the flow to interpose a comment or a mini-essay, and these interruptions correspond, stylistically and ideologically, precisely to Lawrence the essay writer and prophet. Here is a typical example in *The Plumed Serpent*:

> Oh, if there is one thing men need to learn, but the Mexican Indians especially, it is to collect each man his own soul together deep inside him, and to abide by it. The Church, instead of helping men to this, pushes them more and more into a soft, emotional helplessness, with the unpleasant sensuous gratification of feeling themselves victims, victimised, victimised, but at the same time with the lurking sardonic consciousness that in the end a victim is stronger than the victimiser. In the end the victims pull down their victimiser, like a pack of hyenas on an unwary lion. They know it. Cursed are the falsely meek, for they are inheriting the earth.[5]

Passages like this, and there are too many in Lawrence, are a betrayal of what the novel does best, a betrayal of the principle of showing; they are an intrusion of the principle of telling. Very often they are an insult to the reader's intelligence, since he has already worked out for himself what the proper interpretation should be.

There are more insidious forms of narrator's interference when he slides himself into the fabric of the novel's style, especially when he reports the thoughts of a character in a language that is his own. Ultimately, however, this mode of interference is so pervasive that we are forced to accept that style and content are a totality; that the world of the novel is necessarily bound up with the style that evokes it. In this sense the imagined worlds of the novel are distinct from the world we live in, which goes on existing stubbornly and resolutely irrespective of the styles we adopt to grasp hold of it. Curiously, D. H. Lawrence had an excellent grasp of the principles of fiction—it is just that he completely and utterly failed to grasp them in his own work, especially his later work. Perhaps, at that stage, he thought there was something more. In "Morality and the Novel," he speaks a good deal of sense, in forceful and memorable language:

> And morality is that delicate, for ever trembling and changing *balance* between me and my circumambient universe, which precedes and accompanies a true relatedness.
>
> Now here we see the beauty and the great value of the novel. Philosophy, religion, science, they are all of them busy nailing things down, to get a stable equilibrium. Religion, with its nailed-down One God, who says *Thou shalt, Thou shan't,* and hammers home every time; philosophy, with its fixed ideas; science with its "laws": they, all of them, all the time, want to nail us on to some tree or other.
>
> But the novel, no. The novel is the highest example of subtle inter-relatedness that man has discovered. Everything is true in its own time, place, circumstance, and untrue outside of its own place, time, circumstance. If you try to nail anything down, in the novel, either it kills the novel, or the novel gets up and walks away with the nail.
>
> Morality in the novel is the trembling instability of the balance. When the novelist puts his thumb in the scale, to pull down the balance to his own predilection, that is immorality.
>
> The modern novel tends to become more and more immoral, as the novelist tends to press his thumb heavier and heavier in the pan: either on the side of love, pure love: or on the side of licentious "freedom."[6]

In the end, most novelists do interfere with the balance; we tend to complain most when they do it blatantly. As Hardy said, art should be for edification "but the edified should not perceive the edification."[7] Lawrence uses a crucifixion allusion to speak of the deadliness of excessive didacticism; in this he follows the American writer Nathaniel Hawthorne, who in the preface to *The House of the Seven Gables* presents a vivid image of a story impaled on an iron rod of morality "as by sticking a pin through a butterfly—thus at once depriving it of life, and causing it to stiffen in an ungainly and unnatural attitude."[8]

In conclusion, then, sceptical modern views of the random and morally chaotic universe lead us to be impatient with novels based on simple patterns of poetic justice that can lead directly to conduct, so that if we are concerned with value and the novel we must look elsewhere, to the kind of aesthetic reaction outlined by Schiller when he said that the great utility of aesthetic response was that it restored us briefly to a state of indeterminate freedom of choice and analysis. This is very different from the spirit in which Sarah Scudamore in 1758 wrote: "I've lately read over my oracle [Richardson's *Pamela*] again, and already made use of some of Mr. Locke's maxims, made clear and plain by her, upon my little boy, which I highly approve, and intend strictly to adhere to." There are then oversimple uses to which the writing and reading of novels can be put, but these should not prevent one from attempting to identify a true utility, and recognizing that there are more significant functions than amusement.

Notes

1. Kenneth Graham, *English Criticism of the Novel 1865–1900* (Oxford: Clarendon Press, 1965), pp. 85–92.
2. Anon., "Modern Novelists: Sir Edward Bulwer Lytton," *Westminster Review*, N.S. 27 (April, 1865): 482.
3. Edward Dowden, "Fiction and Its Uses," *Fraser's Magazine*, 72 (December, 1865): 759.
4. Anthony Quinton, "The Inner Life," in *The Novelist as Philosopher: Modern Fiction and the History of Ideas*," ed. Peregrine Horden (Oxford: All Souls College, 1983), p. 36.
5. D. H. Lawrence, *The Plumed Serpent* (London: Heinemann, 1955), p. 273.
6. D. H. Lawrence, "Morality and the Novel," in *Phoenix: The Posthumous Papers of D. H. Lawrence*, ed. Edward D. McDonald (London: Heinemann, 1936), pp. 528–29.
7. Florence Emily Hardy, *The Life of Thomas Hardy* (London: Macmillan, 1962), p. 225.
8. Nathaniel Hawthorne, *The House of the Seven Gables* (Columbus: Ohio State University Press, 1965), p. 2.

Bibliography

Abrams, Meyer H., ed. *Literature and Belief: English Institute Essays, 1957*. New York: 1958.

Booth, Wayne C. *The Rhetoric of Fiction*. Chicago: University of Chicago Press, 1961.

Bradbury, Malcolm S. *The Novel Today: Contemporary Writers on Modern Fiction*. Manchester: Manchester University Press, 1977.
Graham, Kenneth. *English Criticism of the Novel, 1865–1900*. Oxford: Clarendon Press, 1965.
Hardy, Florence, E. *The Life of Thomas Hardy*. London: Macmillan, 1962.
Horden, Peregrine, ed. *The Novelist as Philosopher: Modern Fiction and the History of Ideas*. Oxford: All Souls College, 1983.
Jones, Peter H. *Philosophy and the Novel*. Oxford: Clarendon Press, 1975.
Lamarque, Peter. *Philosophy and Fiction*. Aberdeen: Aberdeen University Press, 1983.
Lawrence, D. H. "Morality and the Novel." In *Phoenix: The Posthumous Papers of D. H. Lawrence*, edited by Edward D. McDonald. London: Heinemann, 1936.
MacCarthy, Mary T. *Ideas and the Novel*. London: Weidenfeld & Nicholson, 1981.
Olsen, Stein H. "Thematic Concepts: Where Philosophy Meets Literature." *Royal Institute of Philosophy Lectures* 16. 1983.
Phillips, Dewi Z. *Through a Darkening Glass: Philosophy, Literature, and Cultural Change*. Oxford: Blackwell, 1982.
Quinton, Anthony. *Thoughts and Thinkers*. London: Duckworth, 1982.
Rosenbaum, Stanford P. *English Literature and British Philosophy*. Chicago: University of Chicago Press, 1971.
Scruton, Roger. *The Politics of Culture*. Manchester: Carcanet, 1981.
Taylor, Houghton W. "Modern Fiction and the Doctrine of Uniformity." *Philological Quarterly* 29, 1940: 225–36.
———. "Particular Character." *PMLA* 60, 1945: 161–74.

Language, Literature, and Moral Values

BARBARA COWELL

Introduction

John Wilson in his chapter has stressed the importance of not speaking too generally or holistically about "values." This is a point of particular importance when one is dealing with language and literature. There is a perennial temptation to assimilate to other values the peculiar or *sui generis* values of literature in particular. This is perhaps partly because some of these other values, at particular historical periods, seem to be those of men of preeminent importance; in our own day, one might say, the values inherent in politics or ideology; and in some Western cultures, over several centuries, the values that for many people are summarized by the term *moral*, that term being construed narrowly and connected exclusively with action, the will, and public rules of interpersonal behaviour. But it is also because the peculiar value of literature and aesthetic forms in general is curiously elusive. As Peter Strawson has shown,[1] it appears mysterious to us chiefly because aesthetic forms seem to have no obvious, and certainly no obviously utilitarian, *point* or *purpose*, so that our evaluations seem to be up in the air, as it were, and lacking foundation. Hence there are constant pressures, both in theory and practice, to draw aesthetics into the realm of religion, or politics, or morality (in the narrow sense), or into some utilitarian function. As Bernard Richards says (p. 216), the implicit values of literature are more important than any explicit reference or use that literature may make of other values not peculiar to itself—a point to which I will return.

Language

We are likely to search in vain for specific, *sui generis* value for literature if we draw too sharp a distinction between "literature" and "language"—although these terms are commonly used to enforce such a distinction in schools and other educational institutions. There is a danger of thinking that there is one thing, literature, which has to do with aesthetics or beauty, and another thing, sharply divided from it, which has to do with the strictly formal or utilitarian aspects and uses of language. This is not to deny that there are many different kinds of study involved in learning a foreign language; but we should think rather of a continuum between, for example, Proust and Racine at one end, and cooking recipes or instructions on packets in French at the other. The difficulty of defining literature arises partly through failing to recognize the continuum. The fact is that to learn French (or any other language) is to enter another world which makes demands and has different things to teach, whatever particular context of language use we attend to. Without this recognition, there might be a temptation to say, for instance, that French literature has value because of the moral messages it contains, or because it is a kind of covert psychoanalysis or account of social conditions, a view that fits postromantic novels to some extent, but obviously fails to fit, for example, lyric poetry; and that the French language has only a strictly utilitarian value, being useful for transactions in the Common Market or between cross-cultural marriage partners.

Let me indicate cursorily and in outline form some arguments one might use for the values of the study of a foreign language or, indeed, of one's natural language.

1. We speak of giving the pupil "another world to live in": that is, of course, another conceptual world with its own terms and distinctions and style, which enlarges the pupil's experience and liberates him from the confines of a self largely determined by the conceptual framework of his own language.

   Here it is necessary to distinguish

   A. the general advantage of having *any* other such world to inhabit, and

B. the particular advantage of having the particular world of a particular language (French, classical Greek, or whatever); and it is necessary to specify the *sui generis* merits of each particular language with this in view. (For instance, it is commonly believed that the syntactic, lapidary, and other qualities of classical Latin form a peculiarly important— because sharply different—world from the more paratactic, loosely structured world of English syntax. Note here that one would naturally go on to contrast the classical rules of Latin verse, which strictly determine syllable quantity, with the looser verse stress of English verse, a difference that produces a quite different kind of literature. Here, as so often, it is impossible to keep "language" distinct from "literature.")

2. In general a distinction can be drawn between

   A. arguments for the value of this based on some idea of general enrichment, expansion of consciousness, increased "culture," and so on, with the implication that human beings are, so to speak, basically *all right* but can profit from such enrichment, and

   B. weightier (if sound) arguments based on the more Augustinian or Freudian idea that human beings are in need of not just enrichment but salvation, that they are in some kind of fallen state (due to original sin or the overwhelmingly difficult conditions of early childhood), and that the other world of language is needed to enable them to escape from this state of sin.

3. In trying to enumerate (albeit not exhaustively) the particular advantages of, as it were, putting on new linguistic spectacles, one must constantly fight the (still very common) idea that the world is somehow given, there, and (prelinguistically) understood, and that it remains essentially the same whatever spectacles are worn, whatever words and concepts we use as the furniture of our minds. Of course, there is a point in philosophic discussion at which it is necessary to use terms like *reality* that contrast with any conceptual network used to

throw over the world (although that metaphor is itself misleading); but, on any account, the way in which we perceive reality, if not the nature of reality itself, is in large part conceptually determined. With this in mind, we may distinguish

A. The sharpening of existing concepts by the learning of particular words; thus one may, in some misty way, *have* a concept that might in English be paraphrased as "the extent of a person's power or authority," but this would be considerably sharpened by learning the meaning of the Latin term *imperium*. (And here again, to learn this word properly would mean learning not only quite a lot of Roman history, but also Latin literature, and example of which is:

> Tu regere imperio populos, Romane, memento:
> Hae tibi erunt artes: pacique imponere morem,
> Parcere subiectis et debellare superbos.
> (*Aeneid* 6.851–53)

There is a constant interplay between what may be called "understanding the term *imperium*" and "appreciating Vergil's *Aeneid*.")

B. The gaining of new concepts by learning the words (not always easy to distinguish from [A]). To learn to apply the French phrase *beauté de singe*, for instance, is to learn to put together certain cases of feminine beauty and to identify them, that is, to acquire a new concept. Since concepts can always, in principle, be taught, no doubt it would be possible while sticking to English to teach someone to do this, starting, perhaps with the phrase "monkey-like beauty." But one such way, and perhaps the only proper one (since the French phrase is embedded in a whole background of literary and other uses of it), is to learn French.

C. The gaining of whole new styles of thought by learning to deploy the syntax and sentence structures of another language, distinguishing again

(1) the general syntax and style of French (German, and so on), and

(2) the particular styles of particular authors (Proust, Musil, and so on).

It is peculiarly difficult to describe the way in which this learning affects the mind, but perhaps the parallel with mathematics will help. In learning mathematics, one learns not just *another way of thinking the same thoughts* but another way of thinking: most obviously, a style of argument or of ordering one's thoughts in a certain way according to certain rules. Plato at least thought this of peculiar importance to the soul. The same is true, to a greater or lesser extent—certainly in a more subtle way—of learning a natural language.

D. By taking on and appreciating a language or style, one thereby takes on not just the structure but the feelings, beliefs, and other apparatus that go with the language. A small example occurred to me when hearing a French-dubbed film of Galsworthy's *Forsyte Saga*. When the English text had "Gad, Soames, old chap, jolly witty, what?" the French had *"Mon cher Soames, que tu es spirituel!"* The whole tone, and hence the whole scene, was entirely different. A weightier example, which reinforces the main point, comes from the authorized version of the English Bible. It is quite clear that the position with regard to this version, as against various modern versions (the New English Bible, for instance) is not, as is commonly believed, that the religious belief and tone remains the same, being simply reproduced in different and for modern men more intelligible terms: the *belief and tone change with the language*. The Jehovah who speaks to Job in the authorized version is just not the Jehovah who speaks in modern dress; it is a different god, just as the Aphrodite of Euripides is different from the Aphrodite of his sentimental translator, Gilbert Murray.

E. Learning a language has a direct bearing on three other forms of thought; indeed, it seems in itself to act as a kind of inquiry in these three other forms. (It is perhaps unsurprising that when a leading philosopher of education, Professor Paul Hirst, attempts to categorize various forms of thought he totally omits language learning, except insofar as he can classify it under "the aesthetic": the reason is that learning a foreign language, or any language, cannot be separately categorized in terms of the criteria he uses:[2])

(1) As the example from Vergil may already have shown, it is directly relevant to—a part of— historical inquiry. In learning history we learn to speak with the words of men in the past, because only thus can we appreciate their intentions and purposes.
(2) For any kind of personal knowledge—"psychology" might be a name for this—we need, as it were, to put ourselves in the linguistic shoes of the other person. A psychotherapist, for instance, needs to know what love means to his patient, and this involves knowing how the patient uses the word, as part of knowing how he interprets his experience.
(3) Any serious philosophy must at least begin with the clarification of concepts, which can only be done via the words various people and societies use to mark the concepts. (It is not accidental that many Oxford philosophers were brought up on the translation of English into Greek and Latin, and vice versa.)

There is a clear connection here with morality, on any reasonably wide interpretation of that term. Only this enrichment and liberation enables us to grasp the facts of our own and other people's lives honestly and fully. I believe that it is a failure to have a steady hold of these facts that afflicts the moral person rather than lack of anything we may want to call "will-power" or even "logical argument." One might be willing to grant the whole of Professor Richard Hare's case about the importance of universalizability,[3] claiming indeed that we already know well enough that other people matter, but claiming also that the actual *work* the moral agent has to do involves not just a conscious acceptance of this principle—Who, indeed, does not accept it?—but the *practice* of it by coming to *identify* with the minds and hearts of others in *particular situations*. *Hoc opus, hic labor est*; and language and literature are the chief tools in the task.

Richards has dealt with this point, but it is worth noting that such a view is entirely consistent with the regrettable fact that many highly literate people, well-educated in foreign languages and literature, have nevertheless been capable of the most wicked deeds. That must surely be unsurprising. There are people (Proust has such a character) who see life as a play on a stage, with themselves sitting in the audience—whatever horrors may be there enacted, they must be unreal. It is a task for education to ensure that the insights of language and literature connect with practical action. Such education—the linguistic and literary understanding—is a necessary, not a sufficient, condition for moral virtue.

Literature

Although too rigid a divorce between language and literature would be dangerous, literature may be considered in its own right; to see precisely how it works may be to prevent it from being assimilated to other products.

Richards in his chapter says—and he obviously has in mind the importance of elucidating the *sui generis* value of literature—that it gives us awareness more "than we could otherwise gain by *any* other means" (true, so far) "(except actually living through a similar experience ourselves—and most of us have neither the intensity nor the perception to do that)" (p. 213). Here there is a danger of regarding art or literature as a sort of intense, abbreviated version of life; as if, through lack of time (or "intensity" and "perception"), we could in principle get *the same thing* out of, for example, killing our fathers and sleeping with our mothers as out of reading the *Oedipus Tyrannus*. Of course Richards does not mean to imply any such thing; but the question arises of what the difference is.

This question is intimately connected with the undoubted fact that literature, or any art, must be intrinsically *pleasurable*. By "intrinsically," I do not mean that the work must somehow gild the pill, as if it contained some kind of message or set of perceptions in themselves not particularly pleasurable—indeed, often thoroughly unpleasant—that have to be presented in an attractive guise—rhyme, metre, or other trappings to distract our attention and allow the truth to sneak in unobserved—(which, indeed, is what Freud sometimes seems to say about art). That is, as sometimes happens with overtly didactic poetry, an extrinsic addition of pleasure. Good art is pleasurable in itself, even when—and strangely, particularly when—the subject-matter is unpleasant. *King Lear* is an example of this.

We seem driven to say that literature enables us to do things with our emotions that we cannot otherwise do, and that this process is, if properly performed, pleasurable in itself and, further, that it is only such proper (and therefore pleasurable) performance that enables us actually to *learn* anything, or, if not to learn, to make some internal improvement in our hearts and minds. By in some sense imitating (*mimesis*) the operation of these emotions they are somehow dealt with and set in better order. Vague as this may appear, one may distinguish

(a) the actual unlocking or *resuscitation* of the emotions (often unconscious or deeply buried);
(b) the giving of a certain *shape* or pattern to them (into a story, or some kind of coherent and acceptable entity);
(c) their *celebration* and perhaps legitimation;
(d) their *resolution*.

The emotions are, as it were, freed, shaped, legitimated, glorified, and made acceptable. Tragedy is perhaps a model case of this.

In this process it seems plain that literature does more than remind us of truths, though it certainly does that. We often say, "Yes, that's exactly what self-deception is like," when we are reading perhaps *Persuasion* or *Anna Karenina*. But it also creates new truths for us to see, new possibilities of feeling and seeing and valuing. Our concept of self-deception is (partly) formed or enlarged by these works, because they allow us to admit to consciousness elements we had overlooked or repressed, and to look at them in a given shape.

Understanding this might also be to understand those crucial lines from Shakespeare's *Midsummer Night's Dream*:

> The poet's eye, in a fine frenzy rolling,
> Doth glance from heaven to earth, from earth to
> heaven,
> And as imagination bodies forth
> The forms of things unknown, the poet's pen
> Turns them to shapes, and gives to airy nothings
> A local habitation and a name.
> (V, i, 12 17).

Literature, Fantasy, and Education

Finally I should like to say a little about some possible effects of literature on adolescents and their fantasies. Literature can have good and bad effects on adolescents of quite different kinds, effects having little or nothing to do with whether they learn or remain ignorant. Various books, plays, television programmes, and so forth affect people in different ways: they inspire, ennoble, elevate, corrupt, degrade, and so on. Insofar as educators exercise control or influence over their students, exposure to literature or other media, or make their own views felt—and it is virtually inevitable that this happens—they need to have some grasp of what effect they do have. It is much discussed in the popular press and elsewhere, although the following important points are often ignored:

1. Little or nothing is actually *known* about these effects, although many people have strong views about them.
2. People's views and feelings are likely to be the result of their own prejudices and fantasies rather than of such external influences.
3. Whatever the teacher may think about this, it should not be allowed to stand in the way of his main task—that of using literature to educate students' emotions. For this is the only task that uses literature for what it is, a form of art with its own special educational value.

In discussing the effects of various books and other representations it is possible to distinguish many different kinds of "effect." Let me list briefly *some* of the things that may happen when X reads a certain book or watches a television programme:

1. X copies in real life the overt behaviour of the people in the book.
2. X copies their intentions and purposes, with or without the behaviour.
3. X tries to imitate them in other ways—for instance, to put himself in positions similar to theirs, to acquire their standard of living, and so forth.
4. X may be repelled by the representation and try to *avoid* any kinds of imitation—"I'm not going to behave/talk/think/live like *that*."
5. X may not be motivated to do anything in his real life at all but simply regard the representation as interesting, exciting, boring, informative, and so on. (Seeing the representation as *literature* or *art* is one subcategory of this.)

This list has covered only some of the possibilities regarding X's overt *behaviour*; but of course this is not the only, nor necessarily the chief, "effect" of such things. We have also to consider, for instance:

6. X is upset, shocked, disgusted, terrified.
7. X, as it were, "embraces" the representation because it gives him pleasure; in particular he finds in it a fantasy-world he enjoys.

We are all very familiar with the last instance. Many adults like Westerns, romances, detective stories, travel books, and so on, not as works of art but because of the escape worlds they portray, the heroes and excitement they contain. Adolescents like the world of James Bond, or the comic strips, or the love stories in magazines. The cheap coloured magazines, which often portray sex, violence, or sentimental romance, offer objectified versions of our own fantasies. Many people will realize this consciously; others will appreciate that though they may not allow themselves certain "forbidden" fantasies (perhaps particularly connected with sex and aggression) nevertheless they gain pleasure from more sophisticated or refined versions of these in literature or the arts.

Teachers' concern to develop a proper appreciation of literature may be seen as weaning students from the more primitive, unsophisticated, and "raw" fantasies and encouraging them to take pleasure in works that although ultimately based on similar emotions have *organized* these emotions into a form that is at once more in touch with the real world and gives more lasting aesthetic satisfaction. This weaning is from, for example, the pornographic magazines, the strip cartoons, the elementary representations of violence, justice, sentiment, or romance towards works of *art*—towards genuine literature.

That is the educational task; and it is worth noticing that there is a sense in which it cannot be hurried. It is possible to make every effort to put good literature before students, and to hope that they will be able to find pleasure in it; but they cannot be forced to do so. Teachers should try to encourage them to grow out of their naïve fantasies as quickly as possible; but the process is a long and difficult business which depends a great deal on close communication and understanding. Many fantasies are, in any case, both necessary and inevitable for a particular stage of psychological growth; and if teachers disturb them, try to forbid them, or pour scorn on them, they may simply lose their students' confidence and communication.

For fantasies, whether found in books or in real-life behaviour, fulfill an important psychological purpose for the adolescent's mind; they may form an important defence against his fears, boredom, or other feelings, and incentive to "keep going," and many other functions. They are not the teacher's enemy, but his subject-matter. During adolescence the student *needs* fantasies. Naturally it is an aim of education to make the student realize that he must, often, drop them for the real world, that he should not be allowed to day-dream all the time, or imagine that the real world is like his fantasies. Indeed, perhaps, the most important educational task here is precisely this: to respect the fantasies, but to show the pupil that they *are* fantasies.

Meanwhile, however, there remains the problem of adopting some attitude to fantasies and to the books and programmes that represent and engender them. It may sometimes seem to us as if these fantasies and the vehicles for them are addictive: as if the adolescent is bewitched by them, and subsequently corrupted or degraded by constantly reading, for example, only James Bond, or the comic strips, or sentimental love stories. But these fantasies are *in the student*, for good or ill; we shall not get them out of him by removing the literature. Indeed, if we wish to *educate* the student in any serious way, we have to start where *he* is, not where we are (or like to think we are); and this means that we have to start with his fantasies and feelings as they actually exist. They are, as I have said, our subject-matter.

No undisputed evidence exists on the first five effects of fantasies in the list I gave—that is, on behavioural effects. Indeed, it seems likely that "fantasy fodder" acts as a behavioural safety-valve rather than an incentive, along Aristotelian rather than Platonic lines. The teacher's chief concerns should be with the sixth and seventh effects—especially the sixth, which is something to be seriously considered by the teacher. In part, this will be taken care of if the pupil is allowed freedom of choice—and with this, of course, should go a neutral and detached attitude on the part of the teacher, neither praising nor blaming a student for what he reads or watches but simply perhaps expressing pleasure that he has found something to enjoy.

It is a problem without a determinate solution, because everything depends on the particular case. The popularity of some fairy stories and other works demonstrates that no simple generalizations are possible: we cannot say that all, or even most, children will be upset by, for example, death, or violence, or sexual behaviour, or horror comics. The teacher can only gauge the student's actual reactions, without recourse to any preconceived theory.

Much more important than the *material* itself is the teacher's attitude and expectations. The parallel with sex education is close. If the teacher is calm, detached, not anxious or threatened himself, and expects the same from his students, the possibility of shock or upset is very small. But if the atmosphere is "fraught" (perhaps with the teacher's own anxiety), then the situation is more difficult. The notion that certain things are not to be mentioned, once it gains a hold, is itself the surest way of increasing the temperature and the chances of shock or upset. The *way in which* they are mentioned is, however, important and like the non-directive therapist (a model from which teachers can learn much), the teacher should not force or put pressure on the pupils to open their inmost hearts to public view. Some fantasies are (although none need be) taken by the person who has them as essentially private; the person feels that a part of him would be destroyed if they were made public or communicated.

It is in this general light that the common talk about inspiration, corruption, and so on should be viewed—talk that need not be taken too seriously. The fantasies and the (temporary) psychological needs are there and emerge in the adolescent's choice of literature and other forms of entertainment. At a stage when uncertain adolescents need sometimes to see themselves as brave, potent, or sophisticated, they will inevitably turn to some appropriate hero-figure—Raffles, Bulldog Drummond, the Saint, Philip Marlowe, James Bond. It is important that the vehicles for this need be available, and, if possible well written. In themselves, however, they neither inspire nor corrupt, although they may seem to do so, to anybody who takes such figures as real. But they are not real: they are just the crystallizations of the fantasy need. If it were not for them, we should make up our own heroes, or cast some version of ourselves as heroes in our day-dreams.

Corruption or inspiration, in some sense, may be said to occur in a quite different dimension, the dimension of truth or falsity. We all need some—perhaps, in our early years, much—scope for fantasy; there is no harm and much good in this. The mistake is to take it for reality: *either*, if a person is very simple-minded, for the real world of real people, *or* for the reality of good literature and other works of art. To encourage this mistake is to corrupt; to discourage it, and to lead students to a fuller and more honest understanding, is to inspire. Teachers who use the weight of their authority to make what is false seem true, or what is phoney seem honest, corrupt. Teachers who can help students to see the excitement and interest—indeed the glory—in a true appreciation of great works of literature, and who can pass on to them the desire to purge their minds and attend unselfishly to such works, inspire.

With many students this may take much time and effort. Considerable psychological maturity and powers of detachment are required before a person is able to view something as *literature*, or a work of *art*, at all. Many adolescents may continue to depend on a constant diet of cheap fantasy literature—not because they are corrupted or addicted, but because nobody has helped them towards more solid food. Such general factors as linguistic development, the ability to concentrate and defer gratification, the existence of secure relationships with adults in the real world, self-esteem and self-confidence, and a general feeling of being valued and loved—all these are highly relevant to a person's ability to gain pleasure from sophisticated works of art. It is obvious that this is not so much a matter of academic intelligence or relevance to the modern world; it is a matter of psychological maturity. There are many intelligent and academically successful people whose attitude to literature is still fantasy-based, and the number of people who derive pleasure, much less instruction, from really good literature is very small. The future of both literary and moral education depends very much on how successfully teachers can manipulate these factors for the benefit of a new generation.

Notes

1. Peter Strawson, *Freedom and Resentment* (London: Methuen, 1974).
2. Paul Hirst (with Richard Peters), *The Logic of Education* (London: Routledge & Kegan Paul, 1970).
3. Richard Hare, *Moral Thinking* (Oxford: Oxford University Press, 1981).

Bibliography

Hare, Richard, M. *Moral Thinking*. Oxford: Oxford University Press, 1981.
Hirst, Paul, H., with Richard S. Peters. *The Logic of Education*. London: Routledge & Kegan Paul, 1970.
Murdoch, Iris. *The Sovereignty of Good*. London: Methuen, 1970.
Strawson, Peter, F. *Freedom and Resentment*. London: Methuen, 1974.
Wilson, John, Norman Williams, and Barry Sugarman. *Introduction to Moral Education*. London: Penguin, 1968.
———. *Preface to the Philosophy of Education*. London: Routledge & Kegan Paul, 1979.

Value in Drama
(A Prologue, Three Acts, and an Epilogue)

CHARLES LEPPER

Prologue

In Western Europe, during the last hundred years, creative artists in many of the existing art forms have tried to break free from the realism that had been in vogue since the Renaissance. For example, artists such as Vincent van Gogh and Pablo Picasso, and Henry Moore produced a great deal of non-realistic work. During the same period many composers rebelled against tunefulness (as, for example, in the ballet music of Tchaikovsky) and experimented in more abstract forms. In the field of drama, also, there have been experiments in non-realistic writing; European playwrights such as Eugène Ionesco and Samuel Beckett have written, and inspired others to write, many plays that have won critical acclaim from those members of the audience whom Hamlet described as "the judicious," though it is evident that in this art form, as in the forms of painting and sculpture, the general public prefers realism—though often tempered by tuneful musical scores. Thus *The Sound of Music* has attracted audiences vastly larger than Pinter's famous *The Caretaker* could ever hope for. In drama completely abstract entertainment is particularly difficult to achieve, as the dramatist depends on human beings to present his work, and they can only with great difficulty disguise the fact that they are really man and women. It is perhaps noticeable that many chapters of literary criticism have been written to try to give students realistic explanations of the kind of play that leads audiences to cry out, "What was that all about?" as they leave the theatre.

Drama is thus in line with many of the other disciplines that have been discussed in this volume in that it is essentially a pragmatic rather than an abstract matter. It needs to be considered with reference to real people in real situations rather than in terms of abstract definitions.

People who work in the theatre know that their particular art form is aimed at the audiences who come to see it; a play cannot be considered successful if its audiences fail to enjoy it. However, in this essay I am not considering drama from the point of view of the audience (such an essay would be titled "Value of Drama"), but from the point of view of the dramatist. I concentrate on the material rather than the style, working on the basis that most writers whose work is regarded as of more than passing value have used prose or verse that has sprung naturally from their material. A style that draws attention to itself can do so only at the expense of the ideas which should, in drama, be the point of contact between author and audience.

Act One

For myn entente is nat but for to pleye.

Chaucer's Wife of Bath claimed that her only aim was to entertain, and indeed the provision of entertainment must be the value at the foundation of all theatrical presentations. Of course, this does not mean that every play must give undiluted delight to every person who could conceivably go to a performance of it. All creative artists must be allowed the freedom to be selective in their choice of patrons, and among the rest the dramatist must have the right to decide the type of audience for whom he wishes to write. Success will depend, obviously, on the extent to which the chosen audience has been entertained. If the dramatist wishes to give pleasure only to himself he would select some other literary genre.

Some forms of drama aim at offering improvement to their spectators. But the most popular forms, I believe, are those that simply set out to give undemanding pleasure, in the sense that the spectator need merely sit back and allow the playwright, through the actors and other presenters, to please him. When Hamlet asked the First Player to give him a speech, he recalled that the play "pleased not the million, 'twas caviare to the general," and in a later scene complained of "the groundlings, who for the most part are capable of nothing but inexplicable dumb-shows and noise." The word *inexplicable* suggests that the "groundlings" do not want to be asked to think when they are watching a play. For them the ultimate value of a performance is simply that of entertainment. The prospective London theatre-goer, studying the list of plays being performed on any particular evening, will find a number of undemanding plays of this sort, plays that provide the modern equivalent of "groundlings" with the simple fare they want. Many of these cater primarily for the theatre-goer whose watchword is "I do like to have a good laugh." Often these plays run for several months and are then forgotten; sometimes the supreme theatrical critic, Time, does allow them a permanent place in the repertoire, but this is a rare honour for this sort of play. The laughter is provoked sometimes by visual, sometimes by oral means. Here is an example of simple visual humour taken from a farce, *Charley's Aunt*, that has been revived regularly in various adaptations as well as in its original form since Brandon Thomas wrote it in 1892. At the end of act 1, Lord Fancourt Babberley, disguised as an old lady, and Sir Francis Chesney and Mr. Spettigue, elderly gentlemen who are smitten by "her," are preparing to sit down at the luncheon-table:

> *Sir Francis (Offers left arm to Lord Fancourt)*: Allow me, Donna Lucia.
> *Spettigue*: No allow me. (*Offers right arm*)
> (*Lord Fancourt hesitates—flutters eyelashes at them both, then chooses Spettigue's arm. They go towards chair right end of table. Sir Francis leaves them and goes up to chair right end of table, which he holds ready for Lord Fancourt. Spettigue offers to take chair from Sir Francis, between the two chair is drawn back and Lord Fancourt sits on the floor. The others rise with screams and exclamations)*[1]

Audiences still laugh at the visual comedy of nonsensical sequences like that, as they do at verbal nonsense such as can be found in Oscar Wilde's *The Importance of Being Earnest* (1895). Here, Lady Bracknell thanks her nephew, Algernon, for selecting the music to be played at her reception:

> I'm sure the programme will be delightful, after a few expungations. French songs I cannot possibly allow. People always seem to think that they are improper, and either look shocked, which is vulgar, or laugh, which is worse. But German sounds a thoroughly respectable language, and I believe is so.[2]

It would be wrong to suggest that such plays are easy to write or to perform, or that only "groundlings:" can enjoy them. The so-called *Aldwych Farces* which Ben Travers wrote between the wars drew audiences of all intellectual ranges. It is true, however, that such entertainments make few intellectual demands on the spectators.

Other forms of drama the value of which is simply the pleasure of the hour include musicals (here the effort of listening to words is moderated by the comparative ease of toe-tapping to tunes) and thrillers such as *The Mousetrap*. Periodically, the theatre (although more regularly today the large and small screens) produces chillers, designed to induce actual terror in the audience. In these plays the audience is asked to concentrate on sensational incident rather than on credible character. These plays are often known as melodramas. Some Jacobean tragedies, partly or wholly, qualify for this definition: Webster's Duchess of Malfi (ca. 1632) kisses what she takes to be her brother's hand and finds it is detached from its body. And Giovanni plays the last scence of Ford's *'Tis Pity She's a Whore* (1633) with his sister/mistress's heart "upon his dagger."

Melodrama was particularly popular in the Victorian era; an example is this sequence near the end of C. H. Hazelwood's *Lady Audley's Secret*[3] (ca. 1862):

> *Alicia*: Robert! Robert! My father is dead. Oh, pity me! Pity and protect me!
> *Robert*: Sir Michael dead! Now vengeance, take thy own! Friends, hear me:—I accuse that woman of the murder of my friend, George Talboys.
> *Lady Audley*: How and where?
> *Luke* (*Revives*): I—I will tell that. She pushed him down that well, (*Points to well, all start*) but it will be useless to search there now, for George Talboys is—
> (*Enter George Talboys*)
> *George*: Here!
> *Omnes*: Alive!
> *Lady Audley* (*Petrified*): Alive. Alive. You alive.

Soon she goes mad and dies.[4]

Act Two

To sport with human follies.

There are many plays that sport with human follies the value of which is simply to appeal to the surface emotions of the audience. But there are other plays that arouse laughter, but when examined more deeply, show that the playwright has used comic device to comment seriously on society. Ben Jonson (1573–1630) defined the purpose and value of this sort of comedy:

> ... deeds and language such as men do use,
> And persons such as comedy would choose,
> When she would show and image of the times,
> And sport with human follies, ...

Authors who write in this way are called satirists. The satirist asserts that certain types of behaviour are stupid and are practised only by people who are not using their brains and not obeying laws of common sense. The satirist presents characters who behave in such a way that the audiences will laugh at them and, the author hopes, think seriously about behaviour and avoid committing or condoning similar follies themselves. The ultimate value of satirical comedy is not in the laughter it arouses; it lies in the encouragement of reform offered by the material. The spectator is invited to examine his own behaviour, recognize his own follies, and alter his way of life accordingly. Of course, the satirist does not suggest that the perfect man is one who is a robot-slave of contemporary conventions, but that he should be guided by his intellect, and that the perfect society is one in which its members are ruled by good sense. The audience at a satirical comedy cannot just sit back and allow the author to do all the work. Each member of the audience must be prepared to think seriously and sensibly about the material.

Perhaps the earliest, and one of the greatest, of the world's satirists was Aristophanes (ca. 445–388 B.C.). His basic field of action in *Lysistrata*, for instance, is the male tendency to engage in wars and the female tendency to be annoyed at this. By making the audience laugh at this situation, Aristophanes aims to persuade it to look at war intelligently and to stop waging it. Lysistrata has summoned a conference of women from the other Greek city-states; she explains that their only chance of persuading their husbands to stop fighting is by blackmail—when the men come home on leave they must be denied sexual intercourse.

> *Lysistrata*: Look here. We sit indoors, all tarted
> up,
> In our most transparent things and obviously sexy,
> We get the men worked up, bee-lined for bed,
> And then when it comes to the point—walk out on
> them.
> They'll make a treaty at once—you know they will.
> *Kalonike*: But supposing they simply leave us?
> *Lysistrata*: We must make
> The best of the next best, as the proverb says.
> *Kalonike*: Proverbs aren't lovers. But suppose they
> grab us
> And drag us to bed by force.
> *Lysistrata*: Hang on to the door.
> *Kalonike*: Suppose they knock us about?
> *Lysistrata*: Give in and sulk.
> There's not much fun in raping your wife.[5]

Later satirists, too, have seen themselves as reformers and the ultimate value of their plays as didactic. In *Tartuffe* (1667) Molière examines one of man's eternal characteristics, gullibility, and the ease with which "confidence tricksters" can obtain dominance over credulous fellow humans. Tartuffe has wormed his way into the heart and home of M. Orgon. Accused, with justification, of attempting to seduce Orgon's wife, Elmira, Tartuffe immediately assumes the role of a miserable sinner who deserves to have lies made up about him—and Orgon at once returns to full trust in him:

> *Orgon*: Heavens! What have I heard? Is this credible?
> *Tartuffe*: Yes, brother, I am a wicked, guilty, wretched sinner, full of iniquity, the greatest sinner that ever breathed. Every instant of my life is crowded with stains; 'tis one continued series of crimes and defilements; and I see that Heaven, for my punishment, designs to mortify me on this occasion. Whatever great offence they can lay to my charge, I shall have more humility than to deny it. Believe what they tell you, arm your resentment, and like a criminal, drive me out of your house. I

cannot have so great a share of shame but I have still deserved a much larger.
Orgon (To his son): Ah, traitor! Darest thou, by this falsehood, attempt to tarnish the purity of his virtue?[6]

It is not until Tartuffe has made a further attempt to seduce Elmira while the gullible Orgon is actually listening (hidden under the table) that Orgon sees the truth about the hypocrite—and by then Tartuffe has cheated him out of all his property, even his house!

Before Molière, Ben Jonson had set himself up as a reformer, anticipating many of Molière's uses of comedy. In *The Alchemist* (1610), for example, three confidence tricksters, Subtle, Face, and Doll Common, dupe a number of credulous and greedy people, among whom are two Puritans, Tribulation, Wholesome, and Ananias. Posing as an alchemist who can turn all base metals into gold, Subtle has already persuaded them to hand over three cart-loads of goods belonging to "orphans" under their care. Ben Jonson introduces anti-puritan satire as Subtle points out that once they have "The Philosophers' Stone," they will be able to give up some of their present ways of making money. Subtle confirms that they will not need:

> . . . your holy vizard, to win widows
> To give you legacies, or make zealous wives
> To rob their husbands for the common cause;
> Nor take the start of bonds broke but one day,
> And say they were forfeited by providence.
> Nor shall you need o'ernight to eat huge meals,
> To celebrate your next day's fast the better;
> The whilst the Brethren and the Sisters, humbled,
> Abate the stiffness of the flesh.[7]

Jonson's bitingly funny scenes in which fools and knaves are tricked fill most of his plays, including *Volpone* (1605), which is a scathing attack on unscrupulous greed. There is satire amidst the bawdy of the writers of the Restoration period, and in the warmer comedies of Sheridan. Mockery of people who, to sound impressive, use learned words but use them incorrectly is often found in Shakespeare's plays, but the queen is Sheridan's Mrs. Malaprop in *The Rivals* (1777). Here she shows off her learning to Sir Anthony Absolute:

But, Sir Anthony, I would send her, at nine years old, to a boarding-school, in order to learn a little ingenuity and artifice. Then, sir, she should have a supercilious knowledge in accounts;—and as she grew up, I would have her instructed in geometry, that she might know something of the contagious countries;—but above all, Sir Anthony, she should be mistress of orthodoxy, that she might not misspell, and mispronounce words so shamefully as girls usually do; and likewise that she might reprehend the true meaning of what she is saying. This, Sir Anthony, is what I would have a woman know;—and I don't think there is a superstitious article in it.[8]

Drama in our own century, in Britain, has been enriched by many satirists, from George Bernard Shaw to playwrights such as Tom Stoppard today. Shaw's *Major Barbara* (1905), for example, is centred on the relationship between a girl who has dedicated her life to the good of others to the extent of joining the Salvation Army, and her father, Andrew Undershaft, who is an armaments millionaire. Mrs. Baines, a Salvation Army Commissioner, has told Undershaft that the work of the Army is being hindered by lack of funds; Lord Saxmundham has offered £5,000, and Undershaft now agrees to donate a similar sum:

> *Mrs. Baines (With a touch of caution)*: You will let me have the cheque to show at the meeting, won't you? Jenny: go in and fetch a pen and ink.
> *Undershaft*: Do not disturb Miss Hill: I have a fountain pen.
> *Bill Walker (A bullying down-and-out whose soul Barbara has been trying to save)*: Wot prawce selvytion nah?
> *Barbara*: Stop. Mrs. Baines: are you really going to take this money?
> *Mrs. Baines (astonished)*: Why not, dear?
> *Barbara*: Why not! Do you know what my father is? Have you forgotten that Lord Saxmundham is Bodger the whisky man? Do you remember how we implored the County Council to stop him from writing Bodger's Whisky in letters of fire against the sky; so that the poor drink-ruined creatures on the Embankment could not wake up from their snatches of sleep without being reminded of their deadly thirst by that wicked sky sign? Do you know that the worst thing I have had to fight here is not the devil, but Bodger, Bodger, Bodger with his whisky, his distilleries and his tied houses? Are you going to make our shelter another tied house for him, and ask me to keep it?
> *Mrs. Baines*: Dear Barbara: Lord Saxmundham has a soul to be saved

like any of us. If heaven has found the way to make a good use of his money, are we to set ourselves up against the answer to our prayers?[9]

Currently satire is found principally in such publications as *Private Eye* and in sketches on radio and television, but Tom Stoppard's *Jumpers* (1972) showed that stage satire is by no means dead. In the character of George, Stoppard satirizes one of his favourite targets—philosophers:

> Mathematicians are quick to point out that they are familiar with many series which have no first term—such as the series of proper fractions between nought and one. What, they ask is the first, that is the smallest, of these fractions? A billionth? A trillionth? Obviously not: Cantor's proof that there is no greatest number ensures that there is no smallest fraction. There is no beginning. (*With a certain relish he notches his arrow into the bowstring*) But it was precisely this notion of infinite series which in the sixth century B.C. led the Greek philosopher Zeno to conclude that since an arrow shot towards a target first had to cover half the distance, and then half the remainder, and then half the remainder after that, and so on *ad infinitum*, the result was, as I will now demonstrate, that though an arrow is always approaching its target, it never quite gets there, and Saint Sebastian died of fright.[10]

So the satirist sees himself as a reformer, and the ultimate value of his drama as educative. He has observed what he himself has considered to be stupidity, and he has drawn the audience's attention to this by making them laugh at characters he has created as exemplars of that stupidity. He has invited the audience to laugh, but he intends that they shall respond intellectually as well, his final object being that they should help him to put right what he has found faulty in society. He has asked them not just to laugh, but to think.

Act Three

What a piece of work is a man! (*Hamlet*)

Just as many literary experts see satire as superior in value to the less intellectual forms of drama, so they seem to consider satire, in its turn, as inferior to that kind of drama loosely described as tragedy.

This may reflect an idea that the highest form of drama must appeal not only to man's superficial instincts, not even to his intellect, but to the very depths of his feelings. These experts regard *King Lear* as somehow of greater value than *Twelfth Night*. Most of us spend most of our waking lives in fairly superficial relationships with other people and, less often, in assessing and analysing situations and people with whom we are in contact. So the two types of drama we have looked at so far have asked for responses we have not found difficult to supply. The writer of tragedy asks more of us. He ask us to look far more deeply than is our custom into the very depths of human personality—including our own. Hamlet's mother puts this clearly. She has drifted thoughtlessly on the surface of life; her son has confronted her and accused her of being wicked.

> Thou turn'st my eyes into my very soul,
> And there I see such black and grained spots
> As will not leave their tinct.[11]

The "tragic" writer wants his audiences to turn their eyes into their very souls, so the ultimate value of this sort of drama includes communication between author and spectator at a very deep level. In plays of this sort we find ourselves observing characters who are placed in situations that reveal their innermost essence. This not only intrigues us, it also involves us. Personally we may have experienced only a narrow range of emotions, but, as Aristotle observed, we will be fuller individuals if we add vicarious experiences to personal ones. We shall certainly understand other people better, and probably ourselves too, and perhaps live richer and fuller lives as a result. At this point I should like to express my own dissatisfaction with the term *tragedy*; it seems to me that the word (the dictionary definition of which includes "an unhappy ending") can be applied correctly only if the death of the body is regarded as the end of a person, if there is no further existence once the body is dead. In atheistic societies this may be acceptable, but most religions have postulated some form of continued existence of a person beyond the grave. Thus the death of a person's body cannot be regarded as truly tragic if he is believed to have what we may call a soul, which may enjoy some form of happy continuation after death. I shall hereafter use the term *serious drama* where the word *tragedy* is often used.

We have established that the serious dramatist presents to us studies of the very depths of human personality; he will often tend also to take us out of our relationships with other human beings into what might be considered as "the essence of things." What am I? How did I get here? What am I supposed to do here? How free am I to manage my own life?—these questions are found in the groundwork of serious drama and are clearly connected with man's age-old interest in the matter of free will versus predestination. Since man became capable of philosophical thinking, he has tried in various ways to solve this problem. After all, each of us works on the basis that he is free to run his own life; at the same time each of us knows that he had nothing at all to do with his own birth, and that he cannot possibly prevent his body's death. In many civilizations, an explanation for the conundrum has been supplied in the shape of the supernatural: the gods or God. Serious dramatists throughout the ages have reflected man's ideas about external powers of this sort; in the medieval period astrology was regarded by some as the means by which the gods (more specifically the Christian God) directly affected men's lives. In Shakespeare's play, Romeo and Juliet are described by Chorus as "star-crossed lovers"—implying that they are governed by powers beyond their control.

Central to many of the serious plays which Time has declared to be of lasting importance are these two matters—the examination of the individual in the very depths of his essential nature, and the relationship between the individual and the overall scheme of things. I should like to look in some detail at three serious plays, from widely differing eras, with these two ideas in mind: Euripides' *Bacchae* (ca. 406 B.C.), Shakespeare's *Othello* (1611), and Edward Albee's *Who's Afraid of Virginia Woolf?* (1962). It is noticeable that in each of them there is a strong suggestion of the possibility of an individual's being capable of being "possessed" (that is to say, no longer being in charge of his own behaviour) and of "exorcism" (the returning of the individual to his own control); thus each dramatist finds interest not only in individual character but also in the possibility of some sort of supernatural influence.

Euripides' *Bacchae* is centred on a conflict between a young man (King Pentheus of Thebes) and a God (Dionysus). The young man believes that he is completely self-sufficient, that he is in command of his own fate, and that he knows all that he needs to know about the conduct of his own life and that of his people. He sneers at those who hold views other than his own; particularly, he refuses to join the worshippers of the new cult of the self-proclaimed god Dionysus. When he confronts his grandfather, Cadmus, and the blind prophet, Tiresias, both dressed in the clothing of the cult, he reviles them:

> I see the diviner
> Tiresias in dappled fawnskins,
> And my mother's father making himself ridiculous,
> Playing the bacchant with a thyrsus-rod. I am
>   ashamed, old man,
> To see the foolish senility of the pair of you.[12]

When he meets the disguised god, he not only refuses to accept the validity of his cult but sneers at Dionysus personally:

> Well, stranger, you are not unshapely in your body,
> so far as women are concerned—and it is for this
>   that you are here in Thebes.
> Your locks are long, through keeping clear of
>   wrestling
> and flow right down by your cheeks, full of desire;
> and you keep your complexion fair by careful
>   contrivance—
> not in the sun's rays, but under the shade
> hunting the pleasures of Aphrodite with your
>   beauty.[13]

The god is determined that Pentheus shall join his cult and worship him, and that he shall do this voluntarily, thereby implicitly agreeing that man is not an independent creature, with completely free will, but subject to some force superior to himself and outside his own control.

There is a key moment at which Dionysus finds that Pentheus is inexorably stubborn, utterly unwilling to accept any limitation to his own free will. (l. 810) At this point the god uses powers we should describe as supernatural. He has already "possessed" the women of Thebes, including Pentheus' mother, Agave, because they too have refused to worship him; he then, in full view of the audience, "possesses" Pentheus. The young king, in female clothes, goes out to the mountain to spy on his mother and the other Maenads, and they tear him to pieces; his mother returns to the palace carrying her son's head, imagining it is that of a lion. And then an "exorcism" takes place: Agave's father, Cadmus, rids her of her "possession" by Dionysus, and she faces the hideous truth about what she has done. But this is not the end of the story. Dionysus reappears in all the glory of his godhead and gives commands to Agave and Cadmus that they have no power to disobey. Alone on the stage at the end of the performance is the dismembered corpse of the young man who insisted on his own self-sufficiency.

In one important respect Dionysus is unlike the God of the New Testament: he is not associated with any moral code. For Dionysus and for Euripides' audience the matter was simple: man is not self-created, he must not regard himself as omnipotent, he must be prepared to admit these limitations—and all this is symbolized in his agreeing to worship a being of a superior nature. It is a feature of this play, as indeed of many Greek plays, that the god actually appears in person to deliver his message that man is wrong to rely on himself, and in the last analysis the gods dictate and man must obey them.

Two thousand years later, in Shakespeare's *Othello*, the nature of the supernatural has changed. Whereas in Greek drama various gods oppose one another for reasons other than those of abstract morality, in Christian drama God is invariably associated with the rules of conduct propounded in the New Testament. This "good" God is opposed (from the Garden of Eden, and even earlier) by an evil supernatural capable of magical powers including what we call "demoniacal possession." Exorcism can take place—the evil power can be cast out and the possessed person freed. Scriptural backing for this pattern is readily found in the Gospels: Jesus could hardly cast out devils if they had not had the power to get in!

Shakespeare was very heavily influenced by the only English dramas written before his lifetime, the Mystery, Miracle and Morality plays which must have been performed at Stratford when he was a boy, and which were still regularly played during the Whitsun celebrations throughout his life. This Christian tradition lies behind all Shakespeare's plays, and in *Othello*, for example, we can see Pentheus' case taken a stage further and reproduced in Christian terms. Here the central character is a man who, as a soldier, has complete faith in his own abilities (the Senate considers him "all in all sufficient"). His elopement with Desdemona arouses the understandable fury of her father, who tries to separate them; but Othello is so capable of justifying his own conduct that the Duke of Venice, who is judging the matter, can only say, "I think this tale would win my daughter too."

As Euripides with Pentheus, so Shakespeare with Othello is not satisfied with a human being who seems to act independently of any power outside himself. Hence his creation of Iago. Many references in the text make it clear that Shakespeare intended his audiences to see Iago as an incubus—a fiend disguised in human form (phrases such as "hell and night," "divinity of hell," "this hellish villain" abound). In the course of the play we see the possession of Othello by Iago, until Othello (like Pentheus) is no longer in command of his own thoughts, words, or deeds. After he has murdered his innocent wife, Othello is exorcized (as Agave has been) and realizes the dreadful nature of what he has done—and now follows a notable difference between the pagan Greek ethos and that of the Renaissance Christian: Othello performs an act of penance: "I kiss'd thee ere I kill'd thee, no way but this,/Killing myself, to die upon a kiss."[14]

If we accept Iago's diabolic function, and that the play shows a struggle for the soul of Othello, it follows that Desdemona represents God; and many descriptions of her in the play confirm her sanctity (for example, "the divine Desdemona," "the more angel she," "she was heavenly true"). We may wonder why Shakespeare apparently allows God to be beaten by Satan. The answer lies in the Christian tradition: Othello has been tested as Job had been in the Old Testament, and Griselda in Petrarch's and Chaucer's versions of a medieval story. In these cases, what was being tested was the ability of the individual to withstand and reject evil. Othello fails to pass the test, but a significant difference between his fate and that of Pentheus is that Othello's punishment is seen as a penance; and the audience cannot share his pessimistic view as he stands over his wife's corpse:

> Now: how dost thou look now? O ill-starr'd wench!
> Pale as thy smock! when we shall meet at compt,
> This look of thine will hurl my soul from heaven,
> And fiends will snatch at it.[15]

Physically Othello has been defeated, but spiritually he has triumphed; he has learned his lesson—that the individual cannot be the ultimate authority where his own actions are concerned.

These two plays, pagan and Christian, share as their ultimate value the idea that a human being must be humble enough to accept that there is an authority outside and superior to himself. What about our own time, which seems to lie somewhere between the pagan and the Christian worlds? Edward Albee's original title for *Who's Afraid of Virginia Woolf?* was "The Exorcism," and this remains the title he gives the last Act of his play. This is a clue to a way in which this play resembles the two we have been studying—the "possession" of some person or persons by a supernatural force, and the need for "exorcism." And in the last act, George actually recites the Latin words and succeeds in ridding Martha (and incidentally Nick and Honey and himself) of the demoniacal possession that has brought them all to the verge of ruin (he has tried to strangle his wife on the stage and has been prevented only by Nick's physical intervention). The play presents to us four people each of whom has tried to avoid facing up to the reality of the fact that his or her life has been a failure by creating some form of defence mechanism—such as the houses the three little pigs constructed to keep out the big bad wolf. George has escaped into cynicism, Martha into brash bullying, Honey into vomiting, and Nick into withdrawal from human involvement. Each thinks that he has found the way to save himself from "the big bad wolf," which is, in this play, the truth about his or her situation. Like Euripides and Shakespeare, Albee makes it his purpose to take away from his characters the idea that the individual is self-sufficient. At the end of the play George has revealed the truth about each of the characters, including himself; he has exorcized them; each can now face the future on a proper basis. The homophone Woolf/wolf has, like Dionysus and Shakespeare's God, had the function of making man realize that he is not self-sufficient, that he must accept and submit to influences above and outside himself.

At the beginning of this section, I referred to two values to be found in serious drama. I have dealt at some length with one of these: the place of the individual in the overall scheme of things; I have deliberately postponed an examination of the other: the exploration of the innermost essence of man's nature. I shall cite only two examples of dramatists' attempts in this area, although this matter is at the centre of many of the world's greatest plays.

First is *Peer Gynt* (1867). In what is probably his greatest play, Henrik Ibsen studied the life of a man from boyhood to the grave. Peer has been trying to find the meaning of life. In the last Act he takes an onion and—the symbolism is obvious—strips away one coat after another in order to find what is in the centre; but there is no centre. Peer is desolate, but at the end of the play Ibsen provides him with the answer: he finds again Solveig, whom he has so wronged but who has remained so constant to him. The point and purpose of Peer's existence turns out to be Solveig's continuing love for him:

> I will cradle thee, I will guard thee;—
> Sleep and dream, thou boy of mine.[16]

In *King Lear*, Shakespeare, too, delved deeply into the innermost recesses of man's essential nature. Lear and Gloucester are largely responsible for the disasters that afflict them as well as others; towards the end of the play each thinks he has discovered the answer to life's problems. Gloucester sees the solution as escape through suicide (he asks to be led to the top of a cliff—"from that place I shall no leading need"), and Lear has reached a point of utter pessimism about man ("unaccommodated man is no more but a poor, bare, forked animal"); but each is proved wrong. As does Peer, so Lear and Gloucester discover that the answer lies in the strength of love—Edgar's love for Gloucester and Cordelia's for Lear, and each is enabled to die happy. This solution is found in many of the world's serious dramas. It is really a belief that selfishness leads to misery, and unselfishness to happiness; this message is very simple (it has much in common with the message of Jesus), but the dramatic treatment of the problems of human existence and the false solutions put forward have often been treated in ways that are vivid, moving, subtle, and that affect audiences' deepest sources of feeling and emotion.

Epilogue

I have suggested that plays can have one of three main values: many are content to provide their audiences with a few hours of undemanding pleasure; others demand that their audiences respond not merely with passive acceptance but with an active exercise of the intellect; and others—and these perhaps have the highest value—invite us to look into our souls and out into the universe, not merely passively, not merely intellectually, but with a surrender of our whole being, notably our deepest and sincerest emotional core, to participation in an examination of man's place in the mystery of things, of how each of us can best play his part on the world's stage.

Notes

1. Brandon Thomas, *Charley's Aunt* I (London: Samuel French, undated), pp. 45–46.
2. Oscar Wilde, *The Importance of Being Earnest* I (London: Methuen, 1899), p. 30.
3. C. H. Hazelwood, *Lady Audley's Secret* (in *Nineteenth Century Plays*, ed. George Rowell, London: Oxford University Press, 1953), pp. 265–66.
4. C. H. Hazelwood, *Lady Audley's Secret*, lines 21–24.
5. Aristophanes, *Lysistrata*, translated by Patric Dickinson (in Aristophanes, *Plays II*, London: Oxford University Press, 1957) pp. 85–86.
6. Jean-Baptist Poquelin de Molière, *Tartuffe*, translated by H. Baker and J. Miller (1739), III, vi (London: Dent, Everyman's Library, 1929), pp. 106–7.
7. Ben Jonson, *The Alchemist* III, ii, 69–77 (in *The New Mermaids*, ed. Douglas Brown, London: Ernest Benn, 1966).
8. R. Richard Brinsley Sheridan, *The Rivals* I, ii (in *The Dramatic Works of Richard Brinsley Sheridan*, Oxford: Oxford University Press, 1906), p. 19.
9. George Bernard Shaw, *Major Barbara* II (in *The Complete Plays of Bernard Shaw*, London: Paul Hamlyn, undated) pp. 483–84.
10. Tom Stoppard, *Jumpers* II (London: Faber & Faber, 1972) pp. 483–84.
11. William Shakespeare, *Hamlet* II, ii, 323.
12. Euripides, *The Bacchae* (translated by Geoffrey S. Kirk, Englewood Cliffs, N.J.: Prentice-Hall, 1970), pp. 48–9, lines 248–52.
13. Euripides, *The Bacchae*, pp. 61–2, lines 453–59.
14. William Shakespeare, *Othello* V, ii, 357–58.
15. William Shakespeare, *Othello* V, ii, 271–74.
16. Henrik Ibsen, *Peer Gynt* V, x (translated by R. Ellis Roberts, Oxford: Oxford Univesity Press), p. 269.

Bibliography

Aristophanes. *Plays II*, trans. by Patric Dickinson. Oxford: Oxford University Press, 1970.
Aylen, Leo. *Greek Tragedy and the Modern World*. London: Methuen, 1964.

Brown, Douglas (ed.). *The New Mermaids*. London: Ernest Benn, 1966.
Brown, John Russell. *Effective Theatre*. London: Heinemann, 1969.
Craig, W. J. (ed.). *Shakespeare's Complete Works*. London: Oxford University Press, 1945.
Euripides. *The Bacchae*, trans. Geoffrey S. Kirk. Englewood Cliffs, N.J.: Prentice-Hall, 1970.
Freedley, George, and John A. Reeves. *A History of the Theatre*. New York: Crown Publishers, 1947.
Hartnoll, Phyllis. *The Oxford Companion to the Theatre*. 3d ed. Oxford: Oxford University Press, 1967.
———. *A Concise History of the Theatre*. London: Thames & Hudson, 1968.
———. *Nineteenth Century Plays*. London: Oxford University Press, 1953.
Harwood, Ronald. *All the World's a Stage*. London: Secker & Warburg, 1984.
Ibsen, Henrik. *Peer Gynt*, trans. R. Ellis Roberts. London: Oxford University Press, 1936.
Kitto, H. D. F. *Greek Tragedy*. London: Methuen, 1939.
Knight, G. Wilson. *The Wheel of Fire*. London: Methuen, 1930.
Long, Michael. *The Unnatural Scene*. London: Methuen, 1976.
Molière, Jean-Baptiste de Poquelin. *Tartuffe*, trans. H. Baker and J. Miller. London: Dent Everyman's Library, 1929.
Pope, MacQueen W. *The Curtain Rises*. Edinburgh: Thomas Nelson & Sons, 1961.
Shaw, George Bernard. *The Complete Plays*. London: Paul Hamlyn, undated.
Skeat, Walter W. *Chaucer's Complete Works*. London: Oxford University Press, 1912.
Sheridan, Richard Brinsley. *The Dramatic Works of Richard Brinsley Sheridan*. Oxford: Oxford University Press, 1906.
Stoppard, Tom. *Jumpers*. London: Faber & Faber, 1972.
Taylor, J. Chesney, and G. R. Thompson. *Ritual, Realism and Revolt*. New York: Charles Scribner's Sons, 1972.
Unger-Hamilton, Clive. *The Entertainers*. London: Pitman, 1980.
Vyvyan, John. *The Shakespearean Ethic*. London: Chatto & Windus, 1959.
Wilde, Oscar. *The Importance of Being Earnest*. London: Methuen, 1899.

List of Contributors

Brenda Almond, B.A., M.Phil. is Reader in Philosophy and Education at the University of Hull, and co-editor of the *Journal of Applied Philosophy*.

Barbara Cowell, B.A., M.A., sometime Visiting Professor at Texas Wesleyan University, Fort Worth, and the University of Alberta, is now Research Fellow of the Warborough Trust Research Unit, Oxford, U.K.

J. Duncan M. Derrett, D.C.L. (Oxon.), Ph.D., LL.D, D.D. (London) is Emeritus Professor of Oriental Laws in the University of London.

Gordon Heald M.A. (Cantab.), B.Sc., M.Phil. (London), is managing director of Gallup Polls, London, and was sometime Visiting Fellow of the Oxford University Management Centre.

Edmund S. Ions, M.A., M.Litt. (Oxon.), is the Reader in Politics, University of York, U.K.

Charles Lepper, M.A. (Oxon.) was Head of English and Drama at Bradfield College, Berkshire, from 1967 to 1982.

Alan Montefiore, is a Fellow of Balliol College, Oxford, U.K.

J. K. B. M. Nicholas, M.A., was formerly Professor of Comparative Law in the University of Oxford, and is now Principal of Brasenose College, Oxford, U.K.

Bernard Richards, B.Litt., D.Phil. (Oxon.), M.A. (Philadelphia) is a Fellow of Brasenose College, Oxford, Oxford, U.K.

Paul Seabright, M.A., M.Phil. (Oxon.), is Fellow of Church College, Cambridge, U.K., and Fellow of All Souls' College, Oxford, U.K.

Edward Shils, A.B., serves on the Committee of Social Thought, University of Chicago, and is a Fellow of Peterhouse, Cambridge, U.K.

Bryan Wilson, B.Sc. (Econ.), Ph.D. (London), M.A., D.Litt. (Oxon.) is the Reader in Sociology in the University of Oxford, U.K., and Fellow of All Souls' College, Oxford.

John Wilson, M.A., is Lecturer in the Oxford University Dept. of Educational Studies, Fellow of Mansfield College, Oxford, and at present President of the Philosophical Society of Great Britain.

D. C. M. Yardley, LL.D., M.A., D.Phil. (Oxon.) is Chairman of the Commission for Local Administration in England (the Ombudsman).

Index of Names

Abraham, 69
Albee, Edward, 243, 247
Aristophanes, 237
Aristotle, 98, 107, 193, 242
Arunta (tribe), 35, 36
Atkinson, Lord, 135

Beatles, 62
Beckett, Samuel, 233
Benedict, Ruth, 5
Ben Sirach, 146
Bentham, Jeremy, 110, 124
Berkeley, George, 170
Berlin, Sir Isaiah, 96, 200
Berne Convention, 186
Booth, Wayne C., 214
Buddha, Gautama, 69
Burke, Edmund, 105, 106, 113, 131

Caesar, Julius, 192
Callicot, J. B., 171, 172
Carson, Rachel, 166
Caxton, William, 180
Cézanne, Paul, 211
Chaucer, Geoffrey, 180, 234
Churchill, Sir Winston, 62
Clough, Arthur Hugh, 123
Club of Rome, 167
Cohen, M. R., 170
Comte, Auguste, 99
Compton-Burnett, Ivy, 57
Conrad, Joseph, 212
Crossman, Richard, 142

Dante, Alighieri, 209

Darius, 146
Defoe, Daniel, 169
de Montaigne, M., 64, 208
de Sade, Marquis, 192, 193
Derrett, J. D. M., 8
Diocletian, 107
Donovan, Judge, 139
Dowden, Edward, 211
Duncan, Isadora, 102
Durkheim, Emile, 2, 35, 36, 37

Edgeworth, Francis, 111, 112
Eliot, George, 214
Elizabeth I, 181
Erasmus, Desiderius, 181, 189
Euripides 243, 245, 246, 247
European Economic
   Community, 186
European Patent Office, 183

Ford, John, 236
Ford Motor Company, 187
Frankfurt, Henry, 17
Freud, Sigmund, 226

Gallup International, 76
Gandhi, Mahatma, 94
Galsworthy, John, 223
Gauguin, Paul, 102
Gibbon, Edward, 71
Gogh, Vincent van, 233
Goodin, Robert, 171
Gossen, Hermann, 110
Graham, Kenneth, 211
Gutenberg, Johann, 180

253

Haggart, John P., 9
Harding, W. H., 171
Hardy, Thomas, 210, 216
Hare, Richard M., 224
Hawthorne, Nathaniel, 216
Hazelwood, C. H., 236
Heisenberg, W., 173
Hicks, John R., 111
Hirsch, Fred, 168
Hirst, Paul, 224
Hitler, Adolf, 192
Hobbes, Thomas, 98, 99
House of Lords, 137, 138
Hume, David, 106

Ibsen, Henrik, 247, 248
Iltis, H. H., 167
International Research Association Group, 76
Ionesco, Eugène, 233
Isaac, 69

Jackson, Judge, 120
Jacob, 69
James, Henry, 212, 213, 214
Japanese Patent Office, 187
Jeffrey, Richard, 112
Jefferson, Thomas, 188
Jesus, 69, 94, 248
Jevons, William, 110, 111
Job, 223, 246
Johnson, Samuel, 182, 213
Jonson, Ben, 237, 239

Kannon, viii
Kant, Immanuel, 15, 16, 61, 200
Kingsley, Charles, 214

Lasswell, Harold, 94
Lawrence, D. H., 215
Leopold, Aldo, 164, 167, 172, 175
Locke, John, 217
Luke, Saint, 69
Lytton, Bulwer, 211

Machiavelli, M., 98, 99

McCloskey, H. J., 165, 169
Malinowski, Bronislaw, 5
Malory, Sir Thomas, 181
Marx, Karl, 106, 108, 109, 113
Mauss, Marcel, 115
Midgley, Mary, 169
Milk Marketing Board, 136, 137
Ministry of Agriculture, 137
M O A Foundation, viii, 8
Morton, Archbishop, 179
Molière, J. B. P., 116, 238, 239
Monopolies Commission, 186
Moore, Henry, 233
Morgenstern, Oscar, 112
Moses, 69
Müller, F. Max, 233
Murray, Gilbert, 223

National Opinion Research Centre, 87

Okada, Mokichi, vii, viii

Pareto, Vilfredo, 111
Parsons, Talcott, 99
Passmore, John, 168
Paul, Saint, 69
Picasso, Pablo, 233
Pinter, Harold, 233
Plato, 223
Popper, Karl, 173
Proust, Marcel, 200, 212, 220, 223, 225

Quinton, Anthony, 112, 212

Racine, J., 220
Ramsey, Frank, 112
Rand, Ayn, 165
Richard III, 180
Richards, Bernard, 219, 225
Richardson, Samuel, 217
Robbins, Lionel (Lord), 111, 112
Routley, R. and V., 172

Saint-Simon, Henri, 99

Samuelson, Paul, 111
Savage, L. J., 112
Scudamore, Sarah, 217
Shakespeare, William, 58, 59, 192, 226, 239, 243, 245, 246, 247, 248
Shaw, George Bernard, 240
Sheridan, Richard B., 239
Shils, Edward, 6
Smith, Adam, 106, 107, 108, 109, 113
Snow, Charles P., 148
Spencer, Herbert, 35, 99
Spenser, Edmund, 207
Stoppard, Tom, 241
Strawson, Peter, 219
Swift, Jonathan, 208

Taylor, Charles, 17
Tchaikovsky, P., 233
Thomas, Brandon, 235
Thomas, Dylan, 102

Titmuss, Richard, 114
Tolstoy, Leo, 66
Travers, Ben, 236
Trollope, Anthony, 58

United States Patent Office, 188
Upjohn, Lord, 138

Valerian, 71
Virgil, 222, 224
von Neumann, John, 112
von Schiller, C. F., 216

Wagner, Richard, 197
Warborough Trust, 204
Weber, Max, 33, 40, 99
Webster, John, 236
Wilde, Oscar, 105, 106, 235
Wilson, Bryan, 101
Wilson, John, 14, 219
Wittgenstein, L., 15, 16